THE IDEA OF A FREE PRESS

Medill School of Journalism
VISIONS *of the* AMERICAN PRESS

GENERAL EDITOR
David Abrahamson

Other titles in this series

HERBERT J. GANS
Deciding What's News: A Study of CBS Evening News,
NBC Nightly News, Newsweek, *and* Time

MAURINE H. BEASLEY
First Ladies and the Press: The Unfinished Partnership of the Media Age

PATRICIA BRADLEY
Women and the Press: The Struggle for Equality

MICHAEL SWEENEY
The Military and the Press: An Uneasy Truce

THE IDEA OF
A FREE PRESS
THE ENLIGHTENMENT
AND ITS UNRULY
LEGACY

David A. Copeland

Foreword by Daniel Schorr

MEDILL SCHOOL OF JOURNALISM

Northwestern University Press
Evanston, Illinois

The Foreword by Daniel Schorr is adapted from an essay, "Journalism and the Public Interest," which appeared in Geneva Overholser and Kathleen Hall Jamieson, eds., *The Institutions of American Democracy: The Press* (New York: Oxford University Press, 2005). Reprinted with permission of Oxford University Press.

Northwestern University Press
www.nupress.northwestern.edu

Printed in the United States of America

10   9   8   7   6   5   4   3   2   1

ISBN 0-8101-2329-0

Library of Congress Cataloging-in-Publication Data

Copeland, David A., 1951–
    The idea of a free press : the Enlightenment and its unruly legacy /
David A. Copeland ; foreword by Daniel Schorr.
        p. cm. — (Visions of the American press)
    Includes bibliographical references and index.
    ISBN 0-8101-2329-0 (pbk. : alk. paper)
    1. Freedom of the press—Great Britain—History. 2. Freedom of the
press—United States—History. 3. Freedom of speech—Great Britain—
History. 4. Freedom of speech—United States—History. 5.
Government and the press—Great Britain—History. 6. Government
and the press—United States—History.   I. Schorr, Daniel, 1916–
II. Title. III. Series.
    PN4748.G7C59 2006
    323.4450903—dc22

                                                2006002775

    ♾ The paper used in this publication meets the minimum
requirements of the American National Standard for Information
Sciences—Permanence of Paper for Printed Library Materials,
ANSI Z39.48-1992.

For Robin

CONTENTS

FOREWORD

Daniel Schorr

Freedom of the press and its origins, a tale well told in this history of the idea by David Copeland, proved to be an essential component of America's Bill of Rights. The First Amendment to the U.S. Constitution reads: "Congress shall make no law respecting an establishment of religion, or prohibiting the free exercise thereof; or abridging the freedom of speech, or of the press; or the right of the people peaceably to assemble, and to petition the Government for a redress of grievances."

Ratified in 1791 and its reach extended to the states by the Fourteenth Amendment in 1868, it makes the press the only private industry afforded specific constitutional protection. It was intended to protect printers and pamphleteers like Benjamin Franklin and Thomas Paine against censorship imposed by the politicians they criticized. The framers of the Constitution, who regarded a free press as vital to a democracy, could not have conceived that one day this cloak would embrace vast outlets that stretched the very meaning of journalism.

The press (now more commonly called the news media) continues to insist on constitutional shelter in the public interest while primarily serving substantial private interests, and sometimes being accused of acting against the public interest. This apparent conflict is one that has long interested me.

The guarantee of press freedom has, since the eighteenth century, been subject to attacks, legal and otherwise. The first major test was the controversy set off by passage of the Sedition Act of 1798. Signed into law by President John Adams on July 14, 1798, the act made it a crime for any person "to write, print, utter[,] or publish . . . any false, scandalous, and malicious writing or writings against the government of the United States, or either house of the Congress or the President . . . with intent to defame . . . or to bring them, or either of them, into contempt or disrepute; or to excite against them . . . the hatred of the good people of the United States." Violation of the statute was punishable by a $5,000 fine and five years in prison.

James Madison and Thomas Jefferson were among those who condemned the act as unconstitutional, and they coauthored resolutions against it. In the Virginia Resolutions of 1798, the General Assembly protested that the act "exercises . . . a power not delegated by the Constitution, but, on the contrary, expressly and positively forbidden by one of the amendments thereto—a power which, more than any other, ought to produce universal alarm, because it is leveled against the right of freely examining public characters and measures, and of free communication among the people thereon, which has ever been justly deemed the only effectual guardian of every other right." Opposition to the act fueled the publication and circulation of Republican newspapers and became a major issue in the presidential election of 1800. The newly elected president, Jefferson, pardoned those who had been convicted under the act and remitted their fines, saying: "I considered, and now consider, that law to be a nullity, as absolute and as palpable as if Congress had ordered us to fall down and worship a golden image." The act expired in 1801.

More than a century later, during World War I, the Espionage Act of 1917 prohibited any antigovernment speech that interfered with the success of the military. In 1919 the Supreme Court upheld the espionage conviction of Charles Schenck, a secretary of the Socialist Party, for circulating leaflets opposing the draft to men who had already been drafted. In upholding his conviction, the justices said that Schenck's actions created a "clear and present danger." According to majority opinion: "When a nation is at war many things that might be said in a time of peace are such a hindrance to its effort that their utterance will not be endured so long as men fight and that no Court could regard them as protected by any constitutional right."

In *Near v. Minnesota* in 1931, the court struck down a state law that authorized censorship of scurrilous material published by a local newspaper. While Justice Pierce Butler, in his dissenting opinion, wrote that the Constitution was not intended to "protect malice, scandal, and other defamation when untrue or published with bad motives or without justifiable ends," the majority ruled that even outlandish material was protected. "Charges of reprehensible conduct, and, in particular, of official malfeasance, unquestionably create a public scandal," went the majority opinion, "but the theory of the constitutional guaranty is that even a more serious public evil would be caused by authority to prevent publication."

A truly landmark case in terms of undergirding freedom of the press was *New York Times Co. v. Sullivan* in 1964.

In a 6–3 decision, the Supreme Court struck down a lower court decision that Alabama police commissioner L. B. Sullivan had been libeled in a full-page advertisement in the *New York Times* taken out by civil rights activists. The Court majority held that a public official enjoyed less legal protection than an ordinary citizen. Further, it held that a claim of defamation had to be backed not only with proof that a statement was false, but also with proof that it was intentionally false. The "actual malice" doctrine has served to protect unnumbered defendants in libel suits ever since.

The Pentagon Papers case of 1971 raised in stark terms the issue of press freedom versus national security. A former government employee, Daniel Ellsberg, had conveyed to the *New York Times* and *Washington Post* copies of a classified, seven-thousand-page history of U.S. involvement in the Vietnam War. As soon as the first excerpts appeared in the *Times,* the Nixon administration, in the person of Attorney General John Mitchell, sought from the federal district court an injunction against further publication. Mitchell claimed that further excerpts would cause "irreparable injury" to the national security.

In the end, the Supreme Court held that the restraining order on the *Times* and the *Post* be lifted. Justice Hugo Black said, for the majority, that it was the intention of the framers of the Constitution that the press should be free "so that it could bare the secrets of government to inform the people."

Justices William Douglas and William Brennan were alone in their contention that the First Amendment banned *all* prior restraint. Four justices—Douglas, Potter Stewart, Byron White, and Thurgood Marshall—raised the possibility of criminal prosecution *after* publication. Since then, government officials have, on occasion, threatened prosecution under the espionage statute to keep a newspaper from publishing sensitive information.

In 1985 Central Intelligence Agency Director William Casey made such a threat to Ben Bradlee, editor of the *Washington Post,* over a story that the *Post* was planning to run about the tapping of underwater Soviet cables. Bradlee quoted Casey as saying, "There's no way you can run that story without endangering national security. I'm not threatening you, but you've got to know that if you publish this I would recommend that you be prosecuted." President Ronald Reagan then had *Post* publisher Katharine Graham called out of her shower to warn against publication.

In the end, the *Post* printed the story—and no one from the newspaper went to jail. The issue is a tricky one— the national interest in keeping the citizenry informed versus the national security interest in keeping secrets. In this case, as it turned out, the Soviet authorities already knew that their undersea communications had been compromised and no harm was done by publication.

So, the government could threaten prosecution, but it could not forbid publication as the British government might have done under its Official Secrets Act. This limitation on government powers is due to what may be the key provision of the Pentagon Papers decision dealing with prior restraint. The decision made clear that the right of publication was not absolute. Yet it also held that in this case, the government had not met the "heavy burden" of establishing a threat to the national security so great as to warrant advance censorship. Nor had that heavy burden been met since then. What the Court left open was the possibility of subsequent (postpublication) prosecution or libel action.

Yet the high court had generally heeded the advice of James Madison that "a popular government without popular information or the means to acquiring it is but the prologue to a farce or tragedy." And the advice of Woodrow Wilson, "Everybody knows that corruption thrives in secret places and avoids public places and we believe it a fair assumption that secrecy means impropriety."

Since the terrorist attacks of September 11, 2001, the government has found other ways of influencing the press. One way is to appeal to patriotism at a time when the nation is engaged in a war against terrorism. In October 2001, Condoleezza Rice, President George W. Bush's national security adviser, arranged a telephone conference call with six television news executives to urge them to limit the use of videotaped addresses by al Qaeda leader Osama bin Laden, which might have a negative effect on the American public and might even contain coded messages to al Qaeda followers. Never mind that bin Laden's statements are available to anyone with a satellite receiver. Most of the news executives agreed to cut back on the use of such tapes.

The tension between press and government about keeping secrets is heightened by the knowledge that classification goes far beyond real need, activated more by fear of personal embarrassment than by threats to national security. J. William Leonard, a National Archives official, testified before a House committee, "It is no secret that the government classifies too much information."

Pressures on the media are enormous. Walter Isaacson,

the former president of Cable News Network (CNN), has commented on the media's constant whipsawing between "the Patriotism Police," complaining of a too-compliant attitude toward the government.

"In this war we need to return to our nation's tradition of cooperation and self-defense," said Attorney General John Ashcroft in a speech in June 2003.

The battle between secrecy and disclosure has generated periodic clashes over leaks and confidential sources. For the news media, freedom of press implies freedom to use information from confidential sources. The Supreme Court, in a 1972 decision, recognized a limited reporters' "privilege" but said that it had to yield to the needs of grand juries for information that they could not acquire any other way.

In the early 2000s, two major "sources" issues were being fought out before the courts. In Washington, five reporters, representing the Associated Press, CNN, the *Los Angeles Times,* and the *New York Times,* had been cited for contempt by a federal judge. They refused to answer questions about confidential sources in a civil defamation suit brought by Wen Ho Lee, a Los Alamos Nuclear Laboratory scientist who claimed he was wrongly accused of espionage. In another such controversy, reporters for the *New York Times,* the *Washington Post, Time* magazine, and NBC were subpoenaed by a special prosecutor investigating the leak in 2003 of the identity of Valerie Plame, a CIA undercover employee. Two reporters, Matthew Cooper of *Time* and Judith Miller of the *Times,* were threatened with contempt citations—and Miller actually spent eighty-five days in jail before agreeing to testify before the grand jury.

Hostility to the press often emanates from the Oval

Office itself, and sometimes with good reason. At least three recent presidents could attribute their greatest woes to journalists and journalism.

Richard M. Nixon was embarked on the road to disgrace in June 1972 because of reports in the *Washington Post,* followed by those of other media organizations. The *Post* linked a break-in into the Democratic headquarters in the Watergate office building to the Nixon campaign committee. There followed disclosures about disbursement of campaign money for illicit purposes, and, in the end, a draft bill of impeachment in the House forced Nixon to resign. William Safire, then a Nixon speechwriter, quoted Nixon as saying, "The press is the enemy."

Ronald Reagan, who once said, "I'm up to my keister in leaks," was damaged by the Iran-Contra scandal, which started, oddly, with a story in a little weekly magazine in Beirut, Lebanon, called *al-Shiraa.* Obviously planted by the Iranian authorities to embarrass the Reagan administration, the story revealed that former National Security Adviser Robert McFarlane had flown to Tehran with a planeload of antitank missiles that he hoped to barter for the release of American hostages held by pro-Iranian terrorists in Lebanon. Subsequently it emerged that the proceeds of the arms sale were used to arm the Contra rebels in Nicaragua, something that Congress had specifically forbidden. The prestige of a popular president was shaken by the revelations that started with a little Beirut weekly.

Bill Clinton was started down the road to impeachment by the news media—in this case, the Internet. On the night of January 17, 1998, gossipmonger Matt Drudge posted word on his Web site that *Newsweek* magazine was working on a story about the president's relationship with a White House intern. Drudge was quoted the next morning on ABC television, and within days the story was all over the print and electronic media and the ordeal of President Clinton had begun.

In making presidents accountable for their misdeeds, the press has clearly served the public interest. Yet an old-time journalist finds it a matter of sorrow that the press, at the height of its influence, is at a depth of its public approval. Protected by the Constitution as the guardian of the public interest, the news media are not regarded by most Americans as dedicated to the public interest as they strive for circulation, ratings, and profits.

One Roper–Freedom Forum poll found that fewer than 20 percent of respondents rated journalistic ethics as high. Sixty-five percent thought that there are times when publication or broadcasting should be "prevented" in the public interest. Did we win the fight over prior restraint in the Supreme Court only to lose it in the court of public opinion?

In the television world of today, news has come to occupy a corner of a vast entertainment stage, sharing the techniques and values of entertainment. It is perhaps because of the blurring of the line between reality and fantasy that several journalists have tried to build careers on invented stories.

In 1980 the *Washington Post* had to return a Pulitzer Prize awarded to Janet Cooke for a made-up story about an eight-year-old child hooked on drugs. Two-thirds of the stories written by Stephen Glass for the *New Republic* between 1995 and 1998 turned out to be fabricated. The champion liar was Jayson Blair, who filed many stories for the *New York Times* using datelines naming places Blair had never been. In 2004 Jack Kelley resigned from *USA Today* after producing a series of dramatic but untrue stories on events such as witnessing suicide bombings in Jerusalem.

Opinion polls beginning in the late 1990s have registered growing public distrust of the increasingly concentrated, profit-driven news media. In 2002, forty-six corporations controlled more than 50 percent of the news media—an array that included some 1,800 daily newspapers, 11,000 magazines, 2,000 television stations, and 11,000 radio stations. All of the principal television networks are extensions of large corporations—ABC's parent company is the Walt Disney Company, NBC's is General Electric, Viacom owns CBS, and Time Warner, CNN.

On February 22, 1971, more than a year before Watergate, President Nixon, his words recorded on Oval Office tape, remarked to his counsel, John Dean, "Well, one helluva lot of people don't give one damn about the issue of the suppression of the press, etc." Cynical, but perceptive. Yet no one demonstrated better than Nixon that, for all its faults and failings, the press, at crucial moments, is there to defend the public interest. And it is the origins of this important role that David Copeland's *The Idea of a Free Press* so ably examines.

PREFACE

Journalists love the First Amendment. It holds a special place in the hearts of all those who spend their lives investigating and reporting on all facets of government, from local boards of commissioners to Capitol Hill. But how many of the journalists who rely on the First Amendment every day really know how the concept of "freedom of the press" developed in America? Why did the states and the federal government find it necessary to add clauses to their constitutions to protect this freedom? I admit that, early in my career, I knew little about how this protection came about, even though I worked as a reporter for years, used confidential sources, and wrote with complete confidence that I would never face any repercussions for anything in my stories. I knew that what I printed was the truth, as far as I could be certain of the veracity of my sources. I trusted the idea that in the United States, freedom of the press is guaranteed, but I didn't know how we as a nation had gotten to that point.

That all changed when I met Professor Margaret A. Blanchard. Pursuing a career change in my late thirties, I entered the doctoral program at the University of North Carolina at Chapel Hill. Peggy Blanchard became my adviser and I her research assistant. Doors to knowledge opened. At the time, she was working on her Pulitzer-nominated book, *Revolutionary Sparks,* a history of free expression in the

United States from the 1890s through the 1980s. As I helped her with her research, and as I began doing research of my own for her classes on free expression in America, the seeds were being planted for this project. In its early stages, Peggy's book had encompassed the development of free expression in America in an earlier period—the seventeenth through the nineteenth centuries—and she had done considerable research on that era. The publisher, however, thought that including all of that material in *Revolutionary Sparks* would make the book cumbersome. So she set that portion of her book aside, planning to return to it one day to make it the focus of another publication. Unfortunately, she was never able to do this. While she was alive, most of her energy went toward her graduate students, and her life ended much too prematurely in 2004. Parts of those unpublished chapters, however, have guided this project. I am certain that Peggy would be pleased. Despite her role as a distinguished scholar of free expression in the twentieth century, she was just as knowledgeable about England of the Tudor-Stuart era and the development of free expression in colonial America.

Because Peggy would have loved to have written this book, I was honored as one of her students to be asked to write it for the Medill School of Journalism series, Visions of the American Press. I owe a debt of gratitude to series editor David Abrahamson for the opportunity, and I owe Peggy Blanchard more than passing mention for the foundational knowledge that I acquired from her, which has made completing the task a little easier in so many ways.

Early in my studies with Professor Blanchard, she asked me a question, "What do the sources say?" Her question has guided the completion of this work. As much as possible, I have used primary documents in this book to support and explain the development of free-expression rights. In addition, many outstanding scholars have written about press freedom, and, for me, they are outstanding sources, too. Jeffery Smith and Leonard Levy have argued what press freedom meant for Americans in the eighteenth century. Clyde Duniway provided a comprehensive review of freedom of the press in Massachusetts, and the work of both Frederick Siebert and William Clyde on the development of freedom of the press in England is foundational for any research that examines press freedom in colonial America. These are but a few of the outstanding scholars whose research aided in the completion of this project.

In this book I examine the rise of the era of the printed word in England and its American colonies from the introduction of the press in England through the end of the American Revolution. I focus on people, events, and movements to reveal how use of the printed word, and the demand to be able to express oneself, eventually developed into the concept of a free press that is so cherished by Americans. The rise of a free press in the English-speaking world owes much to religious dissenters who found the interpretation and application of scripture—first by the Roman Catholic Church, and then by Henry VIII's Church of England—inconsistent with their new understanding of God's word. They had gained the ability to interpret holy scripture for themselves with the development of the printing press: Movable type allowed the Bible to be printed in the vernacular, the language of the people, and to be more widely distributed than in the past, when it had been copied by hand in Latin, a dead language that could be read and understood only by those in the uppermost echelons of society. Dissenters believed their ideas should be shared. Those in power, however, believed those ideas should—for the security of the nation—be silenced. The result was a confrontation that would grow beyond the issues of religious freedom to include political freedom. The argument would ultimately encompass the idea that freedom of speech was a God-given right—and one that the state must protect, even if the words attacked the state.

From a twenty-first-century perspective, we often imagine that the right to express oneself, through the printed word, for example, is something noble, an end in itself. From the beginning, though, freedom of speech through the press was a means to an end—liberty of conscience, or the right to believe, interpret scripture, worship God, and live the Christian life according to individual convictions, rather than some ecclesiastical authority. Religious dissenters demanded freedom of the press as a means of achieving these ideals. Early on, nonconformists said that this made sense: It was rational to believe that God would want the crowning achievement of creation—humankind—to be able to do this. This notion was at the heart of the Protestant Reformation.

Many religious thinkers soon adopted the perspective that God would never cause something to happen that man could not understand. They also started to believe that their understanding of God was superior to that of those who had come before them. They were "enlightened." Beginning in the middle of the seventeenth century in England, these thinkers, applying their ideas to the entire realm of human existence, began to develop a political philosophy. Based in their notion of the divine, they advocated a social contract for living in society with a government that drew its authority from the people, the consent of the governed. All of this thought had to be expressed and shared, so freedom of the press became one of the pillars, or "bulwarks of liberty," to quote the famous Letter No. 15 of Cato. Turmoil, struggle, suppression, rebellion, execution, and revolution followed in the next century. The Enlightenment, a movement with deep religious roots and marked by a belief in the ability to apply reason to understanding of the divine and societal life, produced a legacy that people living just a few centuries earlier could not have imagined: a guarantee that people could assemble to discuss issues, that they could petition the government when they felt they had been wronged, and that they could speak out on issues and print and share their thoughts. It sounds simple, but the process whereby a new nation came to guarantee these rights is a legacy worth remembering.

A number of people have made my work easier. As always, my wife, Robin, has been the person on whom I depend most. She is always ready to lend support, read chapters, and point out what's good—and what's not so good—with what I have written. I am also indebted to Elon University for providing a research grant to help me complete this project, and to Dean Paul Parsons and the School of Communications for granting me a schedule conducive to research. I am also grateful to Brooke Barnett and Constance Book in the Elon School of Communications for allowing me to discuss ideas with them, and to Bradley Hamm, dean of the School of Journalism at Indiana University, for always thinking outside the box, challenging me to ponder fresh ideas constantly.

Finally, I thank Peggy Blanchard for opening the door to the world of research for me. I can almost hear her asking, even now, "What are you working on?" "Freedom of expression," I would answer, and I know, even now, she would approve.

DAVID A. COPELAND

ONE

INTRODUCTION

In 1589, a publication from the London press of John Wolfe declared, "I know you in England expect newes with everie happie winde: and happie be that wind which brings you good newes." Wolfe and other English printers were providing the people of London with continuous news of the war in France between Henry of Navarre and the Catholic League. It was a confrontation that attracted unprecedented attention. Thousands of Englishmen had chosen to join the holy fray. Considering England's level of involvement in terms of manpower, the confrontation's Protestant-Catholic nature, and the interest in England in the war's outcome for reasons both political and religious, the fact that an estimated 45,000 news pamphlets on the war circulated through England during the five years of fighting, 1589–1593, may not be surprising to twenty-first-century readers, who are bombarded with thousands of pages and hundreds of news broadcasts monthly concerning political affairs. But the comment that the people "expect newes" was printed in 1589 during the tenure of the

Star Chamber, the Tudor-Stuart monarchy's tool for controlling dissent and information.

More than 160 years later, another printer, this time New Yorker James Parker, described the appeal of news in his time: "This Taste, we Englishmen, have for News, is a very odd one; yet it must be fed." Parker concluded his observation by saying that news was something "we can't be without." The fact that English-speaking people in Britain and America developed a desire for information is logical, considering the political, religious, social, intellectual, and economic changes that occurred in both places in the sixteenth, seventeenth, and eighteenth centuries. Saying in 1589 that people "expect newes," or in 1750 that news is something "we can't be without," is not the same as proclaiming that people have a *right* to speak and print their thoughts, no matter the nature of their words. But those pronouncements certainly reflected people's desire in England and America to obtain as much information and knowledge as possible. At the same time, people were writing that it was, in fact, their right to print their ideas even if they contradicted the ideas sanctioned by governing authorities. The same phenomenon occurred in many other Western European countries—and their New World colonies, too. Yet it was in the former British colonies that became the United States that those who created a new form of government, a republican democracy, declared through legislative fiat that they would "make no law . . . abridging the freedom of speech, or of the press."

How was it possible to reach a time when politicians were willing to guarantee the right of a free press? After centuries of struggle between those who were in power and those who were not, between those of the religious ortho-doxy and those who dissented, a new thought process began to develop. People began to see that when governments con-trolled what was spoken or printed, they limited a natural right of man given by God. If God gave the right, it logi-cally could not be infringed upon by any other person or government. "But how great is the Absurdity to suppose, that Government was ever designed to *enslave* the *Consciences of Men!*" is the way New York lawyer-turned-columnist William Livingston phrased the idea in 1753.

Livingston and most of the other writers and thinkers of his age had been affected by the writings of John Milton, Thomas Hobbes, John Locke, Daniel Defoe, "Cato" (a pseudonym for the eighteenth-century Englishmen John Trenchard and Thomas Gordon), and dozens of other often anonymous writers—many of whom were Puritans and other religious dissenters demanding the inalienable right to act on the dictates of their conscience. These people com-bined their religious beliefs with a new way of looking at the world. They believed that they were more enlightened than those who had lived before them. Humankind, they said, had been given the ability to think; therefore, people could understand the world around them, even man himself—all of which were God's creations—through the ability to think and reason. They believed that God offered a balance—harmony—to the world. Consequently, whatever might be revealed to humankind as "divine revelation" could not, as Henry May has said, "establish truths which were contrary to reason." This way of thinking became known as the "En-lightenment." Those who subscribed to its principles in the seventeenth century and much of the eighteenth did not deny God or God's ability to reveal; they simply said that God could not, would not, reveal, create, or act in any manner contrary to humankind's ability to reason. While not all people in Britain or its American colonies accepted this notion, many did, and it wove itself into the fabric of religion and nearly all aspects of life.

The pages of this book look back to see how the people of England and then America developed the concept that a free press was a right given to the people and how this concept ultimately found its way into the Bill of Rights of the young United States. It is not an attempt to explain what America's Founding Fathers meant by the First Amendment. Rather, it is an effort to see how English-speaking people arrived at the point where they believed that the right to speak and print should be protected by government, and to examine the efforts made along the way to suppress speech for any number of reasons, but principally as a means of protecting and preserving government. In relation to England and America during this period, usually government can be seen as a combination of political and ecclesiastical authorities.

When William Caxton introduced the printing press to England in 1476, no one, no doubt, believed it would ever become an instrument to disseminate "dangerous" or heretical concepts. After all, England was still very much a medieval nation and fervently Roman Catholic in the last quarter of the fifteenth century. Caxton's publications included translations of some of the greatest literature of the ages. He printed religious works and history. When he died in 1491, the great heresy, according to those who held the strings of power, that the printing press would foster—the Protestant Reformation—was still nearly thirty years away.

Because all aspects of life at the beginning of the sixteenth century were written upon indelibly with religion, any questioning of religious orthodoxy brought into question nearly all aspects of life. When Martin Luther nailed his theses to the Wittenberg church door, he openly questioned what had not been questioned in Europe since the end of the fourth century—the authority of the Roman Catholic Church and the monarchies that supported it. Luther's monumental 1520 work, *Address to the Christian Nobility of the German Nation,* introduced the concept of the "priesthood of the believer." One of the basic tenets of the Reformation, this concept posited that all had access to the ear of God. Therefore, one did not need to confess one's sins to a priest. One could go directly to God personally to ask forgiveness.

A young Cambridge-trained scholar named John Frith became one of the first to promote Reformation ideas in England. As early as 1528, Frith proposed that the concept of transubstantiation—the idea that the bread and wine of the Eucharist were literally the body and blood of Christ—was "adiaphora"—that is, made no sense, and therefore should not matter to a person of faith. Frith was not alone in these thoughts—or in his way of thinking—but he introduced the Renaissance concept of rationalism to the growing Reformation debate in England. Human reason, for Frith, was the final arbiter of scripture. Frith's "enlightened" thought removed from the priesthood the power it transmitted in the sacraments and placed it squarely upon God's favor to the believer. If every article of faith were scrutinized in such a manner, then the very foundations of the Roman Catholic Church—and even the monarchy, which ruled through divine right—might be undermined.

What gave the ideas of Luther and Frith such strength was the ability to share them via the printed word. Concepts uttered in a tavern or a classroom at Oxford could be dangerous, but when those words were printed and bulk copies dispersed, they had the ability to produce powerful results. They could take on a life of their own. They could spur more pamphlets and even more wildly heretical thought, according to the crown and church. Frith may have been the first Englishman to publish tracts based on the liberty of conscience—and to die for proposing ideas contrary to the status quo—but he would not be the last.

In England, Henry VIII responded quickly to the writings of Frith and similar thinkers. In 1529, he instituted the first of numerous laws that prohibited the publication of certain books and established trade regulation of books. Henry also instituted a licensing system. The purpose of this system, which was enforced by the Court of the Star Chamber, was to quiet all dissenting voices by requiring governmental approval of all items before they were published. In 1557, Mary Tudor transformed licensing into the Stationers' Company, which established a guild of crown-approved printers who controlled all questions surrounding printing in England. The Stationers had the power to censor printed material, establish printers' wages, and limit the number of employees who could work in a single print shop. The Stationers' Company increased its power in Elizabethan England and continued to operate along with the Star Chamber under the Stuarts—James I and Charles I—into the middle of the seventeenth century. The Stuarts introduced a new legal concept to the mix—seditious libel, which made any criticism of the government, be it true or false, a criminal act.

The Tudor-Stuart reaction to the publication of tracts and pamphlets was explained simply in 1597 by Francis Bacon. In his meditation "Of Heresies," the English philosopher said, "Knowledge itself is power." Before the printing press and publication of information in the vulgar languages, items written in Latin were understood only by the clergy and nobility. To the rest, understanding the mysteries surrounding Christianity—and anything else in print—was left to those who told them what the writings said and, subsequently, how they were to act and respond to the dictates of those words. With printing in the vernacular and calls for reformation in religion, however, the printing press became the weapon of choice. No other way existed to disseminate information as quickly and as widely as this new tool allowed.

THE PURPOSE OF PRINT AND DEBATE

Two traditions developed in England and continued in America that ultimately led to the belief that a free press was a necessity and a right. The first was the desire for information—the rationale behind the news pamphlets of the war in France from 1589 to 1593 and James Parker's declaration that news was something Englishmen could not be without in 1750. This desire for information is hardwired into humans. Of course, people who met along roads, in marketplaces, or nearly anywhere else had been exchanging information for as long as people interacted. Personal letters also served as a means of sharing news, and the writers generally intended for their correspondence to be shared with others in order to impart information. Eventually, personal correspondence turned into newsletters that anyone could buy to learn of occurrences. Handwritten newsletters naturally transformed into printed newssheets. John Campbell's scribed newsletters in Boston, for example, became the *Boston News-Letter* in 1704.

Because the earliest newssheets were, by decree, "published by authority," government agents used them to disseminate information and to shape and direct people's thoughts. This information was news, but it was tailored to fit the needs of those who held political power. In England in the first half of the seventeenth century, however, issues of political and religious importance led to another press, one that printed despite authority (the same would occur in America a century later). As newspapers developed into the form they would assume for the next two hundred years, competition and the gradual weakening and then abolishment of licensing laws created a venue for multiple voices through the printed word. Books, pamphlets, broadsides, newsbooks, and finally newspapers created a metaphysical space, the "public sphere," where ideas and information could be exchanged. A portion of the information shared here was news as we understand it today, although it was still often presented and then understood through lenses colored by the ideology and religion of the writers and readers, who oftentimes were more concerned with passing on a moral lesson than with providing accurate facts. This news included reports on governmental action and policy and events of the community, and it contained essays on subjects political, social, religious, and nonsensical.

Even though the printing press and these early publications together created what we understand newspapers to be, the second element in the development of the concept of the free press—the notion that people have a right to express their beliefs based on liberty of conscience—had appeared before, and it continued to find voice in the printed word from the time of the Protestant Reformation and John Frith through the eighteenth century and beyond. In fact, the exposition of beliefs continued to form a principal use of the printed word into the nineteenth century, when it helped to shape the mass media, and into the twenty and twenty-first centuries, when it took new incarnations in the realms of broadcasting and cyberspace. The human desire to expound on elements of belief was and continues to be so strong that people find ways to express themselves despite governmental injunctions against it. Even death cannot silence principle if more than one person subscribes to it, as attested by the long line of martyrs described by John Foxe in *The Acts and Monuments of the Church* (1563).

Establishing freedom of the press was not the intention of Englishmen who reacted to Roman Catholicism, to Henry's Anglican Church, or to any other authority attempting to place limitations upon the interpretation of scripture. Printing was a means to an end, but it ultimately had to be supported in order for thoughts contrary to the state to be distributed. Liberty of conscience, therefore, became the rationale for a free press in countless publications, including an open letter to Parliament, published in 1688, that said, "it's evident the Freedom of Restraint of the Press depends on this single Question, Whether we ought to be free, or Slaves in our Understandings?" And it is why William Livingston stated that it was an absurdity "that Government was ever designed to *enslave* the *Consciences of Men!*" in 1753.

In the seventy years before Martin Luther, printers were content to publish Bibles and works of history, philosophy, and literature. But three centuries earlier, Thomas Aquinas had written his *Summa Theologiae,* which used Aristotelian logic to establish the validity of the doctrines of the Catholic Church and, more important, the existence of God. The use of rational thought continued to be applied by Renaissance thinkers to find logical ways of explaining the relationship between God and humankind found in the catechism of the church in Rome. The revolt against the church, spawned by Luther and then widened by men such as Ulrich Zwingli and John Calvin, used the same logical thought processes to prove that the Roman Church misrepresented God, holy scripture, and the sacraments. And, unlike Aquinas, they sent their writings to printers. Luther's *Address to the Christian Nobility of the German Nation* sold four thousand copies in two weeks, with subsequent press runs of the book following. The reach of Luther's 1520 treatise had to be beyond the comprehension of people at that time, especially considering the way the products of the printing press had been shared up to that point.

Englishmen such as Frith did the same thing for England that other Reformation fathers were doing throughout the rest of Europe. They printed their thoughts and based their arguments in logic and reason. "I can not in conscience, abiure and sweare, that our Prelates opinion on the sacrament," Frith said, "is an vndoubted article of the fayth." In other words, transubstantiation made no sense. A century later, the Leveller William Walwyn was even more outspoken on the role of reason in understanding the right to worship God and interpret scripture. "God made man righteous," Walwyn wrote, "he made him naturally a rationall creature, judging rightly of all things." Walwyn concluded his tract by telling readers, "Let me prevail with you to free yourselves from this bondage, and to trust to your own considerations in any thing that is usefull for your understandings and consciences." Bondage, for Walwyn, was dependency upon anyone other than oneself for understanding scripture.

Thirty years later, other religious dissenters took rational thought even further. The Baptist Benjamin Keach declared that transubstantiation violated the principles of nature established by God and was, consequently, impossible. "There are some things, which it is no dishonour to God to say he cannot do them," Keach said in a publication entitled *Tropologia*. "God himself cannot make a Man to be alive and dead at the same time . . . and therefore in like manner he cannot make the same Body to be in two several places, for this is not one jot less impossible than the other."

The understanding and interpretation of scripture espoused by men such as Walwyn and Keach did not, of course, develop in a vacuum. Others were using the same enlightened ways of thinking to explain a variety of issues relevant to people in other realms of culture. Many people in Britain and America, of course, had no idea about the writings of Locke, Hobbes, and others who helped spread the ideas of the Enlightenment. Keach and Locke were contemporaries, both dying in 1704, yet Keach never mentioned Locke or any of the other thinkers of the age in his nearly fifty publications; nevertheless, it is clear from his comments on transubstantiation that he believed that man's reason and God's activities had to gel. Keach and other Baptists would never have considered themselves to be writers of

the Enlightenment, and yet Keach's rationale for understanding the Eucharist was certainly rational and in line with how
the great Enlightenment thinkers understood the divine. It
was a view that said that God himself could not do something that was logically impossible according to man's reason.

Like their kinsfolk in England, few Americans of the
seventeenth and eighteenth centuries knew much about the
great thinkers of the age. Nearly all Americans in the colonial period owned a Bible, but they owned little else that was
printed unless they were more affluent or part of the quickly
growing middle class, which sought a lifestyle similar to that
of society's upper crust. They would have said, as Patricia
Bonomi has pointed out, that they had never heard of John
Locke or read anything he had written. Yet, almost all of the
educated elements of society who led both politically and religiously would have. In many ways, colonial Americans
were no different from the people of today. They followed
the direction of society's opinion leaders, which, early in the
period, no doubt included listening to sermons tinged with
Enlightenment concepts, and then later included reading or
listening to newspaper essays on why the colonies should be
free of English control—all of which were based in the same
polemics that concerned the major philosophers of the day.
The writings of the Enlightenment may have been foreign
to everyday folk, but their application was not.

Where Britons and Americans came constantly into
contact with the rationalism of the Enlightenment was in
their eighteenth-century newspapers, especially in the writings of "Cato" and of Joseph Addison and Richard Steele. In
Britain, *The Tatler* and *The Spectator,* the periodicals of Addison and Steele, provided many a topic of conversation in

public places, both at the time of their initial London print-ings in 1709–1714 and for years afterward in collected works, the first of which left the presses in 1721. American printers regularly turned to the Cato essays, which appeared in the *London Journal,* for commentary or justification of a position on a subject. Printers such as Benjamin Franklin readily copied the style of Addison and Steele. Because colonial Americans regularly visited public houses, as did their kin in England, they heard Cato's Letters read, debated, and dis-cussed. Americans quoted Cato when they wanted to justify publishing controversial subject matter, as John Peter Zenger did with a Cato essay on freedom of the press when the *New-York Weekly Journal* began publishing. And the writings of Addison and Steele often delved into the religious. There, Addison, especially, provided readers with the rationalism of Enlightenment thought. "It is very certain, that a Man of sound Reason cannot forbear closing with Religion upon an impartial Examination of it," Addison said in *The Spectator* of August 23, 1712, adding, "The Devout Man does not only believe but feels there is a Deity. He has actual Sensations of him; his Experience concurs with his Reason." So, even if the typical Englishman said he did not know of Enlighten-ment thought, he likely did, without realizing it.

Enlightenment rationalism and religion did not mix for everyone, and the press, naturally, became one of the tools in the confrontation. America's eighteenth-century Great Awakening pitted rational thought against a pietistic religion that its proponents said was disclosed to humankind via scriptural tradition and divine revelation. Humankind did not have to understand it for it to be true. This juxtaposition in ways of understanding God would create divisions in

America that would persist. May said that ultimately in the nineteenth century piety would become Americans' preferred way of understanding and explaining their relationship with the deity, but Enlightenment thought surely shaped the formation of the nation, from the Declaration of Independence to the Constitution, the Bill of Rights, and the First Amendment.

What happened in America in relation to the press, from the time of the Great Awakening through the French and Indian War, and into the period of the Stamp Act crisis and the rebellion against England, ultimately established a mindset that allowed for the creation of the First Amendment protections for expression. The printed word began to focus on issues of importance to almost everyone in the colonies. People from New England to Georgia started to be interested in what happened throughout America. With the French and Indian War, especially, the very existence of the British colonial way of life was threatened. During the war, people readily began to refer to themselves as "Americans," and some even proposed that the colonies join together in a union. One writer called America's resolve to stop the French and the Indians "the old American Spirit"; another writer said, "Ye cannot be saved . . . except ye are at UNION AMONGST YOURSELVES."

When the French and Indian War ended and England sought ways to pay for it by levying taxes on the colonies, the protests succeeded because the press had already established itself as the catalyst for discussion and debate among the people. The number of newspapers being published grew by more than 260 percent during the war, so by 1765, they were readily available and accessible to most Americans, either as reading material or as the stimulus for debate in public places. By 1765, political officials had been abused in print in ways that officials of the seventeenth century could never have imagined. Government often cracked down on printers, but it mattered little. Massachusetts locked up James Franklin, but he paid his bond and continued to make hurling, pointed barbs at government actions. John Peter Zenger spent six months in jail, but his paper continued to attack Governor William Cosby. During the Stamp Act crisis, papers hurled invective after invective at local officials as well as at the London authorities. Nothing could stop them. The colony's lieutenant governor said the press used "every falshood that malice could invent to serve their purpose." But, he realized, "considering the present temper of the People, this is not a proper time to prosecute the Printers & Publishers." In fact, the time to prosecute never again existed in colonial America.

By the last half of the 1760s, the press had become a partisan tool. Writers regularly proclaimed their rights to a free press. Increasingly, however, the Patriots, those in favor of American independence from Great Britain, attempted to silence opposing voices. What seemed to be a contradiction of demands to speak freely for decades, even centuries among Britons, vanished for a time in the colonies, but there was a purpose. It could be found in the ideas of government as proposed by thinkers such as Locke. When Americans won the Revolution and freed themselves from tyranny and oppression, the press resumed its role as a partisan mouthpiece, and most citizens of the new United States adopted the motto they had long ago borrowed from Cato's Letters: "Freedom of speech is the great bulwark of liberty; they prosper and die together."

• • •

The chapters in this book are arranged thematically to a certain extent but also follow a chronological sequence. Chapter 2, "English Origins—Liberty of Conscience," provides an overview of the struggle undertaken by religious dissenters and nonconformists to gain the right to express their religious beliefs in order to worship as they pleased in Tudor-Stuart England. It also describes how the monarchy sought to silence dissent through the Star Chamber, licensing, the Stationers' Company, and seditious libel laws. The chapter introduces the principal players in the struggle that ultimately led to the Act of Toleration in 1689 and the end of licensing in 1694.

Chapter 3, "English Origins—News," traces the development of newsbooks, newssheets, and newspapers that occurred at the same time that the literature on liberty of conscience, discussed in Chapter 2, flourished. The first news sources in England rarely were suppressed because they generally did not discuss topics related directly to the English monarchy and Parliament. In the seventeenth century, especially during the reign of Charles I, this changed. Gradually, newssheets turned to subjects that were matters of internal dissension, and the result was suppression. At two notable times—in the 1640s and again in the 1680s—lapses in English law left the press relatively free of any control. During these periods, newspapers thrived and assumed a partisan tone, setting precedents for what would become common practice in eighteenth-century England and America. Chapter 3 takes us up to the early eighteenth century, when all of the basic official proscriptions on printing ended in Britain, making way for an explosion of public prints.

Chapter 4, "The Marketplace of Ideas and Its Polemi-cists," describes the political philosophy of Enlightenment thinkers, a philosophy that had a powerful influence on political thought throughout the era. The discussion begins with the radical Levellers, who in the 1640s outlined a plan for government by consent, incorporating religious liberty and a free press to stimulate debate. Chief among Leveller spokesmen were John Lilburne, William Walwyn, and Richard Overton, who, along with other Leveller leaders, were locked away in the Tower of London by Oliver Cromwell and his Council of State. The Levellers proposed a democratic society that was at least a century ahead of its time. The rest of Chapter 4 looks at the writings of the thinkers who led Americans to their notions of government, including the necessity of a free press. Included are John Milton, specifically his commentary in *Areopagitica*; Thomas Hobbes, who wrote *Leviathan* and proposed the idea of a social contract; John Locke, with his theories of government that were detailed in the *Two Treatises on Government*; and the letters of Cato as written by Trenchard and Gordon, where the ideas of these thinkers were synthesized. The American press reprinted Cato's Letters completely and often following their initial appearance in London in the early 1720s.

Chapter 5, "American Origins—The Seventeenth Century," reveals early thoughts on expression and how leaders in America justified silencing it. The chapter traces the introduction of the printing press into America and the development of shared information in the colonies. It concludes with a discussion of America's first paper, *Publick Occurrences,* its suppression, and the beginnings of America's first continuously published paper, the *Boston News-Letter,* and the licensing laws that allowed John Campbell to publish it by authority only.

Chapter 6, "Turning Points for Expression," follows the expansion of multiple information sources through two pivotal issues: the trial of John Peter Zenger and the controversy surrounding religious revival and the itinerant British preacher George Whitefield. Competition fueled debate and criticism of government, and the seminal debate in print took place in the home of American printing, Boston. There, in 1721, smallpox and the controversial practice of inoculation initiated the first newspaper war in the colonies. Though the debate centered on inoculation, it was also about religious and political power. From this time, American printers and polemicists turned to Enlightenment writings from England to justify an open press as a medium for public dialogue.

Chapter 7, "Debate and the Public Sphere," focuses first on the pivotal event of the eighteenth century in America, the French and Indian War. The war, which enlisted the press to provide information from throughout North America and, indeed, the world, helped to create a press that was able to cooperate in the sharing and dissemination of information. It prepared printers for what would happen in the years to follow. The war was also a catalyst for much of what followed: The Stamp Act and other taxes were a direct result of Britain's efforts to recoup financial losses caused by the war; the taxes, in turn, set in motion resistance, revolt, and revolution, which led to the formation of the United States, its constitutional form of government, and its Bill of Rights. Chapter 7 also describes how Americans used the press to aid in their quest to obtain independence from Britain. The chapter looks at the changing nature of the press as Americans thoroughly incorporated Enlightenment thought into their framework of understanding for how a government should work. As a result, they believed that the press was the bulwark of liberty, that it should be used as a tool of revolution and independence, and that any other use was contrary to the purposes of liberty. The philosophical understanding of a free press led to the suppression of voices opposing independence because Patriots felt that the ends—an independent America—justified the means—suppression of dissent. Once the break with Britain was obtained, libertarian concepts returned. By taking a look at the writings of the polemicists of the age, it is possible to explain how this paradox was possible, and Chapter 7 will do just that.

Chapter 8, "Conclusion," pulls the developments of nearly three centuries together to explain how unruly concepts—such as the consent of the governed and a free and open press—culminated in legal protections for expression. The chapter looks at explanations of what liberty of the press meant to jurists such as William Blackstone and to the printers and people of the United States in the period just before the Bill of Rights was ratified. It ends by offering ways of looking at the development of a free press in universal terms that could apply not only to the eighteenth century, but also to the twenty-first.

TWO

ENGLISH ORIGINS—LIBERTY OF CONSCIENCE

The belief that freedom of the press was and is a God-given right, granted to humankind through natural rights, developed through a complex process encompassing centuries. The notion of freedom of the press and speech has, of course, never attained a universal consensus that the pair are a right of all; nor is there agreement as to the parameters of the meaning of "free" in this context. What is without debate, however, is the role religion played in their development. As schism occurred within the Catholic Church as a result of the Protestant Reformation, a struggle developed between government authorities, on the one hand, who believed that church and state were essentially one, and that God and scripture should therefore be interpreted in accordance with state goals and ideas by like-minded individuals, and dissenters, on the other, who began to introduce ideas contrary to the state church.

Suppression through law, torture, and death, however, could not stop ideas because, try as government did from the late fifteenth century into the eighteenth, people found ways to publish their thoughts despite government restrictions. Liberty of conscience, according to an anonymous writer, came down to a "single Question, Whether we ought to be free, or Slaves in our Understandings?" At the root of the origins of a free press in the English-speaking world was the desire to know God and to worship according to the dictates of conscience. As William Clyde explained it, the first motive for the development of freedom of the press was "the religious motive."

THE PRESS, PUBLISHING CONTROLS, AND REFORMATION

William Caxton introduced the printing press to England in 1476. In 1487, two years after ascending to England's throne, Henry Tudor, who became Henry VII, instituted the Star Chamber, which, among other things, made it unlawful to create writings that would harm the "good rule of this realm." Henry was responding to years of controversy and upheaval in England that witnessed the Wars of the Roses— the struggle between the houses of York and Lancaster for control of the crown—and to questions surrounding his ascension to the throne after the defeat and death of Richard III on Bosworth Field, not to Caxton's press in Westminster or the other three in operation in England before Henry's coronation. Threats to the crown came in the form of uprisings and covert plots at the end of the fifteenth century, rather than in pamphlet form. But Henry's act, and the fact that it included a prohibition against subversive writings, foreshadowed what lay ahead in England and its colonies in the Western Hemisphere, an imperial acquisition that Henry, no doubt, could not fathom, since Christopher Columbus had yet to sail, and no one even realized that a land mass lay to the west between Europe and the Orient.

Publishing via the printing press was about to take on proportions unimaginable during the tenure of Henry VII. Not even when Henry VIII assumed power following his father's death in 1509 could anyone have imagined that the printed word would initiate the revolution that loomed on the horizon. During the papacy of Pope Gregory I (590–604), the people of the British Isles adopted Christianity, joining almost all of Europe under one church. For centuries, the teachings of the Roman Catholic Church could not be questioned. By the time of Henry VII, kings had been crowned for hundreds of years in England's great cathedrals. Anyone who questioned the authority of the church was silenced—as was John Wyclif, an English priest who translated the Bible into the vernacular, spoke out against the pope, and questioned other aspects of traditional Catholic doctrine. His followers, called the Lollards, were considered heretics and were suppressed especially after 1377.

In 1517, however, a German priest and university professor named Martin Luther openly protested aspects of what he considered a corrupt church. Luther nailed his objections to indulgences to the church door in Wittenberg. Luther believed that indulgences—pardons for sins that one could purchase from Vatican-authorized vendors, who sold them as a means to ease the pains of Purgatory—were not in accord with biblical principles and were in fact a corrupt practice. With his handwritten Ninety-Five Theses, he did not seek to establish a church separate from Rome, but only to eradicate corruption. Luther's complaints about the church were readily received by thousands of people, however, because the list quickly ended up in the shop of a printer who turned out copies that people could read and discuss. Luther added to the public discussion through a series of sermons and lectures, and he published a book, *Resolutions on the Ninety-Five Theses,* in 1518. The Wittenberg doctor published a total of thirty works—more than 300,000 total copies—by 1520 and referred to printing as "God's highest and extremest act of grace." Others discontent with the Roman Catholic Church wrote and published, too. About seventy years after Johann Gutenberg introduced movable type with a press, the printing of ideas was revolutionizing and reforming Europe. Or, as A. G. Dickens said, "For the first time in human history a great reading public judged the validity of revolutionary ideas through a mass-medium which used the vernacular languages together with the arts of the journalist and cartoonist."

Though Henry VIII ruled England firmly, Reformation ideas could not be kept out of the Isles. Not long after Luther began writing in Germany, his works crossed the Channel into England. Henry personally reacted to them in 1521, and he used the same tool the reformers did—the printing press. The king's book, *Defense of the Seven Sacraments,* addressed Luther's complaints about the church, and it earned Henry the title *Fidei Defensores* (Defender of the Faith), a title he would use to create his own church thirteen years later. Henry and his cardinal, Thomas Wolsey, found another way to silence the German reformer: They ordered Luther's worked destroyed. In 1526, Cardinal Wolsey presided as Luther's works burned in Cambridge. But destruction of Luther's writings could not stop the influx of new ideas and information. Later that year, a New Testament translated into English by William Tyndale arrived in England. Just as Wyclif's translation met with disdain from the church, so, too, did Tyndale's, which was based closely on Luther's work. Tyndale hoped that all Englishmen would one day be able to read scripture for themselves, not depend upon priests. Two years later, he published *The Obedience of a Christian Man* and had it smuggled into England. The work attacked Henry's 1527 announcement that he would seek an annulment of his marriage to Catharine of Aragon.

Less than sixty years after the printing press arrived in England, and less than ten after Luther's church-shattering theses appeared, Britons increasingly were turning to the printed word to voice what was on their minds. The concept that people had the right to think and act for themselves surely was not completely new. That they questioned the very fabric that held the nation together—its religion and its ruler—also was not new. But using printed documents to do so certainly was. The danger of the printed word was immediately recognized by Henry and his closest advisers, which is why Henry reacted so strongly to the works of Luther in 1521.

Those who chose to speak what was on their minds and in their hearts also realized the power of the printed word. Those who desired to profess their conscience increasingly believed that publishing freely was a right given by God. This battle between those who wanted to control the press and those who wanted to publish their ideas would influence much of what happened in England for the next two-plus centuries. Printing was more of the means than the ends, but, ultimately, those who wanted to voice their thoughts had to justify the rights of printing, too. The idea of a free press grew because free expression had to be maintained in order to effect societal change.

Even though Tyndale's writings and English biblical translations caught the eye and ire of Henry's government first, the confrontation between Cambridge-educated John Frith and Henry's lord chancellor, Thomas More, best represents the initial significance of the press in the exposition of freedom of conscience and the beginnings of the development of freedom of the press in England. More was the most important person in England following Henry, and he was the king's front person in the fight to keep Reformation thought out of the British Isles. Because of his education and love for writing, More turned to the press as one means of combating what he considered subversive concepts to Catholicism. He also believed in torture and was no doubt one of England's cruelest in silencing dissent.

Frith, the son of an innkeeper, learned of Reformation thought while at Cardinal College at Oxford, where he taught and studied after attending Cambridge. Frith was more in line with Anabaptist teachings than those of Luther, and as a result, Cardinal Wolsey declared Frith a heretic in 1528. After having been locked up at Oxford, Frith gained his freedom and left for Europe. An attack was about to be launched by English reformers, first upon the Catholic Church and its doctrines and then upon the Church of England, and Frith, from his release until Archbishop of Canterbury Thomas Cranmer ordered him to be burned to death in 1533, was foremost among them.

On the continent, Frith sharpened his ideas about what was important in one's relationship with God. He had his writings published and smuggled into England, beginning in 1529 with *A pistle to the Christian reader: the reuelation of antichrist*. In this work, Frith expounded on the ideas of the Protestant reformers about the priesthood of the believer and the actions of God's grace. Frith rejected the concept of transubstantiation but felt the issue was of little consequence. The elements of the meal were spiritual, and each person could receive the grace they imparted through belief in God's atonement without any intercession from a priest. "Knowleg thy self to be a sinner" is the way that Frith termed it. Thomas More, who studied and wrote on theological issues, could not allow Frith to pick apart the state's religion and the church's *mysterium fidei*. More said that Frith "ronneth a great way beyond Luther, and techeth in a few leuys shortely, all the poyson that Wyclyffe, Huyskyn, Tyndale, and Zuinglius have taught." What Frith was saying, More pointed out, was not new. He was, however, extending the heresy of the radicals of the continent by writing for an English audience.

When Frith returned to England in 1532, More had him arrested. Locked in the Tower of London, Frith was still able to smuggle out writings, which were then published and distributed. More responded in print to Frith, and the imprisoned scholar replied with perhaps the first published statement in England regarding liberty of conscience. Just two weeks before Cranmer ordered Frith burned at the stake, Frith wrote from his cell, "The cause of my death is thys, because I can not in conscience, abiure and sweare, that our Prelates opinion on the sacrament . . . is an vndoubted article of the fayth, necessary to bee leleeued vnder payne of dampnacion." The notion that it was a matter of conscience to persist in unleashing ideas that went against the teachings accepted by governing authorities and refuse to allow them to be controlled, even if that meant being put to death, was now in print and distributed throughout the country.

Henry tried to suppress the writings of Frith, Tyndale, and others immediately and in 1529 issued his *Proclamation for resisting and withstanding of most damnable Heresies,* which sought to stop the importation of writings into England by reformers, including Tyndale and Frith, both of whom published their initial works in Europe and smuggled them into England. The law said that "the king's subjects are likely to be corrupted unless his highness (as Defender of the Faith) do put his most gracious help and royal authority" to ensure that "no person or persons do from henceforth presume to bring into this realm, or do sell, receive, take, or detain any book or work . . . made against the faith catholic." To stop what he considered heretical works from being published in England, in 1530 Henry provided an addendum to his proclamation that established a licensing system for works published by English printers. All publications would have to be reviewed by a local diocese. There, someone would have to vouch that the work to be printed contained no information contrary to the teachings of the church and, subsequently, the throne. Printers were ordered to print the names of those authorizing a work within its text.

Of course, Henry's edicts were not foolproof, as Frith's ability to publish his writings from the tower proved. To make sure that heretical writings were further suppressed, Henry's laws also made it illegal to own any such works. And when the king decided to sever ties with the church in Rome and create his own church, the Church of England, through the Act of Supremacy in 1534, writings in the name of freedom of conscience only increased. Now, the monarchy not only had to deal with the works of reformers, but also with the works of those who viewed the casting aside of the Catholic Church as blasphemous.

One of the great ironic results of the Act of Supremacy was that More was beheaded two years and two days after his polemic enemy, Frith, was executed. More, who tortured and killed numerous Britons in the late 1520s and early 1530s for standing firm to the beliefs of their own conscience, now died for the same reason. The irony was not lost on More, who noted in a letter to John Fisher, his friend and the bishop of Rochester, that the Act of Supremacy was a two-edged sword. It required one either to violate principles of conscience or to commit high treason. Ultimately, More, like Frith, chose the latter.

THE LATER TUDORS

The turmoil in England following the death of Henry VIII in 1547 ensured that more Englishmen would think of religion in terms that differed from Anglicanism. Henry's son, Edward VI, an avowed Protestant, was crowned king at the age of nine and died six years later. Although ultimately he assumed the same heavy-handedness as his father in dealing with dissent, at first he followed the advice of those closest to him—especially Edward Seymour, duke of Somerset. As protector, Somerset, for all practical purposes, ruled England during Edward's early years as king, and he supported religious reformation along Protestant lines. As a result, the licensing that Henry so closely monitored disappeared for several years. Reformation literature readily ran on English presses, after Somerset and the Regency Council drew up and had passed the First Treasons Act in 1547. The act negated much of the harsh punishment that Henry had instituted against dissenting voices, especially on matters "concerning religion and opinion," and stated that no longer should "any pains of death, penalty, or forfeiture in any wise ensue" for such expressions.

The young king's advisers cracked down on Reformation printing after Somerset lost power. In 1551, a proclamation stated that "no printer or other person do print nor sel, within this Realme . . . or otherwise dispose abrode any matter" unless "firste allowed by his maiestie, or his priuie counsayl in writing signed with his maiesties most gratiouis hand or the handes of sixe of his sayd priuie counsayl, vpon payne of Imprisonment, without balye or mayneprice." The opening given to Protestants to publish their beliefs would take more than a licensing law to thwart. Edward's death, however, opened the way for the young king's eldest sister, Mary, to assume the throne. The daughter of Henry's first wife, Catharine, Mary was a Catholic like her mother. With Mary on the throne, Catholicism became England's religion again, and hundreds of Protestants left England for the continent. Others were imprisoned or executed.

For those who left England, though, a new revelation awaited—the teachings and writings of John Calvin, which introduced the concept of the elect to Reformation thought. With Mary's death in 1558, Britons in exile returned to their homeland to live under Elizabeth, and many of them thought this was the perfect chance to purify the English church.

Two books appeared early in the reign of Elizabeth that heightened the desire for individual religious thought and, therefore, the need for free expression. The first was the Geneva Bible, Calvin's scriptural translation, complete with the Geneva doctor's theological exposition of the text to guide the reader's understanding. The second was the work of one of those who had left England during Mary's reign, John Foxe. A fellow at Oxford, Foxe had joined the Marian diaspora in 1554 and worked as a proofreader in Switzerland. He started to collect the stories of people who had been martyred in the cause of their faith by the Catholic Church, focusing particularly on the martyrs of the Protestant Reformation both in Europe and in his native land. Foxe's *Acts and Monuments of these latter perilous days,* which was soon referred to as Foxe's "Book of Martyrs," demonstrated for all who read it that a long line of Christians had been brutalized for acting upon their religious convictions. It also emboldened Englishmen of the time to continue to write and expound upon their personal understanding of religion.

In Tudor England during the Elizabethan Settlement, and especially during the Stuart reign, a voluminous output of writings by Puritans and Separatists, Presbyterians, Levellers, Baptists, Quakers, and many others followed the works of Calvin and Foxe. Though Elizabeth reestablished the Anglican Church as England's official worship, many believed the queen's incarnation of national religion contained too much that was similar to Catholicism. They proposed ways to reform Anglicanism along lines more similar to continental Protestant thought. Other groups concluded that reformation of the state church was not the answer. They believed as the Baptist Thomas Helwys did, who wrote in

1612: "For mens religion to God is betwixt God and themselves; the King shall not answere for it, neither may the King
be iudge between God and Man." These Separatists believed
the nation had an obligation to tolerate expression of religious practices that differed from the Church of England because to worship as one pleased was a right that was beyond
government control. And religious minorities increasingly
couched their arguments of freedom in Enlightenment
terms of rationalism and natural law as they gained a certain
amount of prominence in the middle of the seventeenth
century.

What made liberty of conscience and granting the
right to publish those thoughts so difficult in the sixteenth
and seventeenth centuries, however, was, as J. Sears McGee
has pointed out, the fact that every Presbyterian, Baptist, and
Anglican "viewed the other from behind lenses strongly
tinted by a particular ideal conception of true Christianity."
In other words, many of the religious groups that advocated
most strongly for the right to free expression for themselves
were not as willing to provide carte blanche approval for all
ideas once their beliefs became accepted by the state. Consequently, when the monarchy fell and the commonwealth
was established in 1649, Presbyterian Richard Baxter used
the moment to state exactly what was on his mind. "I abhor
unlimited liberty and toleration for all," he said. Of course,
Presbyterianism had replaced Anglicanism as the state church
of England in the 1640s, and Baxter and other Presbyterians
did not feel as inclined to be inclusive now that they were
Parliament's choice for state worship. Though many believed
as Baxter did, returning England to a time when the politics

and religion of the state claimed universal acceptance was impossible.

In the 1570s and 1580s, a series of publications attacked the state church. Perhaps none was more important than an anonymous tract titled *An Admonition to the Parliament*. Officials soon learned, however, that it was written by Puritans John Field and Thomas Wilcox. The admonition was extremely popular with reformists and went through three publications on a press that Elizabethan officials could never find. Field and Wilcox advocated a form of free expression, declaring that in the early and true form of the church, all people's opinions were heard and mattered: "noble or other, tag and rag, learned and unlearned, of the basest sorte of people," they said, their commentaries were "freely receaved." Most Puritans during Elizabeth's reign knew that the House of Commons was sympathetic to their cause, and that is why the admonition was sent there. And after Field and Wilcox were arrested, the pair added another element to the development of free expression via religious controversy: They claimed protection from punishment for what they had written because it was a petition to a sitting body of Parliament and, as such, gave the writers immunity, according to ancient rights of Britons. Even though Elizabeth reacted negatively, the claim that citizens had the right to petition government to redress grievances would become a part of the fabric of free expression, first in England and then in America, where revolutionary leaders used the concept to state grievances against the British government, and finally as one of the five freedoms included in the First Amendment of the United States.

By 1586, Elizabeth and her advisers, particularly Thomas Whitgift, archbishop of Canterbury, had had enough of Puritan publications that attacked the Church of England. Queen Mary had established the Stationers' Company in 1557, which created a list of printers approved by the government as a means of controlling "seditious and heretical books . . . against us, our crown and dignity, but also to the renewal and propagating very great and detestable heresies against the faith and sound catholick doctrine of holy mother the church." The company still existed, but Elizabeth felt she needed more. Archbishop Whitgift wrote that attacks on church doctrine and upon the queen and state (a discussion on marriage and children for the queen had also entered surreptitious public debate) had to stop. The result was *The newe Decrees of the Starre Chamber for orders in printinge,* which laid out a series of regulations governing the right to print in England. The most important element of the decree established the archbishop of Canterbury and the bishop of London as the sole people who could approve what was printed. Printing could only take place in London and at the colleges of Cambridge and Oxford because "dyvers contentyous and disorderlye persons professinge the arte or myterye of Prynting" had produced "abuses and enormities" against the church and queen. Presses owned by Puritans were to be destroyed.

The queen's new decree surely slowed dissident publications, but it did not stop them. A series of anonymous pamphlets began to appear across England that were signed by "Martin Marprelate, gent." Written in an argumentative style meant more for the everyday Englishman than the clergy, the tracts attacked the episcopal organization of the Church of England. Whitgift immediately set out to find the author and the press from which the tracts were being published. Whitgift ordered searches of the homes of known Puritan authors and the destruction of any materials found, but this did not stop the Marprelate tracts because the press that printed them was constantly moved around the countryside. Authorities finally caught up with the press and destroyed it, though Martin Marprelate was never apprehended.

The Marprelate tracts discussed ecclesiastical issues, but their underlying subtext dealt with the right of people to express themselves via the printed word. The Star Chamber disallowed publications attacking the Church of England, and the Stationers' Company permitted printing by government-approved printers only. The fact that so many people assisted in the production of the Marprelate tracts and helped hide, move, and operate the press that produced them points to a great shift in the English mindset at the end of the sixteenth century. The Tudors from Henry VII through Elizabeth erected barriers to printing with the Star Chamber, the licensing system, the Stationers' Company, and a host of other laws. Still, those who dissented from the state church and elements of England's political climate found ways to share their ideas through assorted underground publications. Neither the destruction of pamphlets and presses nor the execution of "heretics" silenced the religious nonconformists. People discussed the content of dissenters' publications in the public sphere, and, as Frederick Siebert observed about the end of the Tudor reign, "faint stirrings of rebellion were discernible" not only among the people but in Parliament, as well. Three decades after the death of the "virgin queen," revolution would encompass the British Isles. The tool of the revolt would be the printing press.

THE STUARTS AND REVOLUTION

When Elizabeth died without an heir, England turned back to the lineage of Henry VII for a new monarch. James VI of Scotland, son of Mary Stuart and great great grandson of Henry and Elizabeth of York, became James I in 1603. By this time, the long line of reformers to the established religious order believed it was possible for Christian England to have church and state operate within separate spheres— connected, yes, but not identical, and without clerics establishing law or politicians creating dogma. James initially offered the Puritans considerable hope that this division could be obtained. Raised in Scotland and as a Presbyterian, the new king let Presbyterianism become Scotland's religion in 1592. Would he bring Presbyterianism to London?

Britons with strong Anglican ties, however, viewed James I differently. They wondered if he really would embrace Anglicanism since his mother, Mary, was a devout Catholic who had been married to the heir to the throne of France and allied with Spain. Mary also had a claim to England's throne and had contended for it against Elizabeth in 1558, but after several Catholic-inspired plots to wrest rule from Elizabeth, Mary was executed in 1587. In addition, one of the first acts James undertook as king was to make peace with Spain. Would the king revert back to the religion of his mother and give Catholics a chance to regain some measure of control in England?

James quickly made his religious policies known. At the 1604 Hampton Court Conference, the new king belittled the Puritans who were allowed to speak. He quickly aligned himself with the Church of England and made it known that all his subjects in England would do the same as he proudly announced, "no bishop, no king." James, however, reverted more to the ideology of Henry VIII and announced that he ruled by divine right, or, as Siebert explained, "From God through the king all blessings flowed, both secular and ecclesiastical." Silencing the reformers was a good thing to many Anglicans, but James's desire to institute church ritual more in line with that of Catholicism created suspicion. As a result, Puritans distrusted him and, increasingly, so did many Anglicans, who joined the Puritans in their efforts to change the church. James, however, felt that Puritans and Catholics alike were his enemies, because in order to be able to worship as they pleased, each increasingly needed for church and state to be separate.

James's dogmatic view of the inseparableness of church and state immediately caused problems. The House of Commons, just as it had been during the end of Elizabeth's reign, was sympathetic to the Puritan cause, but members of Parliament (MPs) also liked the idea of some separation between political and religious matters. They viewed Parliament as the correct place for political policy to be developed. This did not fit with James's concepts of the nature of the state. Now the king would have to combat dissent on two levels, religious and political. Even though some MPs may have viewed the two subjects as independent, they were still nearly inseparable at the beginning of the seventeenth century, and that is the way James viewed them. As a result,

James created—and his son Charles expounded upon—a means of curtailing expression: seditious libel.

In order to create a law that would silence dissent, the Stuart government first returned to medieval law. In 1275, the English crown had created the law of *Scandalum Magnatum,* which prevented any discussion of king and government. This law said that allowing unlimited debate on these topics was dangerous, that anyone found guilty of this type of discussion could be imprisoned, and that only the truth of the statements could prevent prosecution. James expanded upon *Scandalum Magnatum* through the auspices of the Star Chamber and eradicated the truth defense in 1606 when the court heard the case *de Libelous Famosis.* Now, any statement that ridiculed or lowered the public's view of the government was a libel. Truth, in fact, made the statement more libelous, according to the Star Chamber decision, and almost any statement that did not overtly support the Stuart monarchy could be construed as a libel. To add to the crown's ability to control debate, the ruling in *de Libelous Famosis* made publishing offensive material a libelous act. Not only was the author guilty of libel, the person who printed it was, too.

In response to these developments, many of the growing number of Puritans concluded that the purification of the Anglican Church was impossible. They joined the growing ranks of Separatists, many of whom left England for the Netherlands, and continued to write and publish. In 1620, other Britons, thoroughly fed up with the religious intolerance in their homeland, sailed to America to begin a new life free from prescribed Stuart worship. Increasingly, the British colonies in the New World became the refuge for religious dissenters, despite the dangers of life in America.

In the same year that the first ship sailed and landed at Plymouth in America, the House of Commons reacted to James's political alliances in Europe, which heightened the fear that Catholicism would obtain a new foothold in England and initiated debate on the king's actions. James chastised the body, telling it that "freedome of speech . . . are no Theames, or subjects fit for vulgar persons, or common meetings," and that Commons had no right to discuss matters of state. Commons responded by telling the king that every member had the right to speak freely on questions that determined the welfare of the nation. Matters of state and church had been debated on their own merits since the time of Henry VIII. By the first decades of the seventeenth century, however, people began to view discussion of them as part of a basic societal right to speak freely on any subject that affected the people's welfare.

Following the death of James in 1625, his son Charles I assumed power. Charles was very much his father's son. He continued his father's policies and even made it more difficult for Puritans and Separatists to operate openly. As a result, the nonconformists were forced underground, especially when William Laud became archbishop of Canterbury. Charles gave Laud carte blanche approval to act in what the archbishop considered the best interests of England and Anglicanism. Laud decreed that no one could be a lecturer or clergyman in any parish without direct licensure from the bishop. Charles also gave the archbishop control of the stationers and printing. Laud ordered a crackdown on printing by any except the nineteen master printers who were legally appointed as of 1636. The next year, a new Star Chamber decree created the most encompassing control over printing that England had seen. Under Laud's direction, the number of master printers was set, as was the number of presses they could operate. Sanctioned printers had to pay a surety fee to guarantee that all items printed were licensed. Everything published had to pass in front of censors, and a copy of the publication was kept so that it could be compared with random issues that appeared in public. Publications could be sold only by authorized vendors.

Though Charles and Laud created laws that on their surface should have controlled nonconformist publications, they did not. Out of sight officially did not mean out of mind practically. Reformers began publishing books, pamphlets, tracts, and sermons in greater numbers than ever, and foreign printers, especially, found that producing the unlicensed literature created large profits. Works from Presbyterian Scotland flooded the English market, and English printers who were not sanctioned by the Stationers' Company printed clandestinely. The result was what William Haller called "the revolt of the pamphleteers." For more than a century, since the time of Tyndale and Frith, Britons—beginning in small numbers but steadily growing to an eruption of voices in the late 1630s—worked to obtain the right to worship and to interpret scripture according to their consciences. The avenue for speaking became, logically, the printed word.

But as time progressed, liberty of conscience in religious matters expanded to include more. Liberty for Britons surely started with the theological, but in the 1640s the revolution that Puritans so wanted in worship in England expanded to include calls for civil liberties and political revolution. Writers continued to quote scripture and use it to proof text their arguments, be the debate religious or civil, but the pamphleteers of the 1640s also injected rationalism, humanism, and secularism into the written debate. The result was a new breed of writer who was more enlightened than those of the sixteenth century. These new rational explanations would infuse themselves into the religious dialogue, especially that of the more radical Separatists, such as the Baptists, Levellers, and Quakers. In the late seventeenth century and into the eighteenth, Enlightenment thought would guide the nation as the laws against printing dropped away one by one.

As the polemicists presented their arguments on religion and on the nature of the English political order, they increasingly added statements in support of the right to free speech. Within a single tract on religious liberty, a reader could find an apology for religious freedom, admonitions for changes in English civil law, and statements supporting a free press. "'Tis common freedome every man ought to aime at, which is every mans peculiar right," the Leveller William Walwyn wrote in 1644 in support of religious liberty. On Parliament's duty to civil law, Walwyn said, "'tis the principall interest of the Commonwealth, that Authority should have equall respect, and afford protection to all peaceable good men alike." And, on liberty of the press, Walwyn added, at the end of his pamphlet, his hope "That the Presse may be free for any man."

Politically, the late 1630s and the 1640s found England on the verge of more than a polemical revolution. John Lilburne, another nonconformist Leveller sent to the stocks by the Star Chamber for pamphleteering, published the proceedings of his trial, which also gave an account of his punishment by the king's Star Chamber and council. Inside its cover, the anonymous printer added these words: "To speake what I thinke, my minde gives me, that the Lord is now vpon extinguishing the bloody Prelates out of our Land." That is what Parliament did. Reacting to Charles's heavy-handedness, the body, earlier dismissed by the king, reconvened later in 1640 and did not adjourn. The Long Parliament, as it came to be called, remained in session for twenty years. During that time, the Parliamentarians gradually wrested power from the monarchy and changed the state church to Calvinistic Presbyterianism—arresting, trying, and eventually executing Archbishop Laud. Charles continued to cling to the concept of the divine right of kings, which would ultimately ensure that he would keep an appointment with the executioner's blade. Before that happened in 1649, however, a number of events transpired that affected press freedom.

One of the Long Parliament's first acts was to attack the Star Chamber. Since Henry VII's reign, the Star Chamber had served as the monarchy's enforcement arm. It operated outside the purview of England's legislative body, with church officials generally playing a central role in determining what material was offensive. Parliament officially abolished the Star Chamber in July 1641. In conjunction with this, the Stationers' Company, which had established who had the right to print, the number of presses, and other aspects of publishing in England, lost power. Printers were more concerned with their incomes than with administrative squabbles. Consequently, the nation's printers scurried to realign themselves with Parliament. Both acts, the abolishment of the Star Chamber and the stationers' shift of loyalty to

Parliament instead of the crown, left England temporarily without controls on printing. It was, as Frederick Siebert said, a time when "Political and religious controversialists suddenly found the press open to them. The underprivileged printers, who had chafed since the days of Elizabeth under the restrictions of the monopolists, took immediate advantage of the destruction of enforcement agencies."

The great changes in power in England ultimately led to civil war. Charles mustered his army, but too many of his subjects in England, Scotland, and Ireland were tired of the royal prerogative. The Scots readily aided the war effort because of England's adoption of Presbyterianism, and the Irish joined in an effort to break free of London. Puritan forces, as well as those of Scotland and Ireland, organized by Oliver Cromwell, turned back those of the king at Marston Moor in 1644. That victory, for all intents and purposes, ended any power the monarchy held over England. Charles would not surrender, though, and was taken into custody in 1647. Even Parliament was divided on what should happen next, but those who wanted to abolish the monarchy were able to control events. With only members of Commons who were willing to do so allowed to enter sessions, the Rump, as it was called, for the small number of legislators present, abolished the monarchy and the House of Lords in 1648. The king lost his head the next year.

The events of the 1640s had mixed results for printing. Parliament, after gaining control of the state, instituted its own press controls. The king and the Star Chamber were out, but Parliament as the controlling agency was in. Anglican authority was gone, but Presbyterian ideology replaced it. The Stationers' Company was reorganized but continued to control who could print and what could be printed. Part of the problem with civil war, however, is that fighting to unseat the crown required a number of fighters. Many of those who offered to fight with Cromwell were the more radical of the Separatists—Levellers, Ranters, and Baptists. These groups favored a more democratic organization of church and state. They saw no need for bishops, and they believed church and state had to be separate. Levellers, as the name implied, wanted to level society in order to create a country where all people were more equal. Some of the more dynamic writers of the late 1640s were Levellers. The radical nonconformists, because of the role they played in helping to topple the king, became bolder in their assertions and demands.

At the top of the list, for many of the radical Separatists, was a call for political and ecclesiastical separation and freedom of the press. They minced no words in their writings. "That you will open the Press, whereby all trecherous and tyrannical designes may be the easier discovered, and so prevented, which is a liberty of greatest concernment to the Commonwealth, and which such only as intend a tyrannie are engaged to prohibit," John Lilburne wrote in *Englands New Chaines*. It was part of a Leveller demand that Parliament revoke all prohibitions against printing. In a second petition, Lilburne expounded and explained the folly of licensing:

> if Government be just in its Constitution, and equal in its distributions, it will be good, if not absolutely necessary for them to hear all voices and judgments, which they can never do, but by giving freedom to the Press. . . . And therefore all things being duly

> weighed, to refer all Books and Pamphlets to the
> judgment, discretion, or affection of Licensers . . .
> seems altogether inconsistent with the good of the
> Commonwealth, and expressly opposite and dan-
> gerous to the liberties of the people, and to be care-
> fully avoided, as any other exorbitancy of prejudice
> in Government.

Parliament did not buy Lilburne's and the Levellers' claims.
Instead, a new piece of legislation added seditious printing to
the list of items that were treasonous in England. Lilburne
was arrested under the new law but acquitted by a jury. By
1650, Parliament considered itself still in control of what was
printed in England, but too much had been committed to
paper and flowed from the country's presses to ever expect
total control of information again.

In the middle of all the events of the 1640s, John Milton, a Puritan writer disgruntled with state policies concerning divorce, wrote an essay entitled *Areopagitica*. Although it
was not at the top of the reading list during the tumultuous
1640s, Milton still stated eloquently the foundation of why
a free press was needed by civil society and why it would only
enhance it and the lives of the people. Few people know the
names of the radicals who wrote at the time; people know
Milton, though. His words have become a starting point for
any discussion of free expression, no doubt because he was a
more eloquent writer than his contemporaries. And while
most in England never glimpsed *Areopagitica* immediately
after publication, Lilburne and other noncomformists did.
They read *Areopagitica* closely and borrowed from its leaves.
Milton did not intend from his writing to grant the unlimited freedom of expression that Lilburne seems to have

advocated, but taken out of context, that was the meaning derived.

Around the time that England passed the Act of Toleration (1689) and into the eighteenth century, Milton's tract became a principal source to quote or paraphrase when arguing for free expression. Writers pivotal to the arguments for a free press early in the eighteenth century, such as John Trenchard and Thomas Gordon—the authors of the famous "Cato" essays—turned often to Milton. Milton's writing incorporated logic and reason. As *Areopagitica* was "discovered" later in the century, it was probably so accepted by those advocating acceptance of liberty of conscience and free speech because it fit so well with the new and prevailing Enlightenment concepts that other writers, such as John Locke and David Hume, introduced into public dialogue. Milton couched his rationalism in religious terms, which fit the times in which he wrote. The Cambridge-educated writer said that when God created man, "God gave him reason, he gave him freedom to choose, for reason is but choosing." At the same time that God gave humans reason, he created truth, which "came once into the world with her divine Master." For Milton, if God created truth, then it was only rational that, ultimately, God's creation would choose truth when presented with all options. "Give me liberty to know, to utter, and to argue freely according to conscience, above all liberties," Milton wrote, concluding with the lines that are so celebrated: "Let [Truth] and Falsehood grapple; who ever knew Truth put to the worse in a free and open encounter."

As England approached and then entered the period of the Protectorate, the arguments for free expression and liberty of conscience had taken shape. Religion remained at the core of most arguments. Rational thought increasingly aided the dispute. Even though the Star Chamber and other means of controlling printing had either been abolished or curtailed, however, Britons in power, and many who maintained no political clout, could still not conceive of a public sphere that operated in the manner of Lilburne that advocated letting voices be heard. It certainly could not accept the notion of Baptist-turned-Seeker Roger Williams that Roman Catholics, Jews, Muslims, Christians, and even atheists be allowed religious freedom and a voice in society. Milton's idea, which would allow nearly all speech—except that of the most extreme and evil (for Milton, that being Roman Catholics)—was not acceptable, either, but it was more palatable than the ideas of nonconforming religious radicals. The ideas of Lilburne and Williams would eventually gain credence in the United States, but not completely in the period before the passage of the First Amendment— or, in the eyes of many, ever. As a result, the battle for freedom of conscience and religious liberty would continue with Oliver Cromwell and the Protectorate passing new laws to curtail the press.

THE INTERREGNUM TO TOLERATION

By the middle of the 1600s, a number of newsbooks and news pamphlets were regularly being published in London, but they were more concerned with the political elements of the nation, now without a monarchy. Because religion could never be completely separated from politics, these newssheets often attacked nonconformists. So many of the radical nonconformists had fought with Cromwell that he promised them—and they, initially, believed—that England would move into a period of religious toleration. Cromwell disbanded Parliament in 1655 (though this was not recognized by the MPs) and reestablished a form of licensing. The licensing system was aimed more at the proliferation of newssheets than at religious pamphlets, however, and even though it limited the number of printers, Cromwell's government was generally lenient on nonconformists and those who printed pamphlets for them (though some dissenters were punished for their publications). After the lord protector's death in 1658 and the passing of political leadership to his son Richard, however, constraints upon free worship gradually were curtailed. Richard was not as powerful a figure as his father had been and lost control of England to Parliament in 1659. Within a year, the monarchy would be reestablished, with Charles II wearing the crown.

The return of the monarchy and the Stuart line would mean a crackdown on religious toleration in England, not so much because Charles wanted it, however. Charles had strong Catholic leanings and advocated toleration in his April 1660 Declaration of Breda, his statement of resumption of the monarchy. There, he stated: "And because the passion and uncharitableness of the times have produced several opinions in religion, by which men are engaged . . . we do declare a liberty to tender consciences, and that no man shall be disquieted or called in question for differences of opinion in matter of religion, which do not disturb the peace of the kingdom." Because Parliament now wielded more power than ever, and Anglicans and even some Presbyterians believed nonconformists needed to suffer for their actions during the preceding fifteen years, Charles's statement carried little value. The following January, Charles agreed that "all such persons going under the notion of anabaptists, quakers, and other sectaries, henceforward not to meet, under pretence of service." The toleration that seemed likely to create true liberty of conscience and expression for nonconformists in the 1650s was quickly evaporating.

By 1662, a reconfigured Parliament composed almost entirely of Anglicans reinstituted a new licensing act aimed directly at religious dissenters and freedom of conscience. The act stated that "no person or persons whatsoever shall presume to print or cause to be printed . . . any heretical, seditious, schismatical or offensive books or pamphlets, wherein any doctrine or opinion shall be asserted or maintained which is contrary to the Christian faith or the doctrine of discipline of the Church of England." The law did not stop publications by dissenters, however, and enforcement of it often depended more on the degree of bribes and perks that could be obtained by surveyors of the press, appointed to stop heretical and seditious printing, than on the language of the publication. Still, for books or pamphlets that dealt with matters religious, philosophical, or scientific to be published and sold legally, approval from a required licensee—the archbishop of Canterbury, the bishop of London, or a chancellor from Oxford or Cambridge—was required.

The attack on the Baptist minister and apologist Benjamin Keach was one example of implementation of the new licensing act. Keach became a chief spokesman for Calvinistic Separate Baptists from the early 1660s through the rest of the century. In 1664, he published a primer to be used in the home-schooling of Baptist children and others who might believe similarly to Baptists. Because the primer advocated believer baptism, a direct contradiction to Anglican infant baptism, and served as a replacement for the Book of Common Prayer, the chief justice ordered Keach's books confiscated and burned. Guards dragged Keach from his pulpit and ordered him bound and laid in the street, where the horses of the guard were to trample the minister to death. For some reason, the captain of the guard intervened, and for the next fortnight Keach was paraded from town to town and humiliated in public stocks. Later, after he published another primer for children, he went to prison for two years. That Keach's life was spared, and he went on to write and publish more than forty tracts, pamphlets, and confessions of faith attacking tenets of the Church of England and advocating liberty of conscience without again being arrested or hassled to any great degree, demonstrates the sporadic approach to enforcing licensing that existed in the 1660s and 1670s. Other Baptists, Quakers, and even Presbyterians, for example, were regularly jailed for their preaching and pamphlets.

When James II succeeded his brother in 1685, he moved to suspend any impediments to worship of any kind in the Declaration of Indulgence, but this was seen as a means to reestablish Catholicism in England. Only the most radical of nonconformists believed that heretics such as Catholics should be allowed the right to open worship or the ability to hold public office. James soon proved that those who suspected his aim was to elevate Catholicism to the state church were correct. Revolution, again, was in England's future, but this time it would be bloodless. Members of Parliament contacted William of Orange of the Netherlands. William was a Protestant married to James's eldest daughter,

Mary, also a Protestant. He was also the son of Mary, the daughter of Charles I. William's army invaded England; James, whose troops fled as he marched them into battle, decided not to meet his adversary and abdicated.

William and Mary assumed the throne of England. The change produced a series of new laws in 1689. One was *An Act Declaring the Rights and Liberties of the Subjects,* or the Bill of Rights. While it did not provide Britons with a total right to free speech and free press, it did guarantee "That it is the right of the subjects to petition the King, and all commitments and prosecutions for such petitioning are illegal." Redressing grievances was now protected by law. A second decree, the Toleration Act, now made it legal for all to worship freely in England other than Catholics and Unitarians, provided they take an oath to the government. The act even made certain exceptions for groups such as Baptists and Quakers who refused to take such oaths. "At last," according to George M. Trevelyan, "the time had come when English Protestants were ready to let one another worship God. All their parties were exhausted with fifty years of revolution, bloodshed and terror, culminating in the recent narrow escape of their common religion."

Toleration did not mean that all writings would be tolerated, however. England still operated under a printing act that had had various clauses added to it during the Stuart restoration. Parliament renewed the law in 1692 for two years. When it came up for renewal again, sufficient opposition to it in the House of Commons ensured that licensing would end, despite several successive attempts to revive it that occurred even into the eighteenth century. According to Frederick Siebert, the entire purpose of the printing act had been to suppress objectionable printing. That objective, members of Commons said, had failed. Punishments were meted out unevenly. Parliament was no longer arguing about the danger of unlicensed printing. Instead, MPs worried whether one faction of the new two-party system would gain the upper hand. Concerns on liberty of conscience in matters religious were giving way to matters political where members of each party feared the other would obtain political control by means of the press. Censoring by one party meant that the same could occur in reverse at a later date.

England at the end of the seventeenth century did not grant freedom of the press in its Bill of Rights, but the press, in the form of newspapers, was about to erupt. Religious questions would still arise, especially with the pietistic movement of the eighteenth century. Now, however, the question of the development of a free press rested more with the newssheets than with the pamphleteers who fought for liberty of conscience and religious toleration. There, savvy writers would raise political questions that still irked Parliament and the crown and brought on accusations of seditious libel. Writers would also begin to hone the argument for freedom of the press, not purely in religious terms, but along logical and rational lines. Religious writers had not ignored Enlightenment thought in the seventeenth century, but now it would come to the forefront. How newssheets developed and affected the development of a free press, and the arguments of major writers for its validity, constitute the main topics of the next chapters.

THREE

ENGLISH ORIGINS—NEWS

In 1548, during the second year of the reign of Edward VI, a London newsbook proclaimed that there was a "thursty desyer that all our kynde hath to know." The writer of those lines was simply stating what had been obvious for more than two millennia: People want and need to know what is going on around them, whether the information affects their lives and livelihood or just entertains. Long before the printing press, people found ways of knowing. Handwritten scrolls and books, of course, served the purpose, but so, too, did traveling jesters, who wove the information of the day into acts, skits, and stories for those they entertained. The printing press made the process of sharing information simpler, at least in terms of preparation and dissemination.

The development of a free press owed more to the religious dissenters in the sixteenth and seventeenth centuries than to newswriters because religious issues and the right to worship according to the dictates of conscience were critical to living a full life. People did have a "thursty desyer" to know what was happening, but a life aligned with God's will and assurance of a proper afterlife were of more importance to most people. Or, as John Locke would say in *A Letter Concerning Toleration,* "The end of a religious society . . . is the public worship of God, and, by means thereof, the acquisition of eternal life." Knowing what was happening on the continent or in some location other than England was within the realm of possibility for those with power and influence. Still, over time, and as colonialism opened and elevated many both economically and socially within British society, news became important to more and more people. For that reason, those who had controlled information for so many years worked to ensure that they remained privy to knowledge through limits on what could be published, what could be said in publications, and who could print. Success in controlling information, however, was never completely successful.

As the second aspect of the origins of a free press within England and then America, newssheets ultimately became the place where polemicists expounded upon the concept that a free press was a fundamental right. Newsbooks, broadsides, pamphlets, and even printed ballads provided sources of information in England before newssheets became *corantos* (a name derived from the Dutch, for "current," to describe the earliest newspapers), probably during the end of the reign of James I. The eruption of newspapers, however, came after the Act of Toleration in 1689 and following Parliament's refusal to renew licensing when it expired in 1694. Much of papers' polemical content coincided with the spread of Enlightenment thought. News, however, was shared in printed form much earlier than that.

THE FIRST NEWS SOURCES
AND GOVERNMENT CONTROL

The first printed sources of news to run afoul of printing laws hit the streets of London in 1540. Ballads and broadsides attacking Henry VIII's chief minister, Thomas Cromwell, sent their printers to jail. Cromwell's execution and the charges of sedition against the printers, however, were wrapped in the religious controversy of the day—in the upheaval created by Henry's rejection of the Catholic Church and formation of the Church of England. But most printed news sources of the sixteenth century had more to do with moralization than with factual news accounts. According to Sandra Clark, news in the 1500s "placed relatively little stress on precise factual detail: the names, places, dates, and figures which are so essential to modern reporting were often very summarily treated." People also believed sensational occurrences were an example of some truth greater than they could understand. Consequently, specifics were of less importance in the first forms of printed news in England than what the events could reveal about greater cosmic truths.

Because of the nature of the earliest news to appear in England, little effort was made to censor it. Or, perhaps, no one who wanted to produce a newsbook or pamphlet objected greatly to the laws established by the Tudors to control printing, and as a result did not print news that might be considered subversive by the crown. Instead, they printed news exclusively based in events outside of the British Isles. In the sixteenth century, at least in terms of producing newsbooks and the like, few Britons—including printers—had problems with the royal prerogative, which gave the crown control of who could print and what those printers could produce, except John Wolfe. A fishmonger, according to what was known of him, Wolfe wanted to be a printer and was, except he was not a member of the Stationers' Company. Consequently, he was officially banned from printing. Wolfe did not let legality stop him. He printed and even organized other unlicensed printers in protest. Wolfe was not interested in printing any material that might add to the controversy surrounding the rising Puritanism in Queen Elizabeth's realm. He was interested in secular printing. "I am that one man, that must and will reforme the governement in this trade," Wolfe said of his efforts to open the printing trade in England.

Wolfe became a member of the Stationers' Company shortly after his organized protests began, and he appears to have been satisfied once he was a member of the privileged class of printers and ended his protests. But Wolfe's complaints about governmental control of printing provided a genesis for an argument for free speech, just as the Reformation writers did, though perhaps without as much moral foundation as those in the 1580s who were demanding a right to print based on the dictates of conscience. Wolfe was demanding a right to make a living at a trade, and to deny anyone that ability was to deny a person of a basic right. In order to make a living, Wolfe was saying that he had a right to publish. In eighteenth-century America, printer Thomas Fleet claimed the same privilege after publishing material considered offensive by readers. "I had a prospect of getting a Penny by it," Fleet replied in his *Boston Evening-Post*. The right to print would become a part of the fabric of a free press—the idea that for government to say who could publish and what could be published was a violation of basic human rights.

In the 1590s, Wolfe printed the majority of the news-books that appeared in London concerning the Protestant and Catholic wars in France that ultimately put Henry Navarre on the throne. These reports ran to thirty or more pages and consisted of official government information along with letters written from the French battlefields. There was little need for Elizabeth's government to censor content because it provided much of what was printed. In addition, the likelihood that any printer would publish anything pro-Catholic in a newsbook was remote. Still, the fact that news-books were allowed to exist and were so available in London during the 1590s created what one printer called the "greedy purchaser of news," and what Paul Voss described as a "news revolution" in England, where at least one-fourth of all items published dealt with current affairs. When one considers the religious turmoil that was developing at the end of the sixteenth century and official documents that were printed, this is truly a sizable percentage of what English printing presses produced.

Londoners at the turn of the seventeenth century and onward understood the word "news" differently than might be expected. News meant a news publication, and the term was used repeatedly in contemporary literature in that way. The term "newspaper" would not be introduced into the vocabulary until after the restoration of the monarchy in 1660. When William Shakespeare wrote, "What news from France?" in *2 Henry VI,* he was referring to the newssheets that Wolfe and others published, not just information. In fact, Voss said that many of the lines in the Henry VI plays sound like extractions from the news quartos printed at the time. Society readily accepted the newsbooks and sheets, and their terminology became engrained into the language of the day. This, combined with the fact that the news quartos of the Elizabethan period escaped, for the most part, the censor's touch, opened the way for regularly produced single-sheet publications in the 1620s. In fact, by 1624, the idea of obtaining news via newssheets was so common in England that Thomas Lushington, preaching at Oxford, began a sermon by asking, "What's the best News abroad?" He proceeded to frame his sermon in what he considered the nature of England's current information network—"the Chronicle-News." Lushington's question is also important in understanding the focus of information in the early printed news sources in England: They dealt almost exclusively with events that occurred in places other than the British Isles. This, naturally, steered the censors away from them. More-over, the publications by religious dissenters surely kept the Star Chamber busy. The content of English-language newssheets was about to change, however, and with that change came more scrutiny from government.

By the 1620s, the religious controversy that had erupted when Henry dumped the Catholic Church and es-tablished the Church of England, and that had continued with the rise of Puritans and Separatists, began appearing in newssheets. Publications from the Netherlands called *coran-tos,* or currents of news, quickly crossed the English Chan-nel. The Netherlands was home to many disenfranchised Separatists who had left England in order to worship accord-ing to the dictates of their conscience. These dissenters prob-ably had nothing to do with the corantos printed in the Netherlands and exported to England, but the fact that they were free to live and worship there as they pleased reveals something about the nature of the Netherlands at the time. It was a more accepting place that had sympathies with the more radical elements of Protestantism than Stuart England. This was revealed in the way the corantos presented news of the Thirty Years' War in the German Palatinate, which was highly sympathetic to Protestants and raised the ire of James I, who did not think that the people should comment on the affairs of the monarchy.

In response, James issued a proclamation to halt "discourse concerning the state," and the Stationers' Company moved to make the inevitable publication of an English gazette possible only through governmental license. In late 1621, the Stationers gave Nathaniel Butter and Nicholas Bourne sole propriety to publish a coranto in England. With permission came the imprimatur that would be used to control newspapers as much as possible during the seventeenth century in England and the early eighteenth in America. Butter and Bourne could publish a gazette, but it would be "published by authority," meaning its contents were subject to approval of the government. At the same time, the Stationers sought ways to keep the Dutch corantos out of England, but they were unsuccessful.

The political situation in England under Charles I, as seen in Chapter 2, eventually escalated into civil war, the beheading of the king, and the dissolution of monarchy. The rising controversy, naturally, found its way into the gazettes. Butter and Bourne and other publishers were also producing pamphlets sympathetic to the rising opposition to Charles and his advisers. The result was a total suppression of newssheets in 1632, but the law simply sent those who wanted to report on events underground, just as it did the nonconformists who produced religious pamphlets. By 1640, the Long Parliament was in the process of ridding the country of vestiges of monarchial control such as the Star Chamber and the Stationers' Company. As a result, a number of newssheets appeared in London. The new gazettes concentrated on the actions of Parliament and were often referred to as "diurnals."

The vacuum of power created for the first time in England a press that represented two sides of the political upheaval that had the nation on the brink of civil war—papers that supported either parliamentary rule or continued dominion by the royalist monarchy. Because of the dissolution of the Star Chamber and the Stationers' Company, to a certain extent the papers were left to operate in the never-before-experienced realm of free enterprise. The competition, however, was often more between papers of the same faction than between opposing ideologies, since support for parliamentary rule was greater than support for the monarchy.

As important as free competition was to the press, however, it was ideology that shaped the nature of the press in the 1640s. Though the competition would be short-lived because Oliver Cromwell's 1644 defeat of Charles's forces at Marston Moor virtually assured the demise of the monarchy and of the periodicals that might support it, this brief period introduced the idea of a partisan press and calls for a free press. The partisan press of colonial America would, 125 years later, demand the right of free press for itself as it took on what its Patriot mouthpieces considered a dictatorial and oppressive British government. At the same time, those same people who advocated the right to speak freely for themselves worked to silence any opposition, going so far as to destroy Loyalist print shops. American Patriots, just like the majority of their English forefathers, did not totally grasp the notion that a free press meant freedom for multiple voices and factions. That notion, one could argue, took centuries to accomplish if it was ever attained at all. In England in the 1640s, though, *Mercurius Aulicus* (the Court Mercury) and *Mercurius Britanicus* (the Mercury of Britain) carried on a lengthy partisan assault against each other.

Still, 1644 was a pivotal year in the development of freedom of the press. At least twelve papers competed for readers in London, each with a circulation of between 250 and 1,000, leading Joseph Frank to estimate that nearly half of all literate males in London regularly read papers. The fact that this was the same year that John Milton proposed competition in the form of truth and falsehood in public dialogue in *Areopagitica,* and that the Leveller William Walwyn advocated "That the Presse may be free for any man" in his anonymously published *The Compassionate Samaritane,* should not be forgotten. At the same time, John Robinson, who was basically nonpartisan, wrote, "this combat therefore must be fought out upon eaven ground, on equall termes, neither side must expect to have greater liberty of speech, writing, Printing, or whatsoever else, then the other." The year 1644 was important in the development of a free press because the lack of true political control of the nation allowed, for a brief time, open competition among publications for readers and for the exchange of ideas, even though Parliament attempted to control newssheets through some form of licensing. Polemicists readily espoused notions of the significance of a free press. People also had the opportunity to take sides and advocate positions without government restrictions. Even though this openness would end in less than four years, one could see at this time, in both newssheets and pamphlets, how the exchange of ideas might play out in the realm of public opinion where dialogue was not suppressed. The fact that either side would end free discourse once the power vacuum was filled is also important. Britons were not ready to allow complete and open debate on matters political and religious, but the foundation for doing so had been laid. Writers would soon begin to advocate regularly the necessity of this free exchange of ideas, but not before England grappled a bit longer with what a free press entailed and would mean to the nation.

REGAINING CONTROL OF THE PRESS

In September 1647, the openness of the press that had allowed the proliferation of newspapers during the preceding few years was ordered to end. With Charles in the custody of the New Model Army, Sir Thomas Fairfax, its commander, demanded that the House of Lords take control of the country's press. Fairfax's directive said that "Two or Three Sheets may be permitted to come out Weekly, which may be licensed, and have some Stamp of Authority with them." Lords acquiesced and established a new censor for the nation. During the next two years, five different newsbooks received official licensing, but the decree to trim the number of publications that were "scandalous and abusive . . . to the whole Kingdome in general" did not stop nonlicensed newssheets from appearing on London's streets.

Following the beheading of Charles, however, England's new commonwealth government found ways to limit production of newssheets. The 1649 Act of Treason elevated seditious writings to a capital offense, something that had not been law in England for one hundred years. Everything that was published had to be licensed, and Parliament ordered that all newsbooks be suppressed. The government would eventually be successful. The number of individual issues of newsbooks that could be purchased in England fell from 612 in 1648 to 25 in 1657, according to Frederick Siebert, although the number of newsbooks remained strong in 1649, and most were very partisan in their allegiances to Parliament or the monarchy.

By 1649, dozens of Britons had spoken out in support of the right to publish their thoughts based on the premise of liberty of conscience. "To speake what I thinke, my minde gives me" is the way John Lilburne explained the right to publish concerning his religious beliefs. Now with the government limiting the number of legal newssheets that could be printed, some apologists included the corantos in their liturgy of documents that deserved access to a free press. The most unlikely of champions arose for newssheets and political pamphlets—Gilbert Mabbott. Immediately after the House of Lords ordered the licensing and limiting of newsbooks, it appointed Mabbott chief censor of the press. Mabbott had previously worked in printing, and a government position was certainly more secure than the printing trade of the 1640s. Mabbott obviously read a number of the pamphlets and other items that his office was required to license, along with others that published surreptitiously and promoted the right to speak freely on matters of conscience and to discuss political issues openly, estimated at more than 2,500 published on political issues alone in

1647–1648. He increasingly adopted an anticensorship attitude, though he did not give up his job as censor.

In July 1648, Mabbott picked up a second job. He assumed the editorship of a newssheet called *The Moderate.* The paper allowed Mabbott a forum for his ideas on the press, and it served as a platform for John Lilburne, the outspoken Leveller polemicist who had been calling for a free and open press for a number of years and for a more democratic or "level" form for English society. First, Mabbott—in language that preceded that of John Locke and the independence rhetoric of eighteenth-century America—explained that government was a device of the people. Those who served as political leaders did so by the people's will. If they made laws that harmed the people, those laws could be negated, and the people, justly, could remove their leaders from positions of authority. In the November 7, 1648, issue of *The Moderate,* Mabbott proclaimed: "The laws and Government of this land, being Tirannous and Arbitrary, and destructive to the freedome of the people, may be lawfully taken away by the people. . . . All Powers and Authorities, either by King or Parliament, acting against . . . the people are void by the Laws of God, man and nature: the people . . . give these powers and Authorities, expecting they should not abuse their Trust in acting against the good of their Electees . . . because the servant cannot be above his master."

Mabbott continued his rhetoric into 1649, which raised calls for suppression of *The Moderate* from other government officials. Finally, Mabbott resigned his post as chief censor in early May. Two weeks later, he explained why he resigned as he attacked the entire system of licensing and press control in the pages of a number of newssheets, including the May 28 issue of *The Perfect Diurnal,* a paper title that had been used for a number of newssheets since early in the decade. First, having a censor was immoral and illegal, he said, "Because that Imployment . . . is unjust and ilegall as to the end of its first Institution, viz. To stop the Presse for publishing any thing that might discover the Corruption of the Church or State . . . and carry on their Popish, Factious, Trayterous and Tyrannical designes for the enslaving and distruction both of the bodies and soules of all the free people of this Nation." Next, Mabbott said, licensing was the great censor of the voice of the people. "Licensing is as great a Monopoly as ever was in this Nation, in that all mens Judgements, Reasons &c. are to be bound up in the Licensers . . . for if the Author of any Sheet, Book or Treatise writ not to please the fancie, and come within the compasse of the Lycencers Judgement, then he is not to receive any stamp of authority for publishing thereof." Finally, Mabbott said anyone should be able to voice opinions, so long as they were willing to take responsibility for what they wrote, "Because it is lawfull . . . to print any Book, sheet, &c. without Lycencing, so as that the Authors and Printers do subscribe their true names thereunto."

The problem for England—if anyone considered implementing what Mabbott, Lilburne, and others suggested in terms of freedom of the press—lay in the fact that the nation had never experienced a period when the press was free to say anything it wanted. No one really knew if allowing an unrestricted press would be good for the nation or its undoing. Most Britons could not conceive of their country operating as Mabbott suggested in *The Moderate,* with king and Parliament as the servants of the public weal who could be removed if they breached their compact with the people. Participatory government was only just beginning for anyone other than the small class of elite noblemen who had taken part for centuries. Even though the House of Lords would be dissolved following Charles's beheading and a commonwealth initiated, England's rising middle class was still more attuned to the economic than the political. Plus, they had no practical experience in government. That would come later.

In the 1650s, printing via movable type was only two hundred years old, and the tenets of the Protestant Reformation—which constituted the first challenge to strict church-state precepts since the emergence of printing—had existed only slightly more than a 125 years. The English monarchy from Henry VIII forward had established laws curtailing printing that questioned the actions of state and church. So, after a decade in which the nation was in turmoil and printers were essentially allowed to print as they pleased, reining publications in, be they newsbooks or religious pamphlets, would be difficult. Journalism had become, according to Frederick Siebert, "a permanent social and political phenomenon. Once the public had become interested and aware of its craving for information, ways and means were inevitably found to satisfy this demand."

Despite demand, the new leaders of the commonwealth still believed that the supply of printed newssheets needed to be managed by government. The problem was, everyone in England in the 1650s who now had some share of political, religious, social, and economic power had at one time advocated the right to speak freely for themselves. How could they return England to the days of the Star

Chamber? The answer can be found in the fact that—with only a few exceptions—factions both political and religious firmly believed that divine accuracy had been posited solely with them. Those who believed differently were not just providing another interpretation; they were wrong. That is why Milton could say in *Areopagitica,* "Give me liberty to know, to utter, and to argue freely according to conscience, above all liberties" in one paragraph and then a few later state, "that many be tolerated, rather than compelled. I mean not tolerated popery and open superstition, which, as it extirpates all religions and civil supremacies, so itself should be extirpate."

So, early in 1653, the Council of State began reinstituting laws to bring printing under strict government control. Just as had happened decades before, English law established how many printing houses could operate in the country. People who broke the new printing rules would appear before a body to weigh the charges, much as under the Star Chamber. And, to ensure that the proceedings of Parliament were presented only as its members wanted, MPs decreed that Parliament alone would control news about the legislative body. That meant that the Council of State would decide which papers would publish as official state mouthpieces, that is, which would be "published by authority." The law, however, did not significantly slow the London newssheets. When Cromwell became lord protector at the end of the year, however, things changed. As lord protector, Cromwell had monarchial power, and he created a new and more stringent series of laws to control printing, especially newsbooks.

Cromwell established a commission to oversee all

printing in England. The names of all printers, print shop workers, and apprentices were to be collected, along with a tally of the number of presses operating within the realm. Unlicensed printers were to be prosecuted and punished through corporal and pecuniary means. Finally, Cromwell ordered that all newsbooks except those authorized to print by his government were to be shut down, and anyone selling these corantos on the streets of London were to be punished. According to William Clyde, Cromwell succeeded where others had failed. Newsbook after newsbook ceased publication until only two, *Mercury Politicus* and *Publick Intelligencer,* were left. Suppression was not that total, however. Just as nonconformists found ways to print when publication of their pamphlets was outlawed, so, too, did coranto publishers find a way periodically to print. They did not, however, produce the number of unlicensed documents that religious dissenters had. As the Protectorate ended following Cromwell's death in 1658 and fell apart under his son, Richard, newsbooks, licensed or unlicensed, returned to London's streets. At nearly the same time, the Stuart monarchy under Charles II regained control of England, setting up another confrontation between the government and those who believed they had the right to print freely.

MOVING TOWARD A FREE PRESS

The reestablishment of the Stuarts meant that all laws passed during the Interregnum disappeared as Charles II attempted to return England to the time when his father ruled. That meant that laws controlling printing were reinstituted, even those of the Star Chamber, which, however, was not reconvened. Charles simply placed this power in another entity, Parliament. His policies on printing were contained in the Printing Act of 1662. To ensure that the act was properly enforced, he appointed Roger L'Estrange as England's chief censor. L'Estrange's principal target was the massive underground pamphlet business, which produced hundreds of tracts for religious nonconformists and seditious literature for those who still opposed the monarchy. L'Estrange was good at his job because he believed in it and detested the notion of a free press. "The Press has grown so common, and Men take the Boldness to print whatever is brought to them, let it concern who it will; it is high time Examples be made," Lord Chief Justice Robert Hyde said at the trial of the first group of unlicensed printers L'Estrange sent in front of the bench on charges of sedition. L'Estrange and Hyde made sure that one of them, John Twyn, was an example to those who violated the precepts of the new Printing Act. The printer was hanged and then drawn and quartered in late 1663.

Licensing rules under Charles II and the Printing Act specifically hurt news publishers more than they hurt pamphleteers. When Charles returned to England, the number of newssheets was immediately cut to two, both of which were printed by Henry Muddiman, who arranged a deal to be sole printer of news for the monarchy. But L'Estrange usurped Muddiman after proving himself a capable censor. In 1663, L'Estrange held England's newspaper monopoly, publishing, as Muddiman had done, two papers by authority. Muddiman, however, again gained the upper hand in the printing of official newspapers because of two events. The first was the outbreak of the Great Plague in London in the summer of 1665. The second, which occurred the next year in September, was the Great Fire, which destroyed all London printing houses. Because the government removed itself to Oxford during the Great Plague and L'Estrange chose to remain in London and produce newspapers, he could not procure enough information to fill both his papers. Needing a reliable and readily available outlet for information, Charles's counselors allowed another newssheet to publish and summoned Muddiman to the temporary capital. The *Oxford Gazette* quickly assumed the principal role among the three official papers, and when the Great Fire doomed L'Estrange's papers, the *Gazette* became England's only paper, moving to London and changing its name to signify its place of publication.

The year 1679, like 1644, was a pivotal year in the development of a free press. Licensing expired, and Parliament could not come to an agreement on its renewal. As a result, newspaper production was not illegal, and those who opposed the current government reignited opposition newspapers. A printer of Baptist tracts named Benjamin Harris published the first of the nonlicensed papers. *Domestick Intelligence; Or, News both from City and Country* lasted into 1680 when the government arrested Harris and jailed him south of London after a judge declared "to print or publish any news books or pamphlets of news whatsoever is illegal." Harris, who would emigrate to America and begin its first paper when he published *Publick Occurrences Both Forreign and Domestick* in Boston in 1690, got into so much trouble because he focused *Domestick Intelligence* on what his paper's name implied—national affairs—not international news. That, also, is why the Governor's Council of Massachusetts ended the life of *Publick Occurrences* after a single issue.

Before Charles could curtail the eruption of news-sheets, nearly forty different titles appeared on London streets. In 1644, England had briefly experienced a partisan press, but from 1679 to 1682, papers assumed an even more virulent tone, with Whig and Tory papers attacking each other and creating what Frederick Siebert called "the almost hysterical state of public opinion." As in 1644, domestic issues captured most of the columns of newssheets.

Because of Parliament's inaction, Charles personally decided to rein in the press. Doing so was not easy, but by the end of 1682, the second round of partisan newspaper publishing in England ended. All that was left were the sheets published by authority. Nevertheless, as James Sutherland has stated, what "the remarkable outburst of newspapers between 1679 and 1682 had demonstrated beyond all possible doubt was the popular demand for more news, a demand that was scarcely met at all by the official *Gazette.*" Even members of Parliament were beginning to agree. "I think it not natural, nor rational," MP Francis Winnington said in the House of Commons, "that the people, who sent us hither, should not be informed of our actions."

When James II came to the throne in 1685, England was more concerned with the direction the nation would steer in terms of religion than in what newspapers might say. James's actions to promote religious toleration were seen as a smokescreen to enable him to reestablish Catholicism as England's state religion. In what would be termed the Glorious Revolution, James vacated the throne with his daughter Mary and her husband, King William of the Netherlands, assuming monarchial control. Neither attempted to control the press, nor did the last of the Stuarts, Queen Anne, who reigned from 1702 to 1714. Religious toleration became the law of England in 1689, and Parliament let the Licensing Act die rather than renew it in 1694. England's printers were virtually free to print at will. At the beginning of the eighteenth century, the partisan nature of England's papers remained. Regularity in publication, including dailies, made news easily accessible to all in London. Even in the countryside, papers were available. Making a living as a printer, as John Wolfe had demanded in 1582, was now a reality. No publication needed to be licensed in order to be published legally. Even Parliament acquiesced to have its votes appear in papers. Ways to control the press would exist in the eighteenth century, through stamp taxes on paper and political patronage, and, for printers willing to promote the position of the party in power, a good living could be obtained through governmental printing contracts and access to information. The law of seditious libel established by James I remained valid and constituted the harshest of available means to control what was printed if needed.

Britons who believed in the notion of liberty of conscience had published their ideas for nearly two hundred years, from the time of William Tyndale and John Frith in the 1520s, and continued to do so even into the eighteenth century. Newsbooks had existed for nearly as long, but for much of their early history, their writers focused the news on foreign affairs. Only with the Puritan Revolution did newspapers take on domestic issues. At two pivotal points in the seventeenth century, around 1644 and again in 1679, England's situation allowed the press to flourish and assume a natural for-and-against stance on issues and the country's political direction. Members of Parliament increasingly realized that they needed the press to promote their views as the country's two-party system grew. Once this happened, returning the press to any semblance of its early self with only newspapers published by authority was impossible.

The changes in the way England viewed government and the need for a press that was free of most restrictions did not occur solely because of political expediency. A group of writers, some involved in the struggles for toleration and press freedom and others more interested in new notions about government, began to develop a political philosophy about the nature of government. As nonconformists called for religious toleration, and some printers sought ways to publish newssheets that needed no government license, these men philosophized that government should operate in a manner that allowed both. Their writings affected the nature of the press and the political direction of England. And, probably, their ideas had even more influence on the British colonies in North America, where their notions of government and a free press were put into practice in the grand experiment of the United States. What they had to say, and its effect on press freedom, are discussed next.

FOUR

THE MARKETPLACE OF IDEAS
AND ITS POLEMICISTS

The events and developments recounted in the previous two chapters did not, of course, occur within a vacuum. Religious dissenters did not write pamphlets and promote the idea of toleration based on liberty of conscience without knowledge of what other writers were saying about these issues, nor did other Englishmen create newsbooks, broadsides, and newssheets without having conversations with one another about what was happening in government that would affect their livelihood. Those who wrote pamphlets and produced and edited news sources often used the same printers. When Charles II initiated the Printing Act of 1662, fifty-nine master printers were listed for England, though other printers worked outside the official, licensed network. Those who wanted to disseminate ideas often had to turn to the same printers.

As the battle for religious toleration and the development of newspapers was occurring, English writers—as well as others on the continent—began to produce a body of literature that speculated on the notions of individual rights and freedoms along with the way government and religion should operate. These writers accepted God as a foundation for all, and they viewed God's crowning creation as humankind. God gave humans the faculties to think and reason, they said. If this was true, then humankind, out of the basic nature of creation, could only understand God, nature—everything—through the ability to think and to reason. Therefore, everything revealed to humankind was valid only if it was rational, that is, not contrary to the ability to reason, which was God's ultimate gift to humans.

It is only logical that this philosophy would touch upon rights of expression. It also affected the arguments of religious nonconformists and others in England. These writers believed they were more enlightened than their predecessors, and as a result, the period came to be known as the Enlightenment. The thinkers of the Enlightenment did not reject the bedrock of society—its religion and government. Instead, they explained how both should be understood and function based on man's rational ability. Since religion and politics remained very much entwined into the eighteenth century, the new ideas promoted by Thomas Hobbes, John Milton, John Locke, John Lilburne, John Trenchard, Thomas Gordon, and other English writers were woven into people's understanding of basically all aspects of life. Most people in England and America might not have realized that they were being influenced and guided by these apologists, or even known their names, but the people who shaped the direction of England and the American colonies surely did.

Henry May said that the two institutions most universally admired by Enlightenment thinkers were parliamentary supremacy and freedom of the press. Parliamentary supremacy reflected self-government, and a free press was paramount in making sure that those chosen by the body politic knew the will of the people to keep government on the proper course. In the middle of the seventeenth century when Enlightenment writings began to appear, however, self-government was still a notion of which few could conceive, despite the commonwealth and the twenty-year hiatus of the monarchy. In order to express themselves, those who sought to change the course of society needed access to the people via the press. None combined notions on reshaping government with calls for a free press more completely than a group of radicals who proposed democratic reform—the Levellers.

JOHN LILBURNE AND THE LEVELLERS

Of all the factions and sects in England from the first rumblings of civil war in the late 1630s through the demise of licensing in 1694, none espoused the notions of equal rights for all, including freedom of the press, more enthusiastically than the Levellers. Like many other groups to develop in England from the beginning of the Protestant Reformation such as the Baptists and the Quakers, the Levellers advocated a sort of religious democracy for all, or, as William Walwyn wrote, "that every man ought to have Liberty of Conscience of what Opinion soever."

The Levellers and other nonconformists readily joined Oliver Cromwell in the battle to rid England of the monarchy, but unlike Calvinist Presbyterians and most Baptists, who by the 1640s had adopted the theology of the elect, which posited that God had chosen some for salvation through limited atonement to the damnation of others, the Levellers' religious democracy posited that all who practiced liberty of conscience based in holy scripture were of the elect. Since everyone in England—Protestant or Catholic— did that, then they were equal, in the Leveller version of religious equality. That notion, of course, was at odds with the beliefs of every other group that existed at the time and pushed the Levellers to the fringe of what was acceptable religiously during the Interregnum.

The Levellers' political views grew out of their religious views. They did not believe that the elect consisted only of a few and that those few should govern all. Moreover, if men could interpret the divine, and the Levellers believed that they could, then surely they could manage a human invention like government. To the Levellers, it was rational that mankind had the ability to worship according to personal interpretation of scripture: "God hath dealt abundantly well with us," Walwyn said, "there being nothing that is necessary either for the enlightening of our understandings, or the peace of our mindes, but what hee hath plainely declared and mainfestly set forth in his Word: so plainly, that the meanest capacity is fully capable of a right understanding thereof." The Levellers applied their notion of religious liberty to the political sphere and became the first Britons to advocate political democracy, called "heretical democracy" by some, such as the Presbyterian divine Richard Baxter.

The Levellers subscribed to the notion of the "social contract," which proposed an agreement by the people for their own governing. The Levellers advocated the social contract before John Locke and others began talking of it, but the concept was not unique to Britons of the 1640s. The notion sounded much like the covenantal agreement employed by the Puritans, where they joined together in commitment to God and to each other in gathered churches. Within the Puritan system as it was applied in New England two decades earlier, the covenant still had human leaders who commanded through the guidance of God. The Levellers, with John Lilburne as their principal spokesperson, produced *An Agreement of the People.* This document said that the people and the people only had the right to put themselves into a binding legal contract, or government. All the people, if they agreed, would live in the commonwealth under a government to which they elected representatives who produced laws for the people.

Lilburne was very much an Enlightenment thinker, though he would have proclaimed himself a man of the people instead. He based his ideas on religious toleration and the democratic social contract in the law of reason. In step with the ideas of religion that would develop during the next hundred years, Lilburne believed that every person, educated or not, could distinguish good and evil. The law of reason, which was given to man by God, allowed people inherently to know what was best for themselves and for the society in which they lived. Fellow Leveller Richard Overton explained the notion in terms quite similar to those that Locke would use in his treatises on government in 1690 more than forty years later: "For by natural birth all men are equally and alike born to like propriety, liberty and freedom; and as we are delivered of God by the hand of nature into this world, every one with a natural innate freedom and propriety—as it were writ in the table of every man's heart, never to be obliterated—even so are we to live, everyone equally and alike to enjoy his birthright and privilege; even all whereof God by nature has made him free."

Since God had given humans through a natural and innate birthright the ability to think and interpret scripture, they could choose for themselves the best method of worship. If God gave man the ability to know good and evil and what was best for him and those around him, he could govern himself. So, as Lilburne and the Levellers envisioned society, if all people had the right to worship as they pleased and to live under a government of their making, then people would, of course, have the right to petition their government if they believed they had been wronged in any way or if government needed to be steered back on course. This is where the significance of freedom of the press fit into the Levellers' scheme.

First, Lilburne and the Levellers believed in a "level" society: All who joined into the social contract were granted the same rights. For the discussion on the press, that meant, first and foremost, that it was not right for government to take some of these rights away by limiting the livelihood of printers who were not approved by the Stationers' Company. This was the same complaint John Wolfe had voiced in 1582. The government had no right to hinder someone's basic right to earn a living, and government had no right to tell a printer what he could or could not print. Lilburne said that the monopoly of printing established by king and archbishop was "insufferable, unjust and tyrannical" because the Stationers could "print, divulge and disperse whatsoever Books, Pamphlets and Libels they please" and at the same time "breake in, and search honest mens shops" and then "carry them before a Committee, and from thence to Prison" for printing anything that was not approved by the Stationers. To allow the Stationers' Company to exist and limit the free expression of the people, Lilburne went on to explain, violated basic principles of the social contract.

Next, Lilburne demanded a free and open press because one was needed in order to keep the government, which was created by and for the people, on track. A government of the people should "receive all Information and Petitions from any of the Inhabitants there having been many most necessary and usefull things stiffled for want of incouragement in this kind." In 1640s England, Lilburne's writings, as well as those of other Levellers on the rights of Englishmen, were more popular than those of John Milton, but Lilburne, who was a gentleman by birth and an avid reader of anything he could obtain, no doubt read Milton's *Areopagitica* and other works, just as Milton no doubt read Leveller tracts. Both the Levellers and Milton proposed the same marketplace of ideas, though Milton's persuasive words are more popularly remembered. Lilburne demanded, "That you will open the Press, whereby all trecherous and tyranical designes may be the easier discovered. . . . The mouths of Adversaries being best stopped, by the sensible good which the people receive from the actions of such as are in Authority." For the Levellers, the only way to stop the spread of falsehood, which kept the people in religious and political bonds, was to open the press to all so that errors could be discovered. In 1643, Lilburne's compatriot William Walwyn proposed the notion of the open marketplace, where ideas were available for the people's scrutiny, just as eloquently as Milton would the following year. Walwyn said: "let every one freely speake his minde without molestation: and so there may be hope that truth may come to light, that otherwise may be obscured for particular ends: plaine truth will prove all, sufficient for vanquishing of the most artificiall, sophisticall errour that ever was in the world, give her but due and patient audience, and her persuwasions are ten thousand times more powerfull to worke upon the most dull refractory minde, then all the adulterate allurements and deceivings of art."

So, within their writings, the Levellers outlined the basis of self-government and the need for individual rights to ensure basic freedoms for those living within the social contract. The Levellers couched all their arguments in the rationalism that would mark the writings of those considered to be the great Enlightenment thinkers. Their notion of society created a democratic state that allowed for the dissemination of ideas good and bad and demanded that the press be open to all. Unfortunately, seventeenth-century England was not ready for a democratic state along Leveller lines. Cromwell and his Council of State arrested Lilburne, Overton, Walwyn, and other Leveller leaders and locked them in the Tower of London. Though they continued to write, they could not convince most Britons, upper, middle, or lower class, that a level society was in the country's best interests. The political power struggles of the nation led Cromwell to reinstitute press controls. The radical ideas of the Levellers would eventually become the foundation of American government and the American notion of a free press, but their writings would not be the instruments for acceptance. That acceptance would, instead, come through the works of others.

THE POLITICAL PHILOSOPHERS

A number of political philosophers helped formulate the notion of self government and the need for open debate on issues that ultimately led to the political system in America and the notion of a free and open press. Some of them, such as the Levellers Lilburne, Walwyn, and Overton, outlined the foundation for a country with religious toleration, a government of and for the people, and a free and open press to debate issues of importance to religion and government. While their writings have not been lost, they were not the ones to whom people turned toward the end of the seventeenth century in England or in the eighteenth century in America. Instead, the educated sought out Milton, Hobbes, and Locke. In England, those who wrote for the growing press combined the ideas of these men into essays that were printed and reprinted throughout the eighteenth century, especially in America. The newspaper polemicists— especially the writings of "Cato," that is, John Trenchard and Thomas Gordon—ultimately became the voices for democratic government and free press for Americans.

John Milton's *Areopagitica* was the first work of the three important English political philosophers to be printed. Milton focused on the idea of free and open debate and its importance in shaping and directing government. Born in 1608 in London to a father who created a sizable fortune working in a law office and as a moneylender, Milton received a top-notch education with bachelor's and master's degrees from King's College. But Milton entered the debate on a free press by accident. In 1642, at the age of thirty-three, he married Mary Powell, who was nearly half his age at seventeen. The pair had been married for about a month when Mary left Milton and returned to Oxfordshire to live in the home of her wealthy justice-of-the-peace father.

As much as age and social status divided Milton and Mary, it was probably their political differences that created the marriage breaker. Her family was very much in the royalist camp, while Milton was a Puritan. Mary refused to return to live with her husband, and Milton, realizing the mistake of his matrimony, wanted the marriage to end. Divorce, however, was impossible in seventeenth-century England unless adultery could be proven. Milton believed that marriage was a legal contract, not a religious one. Plus, he was extremely angry that he had made the mistake of marrying such an incompatible person. He immediately produced a pair of pamphlets on divorce and rushed them to a printer. Though the nation was in a state of political uproar, pamphlets were still expected to be licensed, and Milton had neglected to obtain a license. In the House of Commons, Herbert Palmer preached a sermon against Milton and his tracts. The combination of the two things—the admonition for not licensing his work and the sermon against his propositions on divorce—pushed the Cambridge-educated writer in a new direction in his writing. He penned a monograph to Parliament on censorship, licensing, and public debate.

When *Areopagitica* appeared in November 1644, the people of London did not clamor to find copies to read. It was not a best-seller. In fact, according to William Haller, the unlicensed booklet, which did not carry a printer's name, went completely unnoticed in the uproar of the times. This analysis is not completely correct, because Lilburne and other Levellers obviously read it. And the fact that hardly anyone paid attention to *Areopagitica* should not diminish its significance. A generation later, in the 1680s and 1690s, those who were fighting for toleration and an open press returned to its lines to bolster their arguments. A 1681 pamphlet entitled *An Apology for the Liberty of the Press,* for example, copied Milton's work as it outlined why England should institute freedom of the press, and Matthew Tindal used Milton's 1644 analogy of truth defeating falsehood in open debate in his treatise on why limiting the press threatened the liberties of the entire nation. The concepts in *Areopagitica* became important in America as well. It was republished shortly after the 1735 New York libel trial of John Peter Zenger as rationale and validation for the printer's not-guilty verdict, and it was also used, as we will see shortly, as justification in Zenger's paper for the attack that was about to take place on Governor William Cosby. American revolutionaries in the 1770s turned to Milton's ideas to justify their writings and actions, too. According to Leonard Levy, "To Americans of the Framers' generation, only John Locke's reputation as a libertarian rivaled Milton's."

Milton's call for open debate was not a call for total freedom of the press. He framed the entire argument in light of his faith. Protestantism necessitated free and open debate, while heresy—which to Milton included Roman Catholicism—was excluded from participating in the public sphere. Milton said that Catholicism "extirpats all religions and civill supremacies," meaning that loyalty to the pope superseded loyalty to anything else and for that reason would extirpate public debate and loyalty to government. Since Protestantism, Milton believed, was based in the same biblical fundamentals for all groups and sects as well as his country's government, tolerating all that Protestants of varying sects had to say was not only needed but expected, according to scripture. "Read any books what ever come to thy hands, for thou are sufficient both to judge aright, and to examine each matter," Milton pointed out, "because it was answerable to that of the Apostle to the Thessalonians, Prove all things, hold fast that which is good."

Having set his parameters for open debate and printing, Milton attacked licensing of publications, which was censorship, or prior restraint, saying that all should be allowed into discussion, and if print was to be regulated then everything that people did needed to be controlled by the censor. "If we think to regulat Printing," he said, "we must regulat all recreations and pastimes." Besides, there was no need to regulate what was printed because "when God gave him [man] reason, he gave him freedom to choose." People, through God, were given the ability to think and to know the truth. Milton, the enlightened thinker, believed that this one fact would ensure that people would not be led astray by any heretical thought, which leaves one to wonder why opening debate to Catholics would keep the truth from being discerned from falsehood.

Milton concluded his argument by saying, "Give me the liberty to know, to utter, and to argue freely according to conscience, above all liberties. . . . And though all the windes of doctrin were let loose to play upon the earth, so Truth be in the field, we do injuriously by licensing and prohibiting to misdoubt her strength. Let her and Falshood grapple; who ever knew Truth put to the wors, in a free and open encounter. Her [falsehood] confuting is the best and surest suppressing." For Milton, if public debate were open to all ideas, man, through his God-given reason, would naturally be led to God-revealed truths, and that was the only true way of suppressing erroneous ideas.

In Milton's world, church and state could never be totally separated, but one did not have to dictate completely the actions of the other. Liberty of conscience and free will both operated under the umbrella of reason. That may be why *Areopagitica* resonated so strongly with colonial Americans of the eighteenth century. It never denied the role of God in the activities of man, and it never denied that man had the ability to use reason to glean the truth in whatever was presented to him. This concept was perfect for understanding how government should operate. So, according to Susan Achinstein, "For Milton, conscience could function as a radical brace preserving individual liberty against coercive state authority, but it was also radically open to the workings of divine impulse."

This is exactly how the *New-York Weekly Journal* framed its initial attack on Governor Cosby in 1733 that resulted in Zenger's famous libel trial. Paying homage to Milton without naming him, the November 12 issue said, "it would not be improper to communicate to the Publick the Sentiments of a late excellent Writer," which was followed by the great statement of *Areopagitica:* "Truth will always prevail over Falshood." In the continuation of the essay in the next *Journal,* the writer explained, "No nation Antient or Modern ever lost the Liberty of freely Speaking, Writing, or Publishing their Sentiments, but forthwith lost their Liberty in general and became Slaves." Not to lose Milton's notion of divine guidance, the essay reminded readers that whoever attacked corrupt government in the press must be "one whose Principles lead him to be firmly attached to the present happy

Establishment, both in Church and State." Americans, at least by the 1730s, had truly incorporated Milton's ideas into the framework of how the press should operate in relation to the state. And by this time they had also adopted the notion of the social contract. The *Journal* writer insisted that in order to attack a corrupt government, one had to be "firmly attached" to it. Those who had consented to be governed were the only ones who could criticize authority and change it. Here, the ideas of two other important political philosophers—Hobbes and Locke—combined with those of Milton.

Thomas Hobbes proposed elements of the social contract in his opus, *Leviathan,* which was published in 1651, eleven years after he fled England for France. Hobbes had found it necessary to leave England because, in 1640, he had written and distributed *Elements of Law,* which emphasized the need for absolute sovereignty. Unfortunately for Hobbes, the political situation in England deteriorated almost immediately; Charles I dissolved Parliament only to have the MPs return and begin the Long Parliament. This was the first step toward civil war, and Hobbes knew it. As a result, he decided that it would be in his best interests to leave England. He returned shortly after completing *Leviathan.*

Hobbes called *Leviathan* "my discourse of Commonwealth" and explained that the state, or commonwealth, was the "great Leviathan," the name of a sea monster in the Old Testament book of Job. The entire title of Hobbes's work, *Leviathan or the Matter, forme and Power of a Commonwealth Ecclesiasticall and Civil,* gets to the heart of what he was trying to say. Hobbes very much understood the dual nature of government in his time: It was both ecclesiastical and civil.

But he believed that God was more deistic in nature—that is, God created the universe and set it in motion but left it to operate on natural laws. He created man, and in the natural state of creation, man was free to act because he had been imbued with reason by God. Consequently, rulers—even kings—did not assume that position by any divine right, but by the consent of the people. This portion of Hobbes's thought became important in America in the unruly era of revolt. God remained part of what was happening, but it was man, as God's rational creature, that had to act and make sure that society was formed in the best possible way.

With the idea of how man and God interacted established, Hobbes said that people form a commonwealth—the seventeenth-century term for the political state—"when a *multitude* of men do agree and *covenant, every one with every one,* that to whatsoever man or *assembly of men* shall be given by the major part the *right* to *present* the person of them all . . . every one, as well he that *voted for it* as he that *voted against it* [and] to live peaceably amongst themselves and be protected against other men." Hobbes in *Leviathan* did not change his position on absolute sovereignty that had caused him so much trouble in 1640. He said that when people entered into the covenant, they were obliged to follow the laws its leaders created, something that Oliver Cromwell no doubt relished reading. Hobbes said that "there can happen no breach of covenant on the part of the sovereign; and consequently none of his subjects, by any pretence of forfeiture, can be freed from his subjection." Because the people have joined together in contract, neither subject nor ruler can break the covenant. The ruler can do nothing to harm the people, and the people agree to obey the laws created by the sovereign. This makes the covenanted commonwealth indivisible, according to Hobbes.

Hobbes's notion of the covenant of government would work well in America and would be expounded upon by Locke. But Hobbes also believed that the dissolution of the covenant should be mutual, and that government had the right to censor any who tried through subversive writings to undermine the commonwealth. While his position would have been readily accepted by those of the ruling class, it was not a position that revolutionary Americans, or English writers of the 1690s and later, would have adopted. "I cannot imagine how anything can be more prejudicial to a monarchy than the allowing such books to be publicly read without applying such correctives of discreet masters as are fit to take away their venom," Hobbes wrote. And yet he also said that censoring other types of writings "are injustice both before God and man." Though he subscribed to the natural rights of man, he believed that anything that might usurp the commonwealth or cause it to be disbanded on any grounds other than mutual dissolution was wrong. Here, revolutionary America would ultimately reject Hobbes. Americans, instead, found the perfect blend of individualism and the commonweal in another English writer.

The most important of the English political theorists to the formation of America's type of government and its ideas concerning inalienable rights, such as those that would be found in the First Amendment, was John Locke. According to Thomas Peardon, Locke best represented all the theorists of the Anglo-American political tradition. In addition, Peardon said, Locke was the principal source of ideas for the American Revolution and the theorist of the English Revolution of 1688. As we have already seen, the ideas proposed by Locke were not new. The Levellers advocated nearly all of his ideas in their publications from 1643 through 1649, and Hobbes had already expounded upon the social contract, though both he, Locke, and the Levellers probably got that idea from Richard Hooker's *The Laws of Ecclesiastical Polity,* published in parts in 1594 and 1597, and from the anonymously authored *Vindiciae contra tyrannos,* released in 1579. Still, if one reads the Declaration of Independence and then Locke's *Second Treatise of Government,* one discovers that Locke's concepts are present, and that Thomas Jefferson borrowed from Locke's phrasing. Some even say that the man who would become the nation's third president copied wholesale from Locke.

Locke started from the point that all humans existed in nature as free individuals, and he made the assumption—as the other groups and people described in this chapter did—that God endowed man with the ability to think and rationalize the world around him. God would not, could not, create anything that his highest creation could not comprehend. Because they were rational, people quickly determined that they needed to form government, for security first, and also for the pleasures that living within community could offer. Locke and Hobbes agreed that people needed to form a social contract, but Locke based his understanding of it on the rights of the individuals within the collective, not on the absolutism of authority. What Locke proposed for society was government based on the consent of the governed. "No one," Locke explained, "can be . . . subjected to the political power of another without his consent." If consent could be granted by individuals only, then individuals possessed what Jefferson, in the Declaration of Independence, would call "inalienable rights," which he based on Locke's notion of the rights of the individual, that is, a person's "life, liberty and estate [property]."

Even if there were certain inalienable rights that individuals possessed, they were still joined together through a social contract that created a government to set rules and regulations for them. For Locke, those rules were established by the "consent of the majority," and those who joined together in the social contract were obliged to live by those laws. However, if laws were made without authority of the majority, Locke said, "the people are not therefore bound to obey." Locke then stated that "The end of government is the good of mankind" and that "rulers should be sometimes liable to be opposed when they grow exorbitant in the use of their power." People thus must be in a position to judge the actions of those in power. Though Locke did not say so, his ideas about judging the actions of those in power aligned themselves closely with the notion of redress of grievances as proposed first by the Levellers and then eloquently by Milton in *Areopagitica*: Actions of the governing could be judged by the governed through the exchange of ideas via the printed word in the marketplace. And, according to Frederick Siebert, Locke would have agreed that a free and open press was the way to usurp tyranny, because it was Locke who provided the House of Commons with a list of eighteen reasons for allowing licensing to expire instead of renewing it in 1694. For Locke, the idea of debate was entailed in informed consent. In order to allow themselves to be governed, people needed to have as much knowledge about government as possible, even if the information was wrong, selective, biased, false, or incomplete. Ultimately, Gillian Brown said, Locke's ideas on government and individual rights came to fruition as colonial Americans applied Locke's idea of self-determination to themselves.

In England, though, the teachings of the country's political philosophers were officially condemned by Oxford University and burned publicly in 1683. Charles II, the same year, regained control of the press through licensing, so newssheets and other publications, which had been printed with little governmental intervention from 1679 through 1682, were once again under control of the licenser. That meant that public discussion, at least through the press, was limited. As a result, coffeehouses popped up as a new phenomenon and served as places where public debate and dialogue could take place. These gathering spots sprang up in London in the 1650s and quickly became centers for conversation on assorted concepts and issues. The ideas of the Enlightenment writers were especially popular for discussion, and for that reason, Charles closed the coffeehouses down.

The problem for Charles and for other monarchs and rulers from this time forward in the Anglo-American world, however, was that there was no way to turn back the clock. Open discussion was one of the great legacies of the rational thinkers of sixteenth century. Once printing unleashed ideas, there was no way to control where those thoughts would take people. This had been happening as far back as Martin Luther in Germany, and then in England from Frith and Tyndale, and it continued through the Puritan Revolution and the writings of the political philosophers. Until the introduction of coffeehouses, the great debate in society almost always took place in the pamphlets and in the gathering places of religious nonconformists who were seeking freedom of conscience for those of like mind. God was central to the arguments, even when press freedom was part of the discussion.

Now, with coffeehouses and taverns becoming the locus of discussion, what people debated took on a decidedly more secularized tone. Religion was still important, and after the Act of Toleration, many of the dissenter groups in England faced more intolerance. But Milton, Hobbes, and Locke, while they grounded their arguments in belief that God created all, saw man as the means to an orderly society. "It was God's ordinance that the supremacy should be unlimited in Adam," Locke said in his *First Treatise of Government*. And in the *Second Treatise,* Locke explained that "the law of reason" was what all of Adam's posterity would use to act. Increasingly, as Locke discussed government, individuals ascended in importance, and society remained vital because people needed it to exist peacefully and in harmony with each other—but nowhere in his conclusion does Locke mention God.

With toleration, the end of licensing, the growth of newspapers at the end of the seventeenth century and into the eighteenth, and the proliferation of other types of publishing, debate continued in the realm to which Locke had taken it. Now, however, a new set of writers were set to lead the debate. Their principal medium was the newspaper, and they advocated free and open discussions as a mandatory corollary to the social contract. These writers took the concepts of Milton, Locke, and others and synthesized their thinking for all levels of society that had access to what they wrote. As we have noted, most Americans in the middle of the eighteenth century would have said they knew nothing of John Locke, but they would have known the writings of "Cato."

THE NEWSPAPER POLEMICISTS

Following the end of licensing in 1694–1695, printers were free to produce newspapers without concern for licensing. The *London Gazette* was the only paper printed in England when licensing ended, but others quickly sprang to life. Early in the eighteenth century, newspapers superseded pamphlets as the dominant printed form of political discourse in England. They were cheaper to produce and disseminate than pamphlets. Plus, printers could support them with advertising. America lagged behind the mother country by about three decades in the content of newspapers and much more than that in their production. This was as much for financial reasons as anything else. America's towns at the beginning of the eighteenth century could not support the level of competition among newspapers that could be found in London. Also, colonial governments still wielded considerable power, with licensing still on the books. Use of this authority can be seen, for example, in the immediate closing of *Publick Occurrences* in 1690 and in governmental oversight of the *Boston News-Letter* when John Campbell began publishing it in 1704.

The mercurial rise in British newspapers in the early eighteenth century can be chronicled in circulation figures. In 1704, the *London Gazette* was selling six thousand copies per issue, and other papers were selling anywhere from four hundred to four thousand copies per issue. By 1712, London's daily papers were selling, on average, more than two thousand issues per day, while weekly newssheets sold up to ten thousand papers per printing. Some papers, such as *The Tatler,* even produced multiple editions of the same issue, sometimes resetting copy to improve it or update it. By 1711, there were at least sixty-six different periodicals readily available for readers to purchase.

The newspapers of the early eighteenth century discussed a variety of topics ranging from the politics of the day to the nonsensical. One thing that newspaper printers had in common was that they wanted their papers to be "in demand" by readers. They therefore produced essays that offered subjects for discussion and debate in local congregating spots. People, as they had done since the 1650s when they had gathered in the coffeehouses, read the essays aloud and then discussed their merits. Since papers were produced anywhere from once a day to once per week, ideas for debate were always readily available, and the ideas of Locke and other political philosophers often turned these conversations toward the nature of the individual and his rights in relationship to governance and society. Again, the dialogue was difficult to control, but toward the end of Queen Anne's reign, she attempted to find ways to curtail discussion and debate. This move angered many because, at the same time, Parliament declared that it had a right to free and open debate within its walls. Matthew Tindal, in a stinging attack on this concept, said that all people had "a natural Right in all matters of learning and Knowledge." If open debate was allowed in Parliament, the people deserved the same. "If the Honourable House of Commons have upon a solemn Debate thought fit to publish their proceedings to prevent being misrepresented," Tindal asked, "why should they deny those they Represent the same Liberty?"

Despite such statements, Parliament in 1712 instituted the first stamp tax on paper. Its target was the country's periodicals, since books were exempt. The tax spurred Joseph Addison to write in *The Spectator,* "This is the Day on which many eminent Authors will probably Publish their Last Words." Other methods of controlling the press were also employed. Subsidization, or political patronage, was one of these, and seditious libel was still valid law. Despite Addison's dire warning, though, papers continued to print, and people continued to purchase them.

Around 1720, a pair of writers who had thoroughly incorporated Locke's ideas of natural selection and consent of the governed combined them with Milton's marketplace concept to produce a series of essays explaining that a free and open press was a natural right of all who lived in a state where government created laws to meet the will of the majority. By 1723, Trenchard and Gordon, using the pseudonym "Cato," a name they borrowed from the famous Roman statesman known for his honesty and virtue, had written 138 essays. They were then collected and printed in four volumes. By 1755, Cato's Letters had gone through six editions, and in 1720 they began appearing in the *London Journal.* Trenchard and Gordon believed that the only way society could achieve what Locke and Milton proposed was to allow full and open debate of all issues of importance to the people. "Whilst all Opinions are equally indulged, and all Parties equally allow'd to speak their Minds, the Truth will come out," Cato explained, "and we see every Day that she breaks the Bonds of Tyranny and Fraud, and shines through the Mists of Superstition."

What Trenchard and Gordon were attempting to do in their essays on freedom of the press was to establish the importance of the public dialogue through printing to the operation of government. Public comment would provide a means for the people's redress of grievances. The Puritans had claimed the right to a redress of grievances during Elizabeth's reign, and the Levellers had applied the concept to the necessity of a free press in the 1640s. The English Bill of Rights of 1689 granted "That it is a right of the subject to petition the King" and "That the freedom of speech and debates or proceedings in Parliament ought not to be impeached," but it said nothing about a free press. Cato believed that only through a free and open press could government operate correctly, because in no other way could a king or a legislature know what the people thought. "Without freedom of thought, there can be no such thing as wisdom; and no such thing as publick liberty, without freedom of speech," Cato stated in the February 4, 1720/1721, *London Journal,* adding, "The administration of government, is nothing else but the attendance of the trustees of the people upon the interest and affairs of the people. And . . . it is the part and business of the people, for whose sake alone all public matters are or ought to be transacted, to see whether they be well or ill transacted." Trenchard and Gordon placed free speech as the foundation upon which Locke's government ideas had to be built. "Freedom of Speech," Cato declared, "is the great bulwark of liberty; they prosper and die together." Cato concluded the essay "Of Freedom of Speech: That the Same Is Inseparable from Public Liberty" by saying,

"Freedom of Speech, therefore, being of such infinite Importance to the Preservation of Liberty, every one who loves Liberty ought to encourage Freedom of Speech."

Cato's idea of the press as the bulwark of liberty called into question any governmental action that might inhibit free discourse, such as a stamp tax or subsidies for patronage printing. In Essay 32, though, Trenchard and Gordon attacked British libel laws, and there is little wonder that the *New-York Weekly Journal* used their logic when preparing to attack the governor in 1733, or that it ascribed its own essays to Cato.

For Cato, when the welfare of the state was in jeopardy, and when the statements made benefited the state, there could be no libel. "The exposing therefore of publick wickedness, as it is a duty which every man owes to truth and his country, can never be a libel in the nature of things," Cato explained. "Whoever calls publick and necessary truths, libels, does but apprize us of his own character, and arm us with caution against his designs." A free and open press, Cato went on to explain, would, out of its very nature, sometimes libel people, but that was an unfortunate byproduct of a free press. In order to make sure that government functioned according to the consent of the governed, open debate in an unrestricted marketplace was essential. Cato said, "I must own, that I would rather many libels should escape, than the liberty of the press should be infringed." That is because Cato viewed the press as a watchdog of government, to borrow twentieth-century terminology. Protecting the governed, not the governors, was paramount to preserving liberty. "I know not what treason is, if sapping and betraying the liberties of a people be not treason, in the eternal and original nature of things," Cato proclaimed. "Let it be remembered for whose sake government is, or could be, appointed; then let it be considered, who are more to be regarded, the governors or the governed."

Trenchard's and Gordon's synthesis of seventeenth-century political philosophy into Cato's Letters greatly affected the political direction of England, and especially America, in the eighteenth century. Their *London Journal's* circulation reached ten thousand per issue by the summer of 1721. In America, the essays appeared in a multitude of newspapers, and essayists adopted the Cato moniker whenever questions of individual and societal rights versus government authority arose. Though it may sound as if the clarion call of Milton's marketplace of ideas, where truth prevails over falsehood, and Locke's social contract, where society is ruled by the consent of the governed, was accepted wholeheartedly by all right-thinking people, that was not the case, however. Well before William Walwyn or John Milton called for a place of open debate, which in the twentieth century came to be called "the marketplace of ideas," others envisioned such a place of debate but doubted the possibility of the truth always rising to the top. "If ten mens voyces be louder then one, then would the noyse of Errour drown the voyce of Truth," Richard Baxter posited five years before Milton wrote *Areopagitica*.

Other writers required time to be won over to the notion of a place of free debate and press. In 1699, Daniel Defoe supported renewed licensing because he believed that truth did not always prevail against falsehood in open encounter. By 1712, however, Defoe sounded much like Milton. "A design to suppress printing on either side can be nothing but a design to suppress truth," Defoe wrote in *The Review.* "But to lay a universal load upon everything, or, in English, to silence mankind, is a plot against truth, against the friends of virtue, learning, and religion."

The writings of Enlightenment thinkers paved the way for debate and public discussion, what German sociologist Jürgen Habermas labeled the "public sphere," a place where open debate could take place. The catalyst for these discussions was the printed word—newspapers, books, pamphlets, or anything that provided subjects for open dialogue—and anyone with access to printed material could take part in the discussion. For Habermas, the public sphere came about because of a rising middle class and its desire to join into national dialogue, and in that respect it is nearly identical to Milton's marketplace.

What made the debate and writings of Enlightenment thinkers so powerful and unruly in the eighteenth century was the fact that no one knew exactly where the ideas might go. Revolution in France and America produced radically different results, even though both were based in the concept of government for and by the people. By early in the eighteenth century, gangs of hawkers sold dozens of newspapers on London's streets, and some of those papers sold ten thousand issues per printing. Newspapers and other printed materials were a staple of life.

The press, however, was not completely free in England because of taxes and libel laws, and in the first century of British colonization in America, printing was very much under the control of government. In many ways, American press control mirrored what had happened in England, but the timeline for change in America moved much more swiftly than in England because of the theories of government and press provided by Enlightenment thinkers. That America received Cato's Letters at a much earlier point in press development than England did certainly made a difference. But what happened before Cato's Letters reached the eyes and hearts of Americans? How the press was controlled in America from the introduction of the printing press in 1638 through the first two decades of the eighteenth century is the subject of the next chapter.

FIVE

AMERICAN ORIGINS—THE SEVENTEENTH CENTURY

By the time the first printing press arrived in America in 1638, nearly twenty thousand English emigrants lived in what John Winthrop called "a City upon a Hill"—the colonies of British colonial America. These New World settlers were among a massive migration of Britons, estimated at nearly eighty thousand, or 2 percent of the English population, who left because of the turmoil and uproar that the actions of the Stuart monarchy created. Charles dismissed Parliament. Archbishop William Laud demanded a loyalty oath to the king for all clergy and wiped away any vestige of Puritan changes to the Church of England. Many Puritans who remained active in the state church believed that Laud was positioning England for a return to Catholicism. In addition, England suffered from economic depression, and epidemic disease ran through some sections of the country.

Initially, the brave souls who left England during the reign of Elizabeth and then in the early years of the tenure of James I did so as part of the colonial and economic expansion of the nation. The Virginia Company's efforts were part of England's initial imperialist efforts. The colonies in Virginia were aimed at providing monetary gain for investors and propagating English ideals. Living in swamps along the Chesapeake Bay and James River, however, was not conducive to any kind of success. By 1624, seventeen years after the first settlers arrived and established a permanent settlement at Jamestown, only slightly more than 1,100 Britons lived in Virginia, though more than 14,000 had tried. Most of them had died from disease or from warfare with the Indians.

Many of those who decided to try a new life in Virginia did so because of the printing press. As a means of enticing people to go to America, the Virginia Company, and later other land companies, created colonization literature that extolled—beyond any concept of reality—the wonders of living in America. "And here are no hard Landlords to racke us with high rents, or extorted fines to consume us, no tedious pleas in law to consume us," Virginia's most famous early inhabitant, John Smith, claimed, adding that "here every [man] may be master and owner of his own labour and land; or the greatest part in a small time. If hee have nothing but his hands, he may set up his trade: and by industrie quickly grown rich."

Printing was by the time of colonization efforts an integral part of English life, but it was something that the monarchy still believed it possessed a divine right to control. Protestant Britons had left England by the thousands when Mary Tudor assumed the throne in 1553 because they were in fear—rightly—of reprisals against them as she reinstituted Catholicism as the state religion. In Europe and surreptitiously in England, they began to publish pamphlets calling for religious freedom based on the dictates of conscience. When James I came to power in 1603, he sought ways to curtail these religious tracts. He placed new restrictions on printing through the law of seditious libel. Since church and state were one, such publications were seditious, and James made sure all understood it when he stated "no bishop, no king" at the 1604 Hampton Court conference. Charles continued his father's policies and put even more pressure on Puritans and other groups.

In the second religious diaspora from the Isles, nonconformist Protestants desperately sought a place in which they could begin a new life free of the fetters that constrained their notions of worship, a place that would offer each the chance to be "master and owner of his own labour and land," to use Smith's words. At the height of the migration away from England in the 1630s, Puritan polemicists were producing hundreds of pamphlets yearly despite Stuart law, and during the 1640s, estimates put the number of titles at more than twenty thousand. The central message in most of them was that, in terms of religion, each person must be allowed to "speake what I thinke, my minde gives me." As a result, when Puritans and others sailed west across the Atlantic with the baggage required to begin a new life, they also brought with them all that had transpired in the development of liberty of conscience up to that point. The printed word had become vital to their lives, first as holy scripture and second as justification for their right to worship according to the dictates of their divinely guided understanding of the Bible. In England, demands to speak and think freely were necessary within a system that prescribed state worship. Liberty of conscience, just as it had been in

England, was the foremost reason for expression in the first century of British colonial America.

In the New World, if John Winthrop was correct in seeing it as a New Jerusalem, the Puritans would have the chance to establish society on their own terms in relation to God. Since they and other English religious dissenters believed they had found the true understanding of God's word, would dissenting voices be allowed? According to David Hackett Fischer, the Puritans did not hope to establish a new world filled with religious freedom, but one granting freedom for the true faith. That meant that anyone who did not subscribe to Puritan religious orthodoxy lacked a true understanding of what God revealed in scripture. The English Civil War, at least for religious nonconformists, was about liberty of conscience. But in terms of religious power, it simply moved state-sanctioned worship from Anglicanism to Presbyterianism, and Presbyterian leaders, such as Richard Baxter, strongly denounced religious toleration. Puritans agreed with Baxter. "He that is willing to tolerate any religion, or discrepant way of religion, beside his own," Puritan Nathaniel Ward wrote, "either doubts of his own, or is not sincere in it."

As we have seen, groups such as the Levellers advocated a much more democratic version of society, but their ideology was not that of those who first settled America, though some, such as John Eliot, proposed instituting their ideals only to find themselves either censored or banished. Leveller philosophy would become part of the Enlightenment rhetoric of Locke, Cato, and the Founding Fathers of the United States in the eighteenth century. In the seventeenth century, though, the very nature of America created tighter controls on society, initially, for survival. People valued the printed word, and it served specific purposes. Religious toleration, however, was not one of them. Any publication that promoted democratic ideals was certain to be suppressed.

PRINTING AND READING IN AMERICA

Any number of reasons existed for the introduction of a printing press to the growing Massachusetts Bay colony. With a steadily rising population, colonial leaders no doubt believed they needed a means of printing official government documents. As a society deeply imbued with religious ideals, the propagation of the gospel to Native Americans figured into the need for a printing press. The Reverend Jose Glover—like William Caxton in 1476, John Wolfe in 1582, and dozens of other printers since—no doubt believed ownership of a printing press would provide a means of making money. For all these reasons, Glover sailed to England to buy a press, find a printer, and bring both back to Massachusetts. Glover died on the return voyage, but printer Stephen Daye completed the voyage safely with the press and produced on it an oath for use by the Massachusetts Bay government, a Psalm book, and other religious publications, including a Bible for Indians, and an almanac for general public consumption. His press was, therefore, serving political, religious, and economic functions.

Even though America's population reached about 20,000 shortly after the first press arrived in Cambridge, Massachusetts, the colonial population in the seventeenth century was not great enough to support widespread printing. London and the surrounding cities of Westminster and

Southwark had a population of around 375,000 by 1650, and 750 other English towns could boast populations ranging from 400 to 20,000 people each. In addition, only 17 percent of the England's people even lived in towns or cities. America's population, by contrast, totaled slightly more than 50,000 by 1650, with settlements ranging from Maine to Carolina, a distance of more than 1,000 miles. Only Massachusetts Bay and Virginia had populations of at least 20,000. Other colonies, such as Pennsylvania, had yet to be settled. By 1700, America's population had grown five-fold to slightly more than 250,000, but it was still only a little more than 40 percent of London's, which reached 600,000 by the beginning of the eighteenth century. Printing, to be profitable, needed a large, centralized audience.

The Britons who came to America in the seventeenth century were literate for the most part, so reading material was important to them. Nevertheless, by the beginning of the eighteenth century, only five presses were operating in America, and three of them were in Massachusetts. The small number of printing houses made it easy for colonial governments to control what was printed. Governmental printing was the principal means of making money. All American colonies, as their populations grew, realized a need for a printer within the colony to produce official documents, money, and legislative proceedings. South Carolina, for example, advertised for a printer for the colony in 1731 and eventually was able to attract one through a partnership with Philadelphia's Benjamin Franklin. With printers dependent upon their local governments for business to maintain their livelihoods, they rarely printed anything that intentionally challenged local authority. Confrontations, of course, did occur, and once competition among printers for newspaper readers—and ideological differences—developed in the eighteenth century, governmental support was of less importance. In the seventeenth century, though, the lack of a critical mass of consumers and the lack of competition tended to give government greater control over what was printed. That type of control, however, was not the same as controlling what people read and what they might say.

Most of the reading material in seventeenth-century America was imported from the mother country. Theological writings, as might be expected, were vitally important, but so, too, were books on history, law, medicine, and literature and poetry. Political writings also crossed the Atlantic during the tumultuous 1640s and 1650s. The importance of education in the colonies no doubt also made books important. By 1671, most New England colonies had passed laws that required all children to be taught to read, either by their parents or a schoolmaster. The desire to have all children become readers was tied closely to the Reformation tenet that people needed no intermediary between themselves and God. "Knowledge of the scriptures" was, according to the "Old Deluder Law" of Massachusetts, the only way to ensure the success of their New World endeavor. This insistence upon education would eventually open New England to Enlightenment thought.

Suppression of printed material depended upon where one was. In Virginia, which was a royal colony, political writings were of prime concern. After the beheading of Charles I, the governor and assembly ruled that anyone circulating works that discussed the end of the monarchy or that might suggest a change in government for Virginia committed a capital offense. The colony removed the death penalty from the statute eight years later but still made publications that questioned royal lineage or status-quo rule in Virginia a crime. In New England, the removal of the king was not considered a bad thing, but writings distributed by Baptists were. To eradicate the heretical literature these radical nonconformists brought with them, Massachusetts banished Baptists from the colony. The Massachusetts Bay colony did the same to Roger Williams in one of the more famous examples of early American intolerance. Puritan leaders banished Williams in 1635, saying that he "hath broached & dyvulged dyvers newe & dangerous opinions, against the aucthoritie of magistrates" and "shall dept out of this jurisdiccon within sixe weekes now nexte ensuing." Williams's writings were printed in England and brought back to America. His 1644 work *The Bloudy Tenent of Persecution,* especially, raised the ire of most people in England and America because it advocated religious tolerance for all, even Jews, Muslims, and atheists.

Works printed on the presses of America could face even more scrutiny than imported writings, but there was little concern that America's initial printings would produce seditious or heretical material as long as they related to the goals of the colonies. Almost all of what was printed for much of the seventeenth century related to the religion of the colonies. Because the New England Puritans were removed from England by only a decade or two at the most in the 1640s, they knew firsthand the value of the printed word. Pamphlets, broadsides, and books had been the tools to effect change by nonconformists in England for at least one hundred years by the time the Puritans settled in the

New World. Puritan writers from Queen Elizabeth's rule forward had turned to the printing press to state their case for changes in the English state church. Those publications erupted in the late 1630s as differences between the Stuart monarchy and the will of Parliament pushed the country into civil war.

In New England, the turmoil that affected the English government was not nearly as important as the religious state of the people. After all, they had left England not "to obtain riches quickly," as one Puritan emigrant explained, but "that they might enjoy Christ and his Ordinances in their primitive purity." Since the press at Cambridge was controlled by Harvard College and subsequently by the ruling body of the colony, its principal function would be to promote the goals of the colony—the education and religious edification of its inhabitants and the propagation of the gospel among the Indians.

One of the best examples of the use of printing in New England to meet the religious goals of the colony was the work of John Eliot. Eliot, upon arriving in New England, began working to Christianize the Indians. The English for more than a century had believed that it was the duty of the civilized Christians of Europe to proselytize Native Americans. In 1519, John Rastell wrote that the inhabitants of the New World "nother knowe God . . . nor never harde tell of wrytynge nor other scripture." Rastell then said that it would be "a great meritoryouse dede" if Europeans could teach the heathen about God. Eliot set about to accomplish this task, which meant that he first had to learn the language of the Indians. He mastered Algonquin and proceeded on the colony's proselytizing mission. Because the

Puritans believed that the true way for anyone to know God was though firsthand experience with God's word, Eliot translated the Bible into a printed version of the Indian language, and he did the same with other Christian writings he felt were important.

Eliot, however, was also a victim of the tight censorship of Massachusetts Bay. Despite his meritorious work in propagating the gospel to the Indians, Eliot crossed the line when he published *The Christian Commonwealth*. Printed in England in 1659, the General Court of Massachusetts ordered that Eliot's book "be totally suppressed." In addition, the court ordered that anyone owning one of Eliot's heretical books should destroy it. Eliot had proposed the Leveller idea of democratically elected officials.

Until the time of Eliot's trial in 1661, however, nothing that was produced on America's sole printing press in Cambridge needed to be suppressed because, as Clyde Duniway pointed out, everything that the press produced was done so under the close supervision of Harvard presidents Henry Dunster and Charles Chauncey. Just as in England, there was no general notion that freedom of the press was a right of the people. Multiple writers, including John Lilburne, John Milton, and William Walwyn, advocated versions of a free press in the mid-1640s, but the Commonwealth Parliament and then Oliver Cromwell in the Protectorate passed laws to control printing. When the Stuarts returned to control of England in the 1660s, Charles II successfully curtailed the growing newssheet trade. The Puritans of New England reacted no differently to printing than their homeland counterparts did. Controlling printing, however, did not mean elimination of debate and discussion on dozens of subjects. In England, government—whether it was monarchial or that of the Interregnum—never completely halted printing by nonconformists. In America, total control of what was printed through the mid-1660s was much simpler, since only one press operated, and it was under tight Puritan supervision. The same cannot be said of discussion and debate. While the Puritans did not acknowledge any right to freedom of expression and sought to stop it, the task was impossible. The same ideas that led Puritans in England and America to seek ways either to purify the church or to create a New Jerusalem were the products of independent thinking—liberty of conscience. Only a people who believed that they had come up with the ultimate answers would think that no more discussion of ideas was necessary. In America, as in England, debate would continue.

DEBATE AND DISCUSSION

In 1645, John Winthrop addressed his fellow colonists on a matter of great importance to them. In England, the Anglican Church had been displaced as the state church and Presbyterianism put in its place. The turmoil from 1643 had produced a body of literature that advocated religious toleration beyond anything that had ever been proposed in England previously. The Levellers, under Lilburne's guidance, were proposing that the entire country operate under a social contract similar to the religious one that Winthrop and the Puritans had devised for the New World. Only, under Lilburne's proposal, self-government was based not in religion, but in a society that allowed all who believed in scripture, no matter the interpretation, a voice. Cognizant of the debate in England on the direction and fate of government, some New England colonists began to advocate a relaxation of the tight entwining of government and church in Massachusetts. In Plymouth, a call for a "full and free tollerance of religion to all men that would preserve the civill peace" was quashed by the town's magistrates. Radical ideas such as these were creeping into discussions in Massachusetts, and Winthrop needed to address them.

Winthrop said that people were free to act because God had given them a natural liberty at the time of creation. But in order to exist in society as God would have people do in order to survive, they had to submit to civil liberty or authority. People give up individual rights for the well-being of the whole. Winthrop said, "It is the same kind of liberty wherewith Christ hath made us free." We may be free to act individually, but in order to survive, we submit to authority, Winthrop explained. If people could not do this, they had to be made to do it or be banished from the covenanted community, as the Puritans had done to Roger Williams and Anne Hutchinson after him. Winthrop said that if people believed their leaders were acting in a Christ-like manner, then the people should "quietly and cheerfully submit unto that authority which is set over you." But in his last sentence, Winthrop acknowledged that rulers, as fallible humans, might sometimes need a corrective. "[I]f we fail at any time, we hope we shall be willing," he said, "to hearken to good advice from any of you, or in any other way of God; so shall your liberties be preserved, in upholding the honor and power of authority amongst you."

Winthrop's statement referred to the notion of petitioning government, and it was not new. Puritans had done this during Elizabeth's reign and would continue to advocate it in England until it became part of the English Bill of Rights in 1689. But in 1645, Winthrop opened the door for debate, though he would never have acknowledged doing so except for members of the elect within his gathered colony. In America in the seventeenth century, though, discussion anywhere that questioned authority raised the ire and prosecutorial hackles of authorities. The rapidly changing nature of the mother country and fast growth of the colonies, whose population grew by more than 800 percent from 1640 to 1700, ensured that dialogue on ideas contrary to the status quo would occur as Catholics, Quakers, and Baptists, and people from other European countries besides England, moved to America.

Still, petitioning the government remained open to people within the colonies, but only within certain confines. People could appeal to the government once a decision had been made, or they could petition the government to act on a request or to accept what they viewed as viable alternatives to laws. For example, in Massachusetts in 1673, a man appealed a ruling by a county court that had fined him for slandering its members. On appeal, he won. A decade later, Massachusetts residents petitioned the government to allow taxes to be paid with agricultural products rather than money. The government agreed. But, as might be expected, the longer people lived in America, the more likely they were to use the right of petition to complain about governmental actions. In 1680, the Virginia House of Burgesses changed its rules of petition because the members believed people were using the privilege not to petition the assembly for anything credible, but as a way to put into circulation "scandalous and seditious papers, and to entitle and call them the grievances of the inhabitants."

Virginia may have instituted the 1680 law more as a reaction to what happened there and in neighboring North Carolina than for any other reason. A colony with marginal access to the ocean at best, and with land even more swampy than that surrounding Jamestown, Albemarle, the Carolina county closest to Virginia, had difficulty surviving. In 1677, the Lord's Proprietors, who owned Carolina, sent an acting governor to the Albemarle. Thomas Miller was supposed to create stability there, before Governor Thomas Eastchurch arrived, but, instead, he caused a rebellion to spring up. In December, the ship *Carolina* returned from England. Miller discovered that on board the ship was George Durant, who had gone to England to petition for a change in the colony's government, especially its taxation policies. Miller considered what Durant had said to be seditious libel and secretly boarded the ship in an effort to arrest Durant. Instead, the move backfired, and irate Carolinians soon were in open rebellion against Miller and his government.

Within two weeks, all officials of Miller's government had been arrested. The insurrectionists petitioned the court to remove all political leaders for a number of reasons, the most important of which was that Miller's actions since arriving in the colony had been illegal. Culpeper's Rebellion, as the uprising was called, eventually fell apart, but not before the rebels had established their own government, which ran Albemarle County until 1683. After petitioning the government both in England and at home, citizens had revolted; for the first time in America, a governmental body had been usurped by the people.

The year before Culpeper's Rebellion, Virginia Governor William Berkeley faced similar petitions about government practices. Nathanial Bacon, elected to the colony's assembly, brought the people's concerns to light through a series of handwritten manifestos distributed to the public and in the House of Burgesses. Berkeley made sure that the requests were ignored. Incensed, the people revolted, but Bacon died shortly after the rebellion started. Berkeley rounded up colonists who supported the revolt and forced them to apologize publicly for their actions. Virginia leaders no doubt considered Bacon's revolt and Culpeper's Rebellion when revising the colony's laws on petitioning government in 1680, but interestingly, King Charles II recognized the Virginians' petition as valid and recalled Berkeley to England.

One way that colonial governments sought to suppress debate that might lead to uprisings like Culpeper's Rebellion and the Bacon revolt was through loyalty oaths. During Bacon's rebellion, both the governor and Bacon's forces required loyalty oaths of people. Any person leaving England for Jamestown in 1607 had to first take an oath of loyalty to James I. Anyone discovered in the English New World settlement who had not signed a loyalty agreement was sent back to England. The covenantal arrangement in New England was a type of loyalty oath, and the Freeman's Oath—the first document produced on the Cambridge printing press—required settlers to swear allegiance to the government of the colony and to report any who might question it. In Virginia, colonists were required to take another loyalty oath in 1641, just two years after Lord Baltimore and his group of Catholics settled Maryland. Many people in England and in America alike believed that Charles I, through Archbishop Laud, wanted to reinstitute Catholicism as the state church during the turmoil of the 1640s. With Catholics close by, Virginians were required to swear loyalty to the Anglican Church. Those who didn't could be fined one thousand pounds of tobacco, and those who held a political position could lose it. With stakes as high as these, Virginia could stifle any debate about religious toleration and ensure that its citizens would remain loyal to colony and crown.

While fealty to government officials was the prime reason for loyalty oaths in Virginia and the reason for the actions by the House of Burgesses, protection of the religious order was the reason public debate needed to be quelled in New England. Separation of religion and government was much harder to distinguish there than in the Southern colonies, and the leaders in New England believed any public discussion that criticized its laws or authority had to be curtailed, including public sermons.

As mentioned earlier, Massachusetts passed laws that banished Baptists from the colony in 1644, but this did not stop the radical nonconformists who denounced infant baptism from continuing their proselytizing efforts among the Puritan elect. After his expulsion from Massachusetts, Roger Williams established the Rhode Island colony. For a time, Williams worshipped as a Baptist, but he set up his small settlement as a place that would operate under total religious toleration. In 1651, three Rhode Island Baptists came to Massachusetts. Harvard's first president, Henry

Dunster, listened to them and then decided not to baptize his just-born child. To make matters worse, Dunster preached sermons denouncing infant baptism. To the Puritans, infant baptism marked entry into God's body of the elect and the covenantal community. Dunster's words threatened the very fabric of the colony, both religious and civil. Dunster was banned from public speaking and removed as president of the college. In addition, the colony created a new law that required anyone who taught to be thoroughly questioned to make sure they followed Puritan religious doctrines completely.

Throughout the seventeenth century, people were arrested and punished for all manner of public speech. Protecting government, as we have seen, was the basis for nearly every action to suppress debate and discussion. That meant, in most cases, that religious debate was a threat to the standing order, too. People who spread false news threatened colonial welfare, as did anyone making a public comment about a public official. According to Larry Eldridge, America's first public officials felt they had to curtail any kind of debate outside the narrowest of confines because it "inevitably endangered the moral and social values that government protected, the public peace it sought to maintain, and the institutions it erected and protected to serve those ends. Punishing such words, in simple terms, preserved society." Officials were not doing anything different from their counterparts in England, but changes in England in the last quarter of the seventeenth century, the growing American population, and the introduction of new presses and alternate ways of spreading information meant that conflict between expression and government would continue.

THE RISE OF PRINT

A glut of publications never overran the colonies the way they did England since there were only five presses operating in America by the end of the seventeenth century. But American law still mirrored English law, especially from the restoration of the monarchy on. The last efforts at suppression of the press in England helped in the publication of America's first newspaper, too, but the newspaper explosion that occurred in England following the demise of licensing in 1694 would have to wait decades to take place in America. Assorted laws were put in place to ensure that America would not face this explosion of papers at the beginning of the eighteenth century. The sharing of information, however, became increasingly important to colonials. The development of newsletters and newspapers to pass along what people were talking about was inevitable.

Before 1660 in America, there was no real need to worry about what the Harvard College printing press produced because all was closely overseen by the school's presidents. That, however, did not stop the General Court of the colony from requesting in 1649 that the governor establish a licensing system. In its appeal, the judges noted that "ffor as much as Seuerall inconueniencys may acrew to the Commonwealth by ye liberty of ye pres this Cort doth heerby order y^t noe booke or wrighting shall bee Imprinted wthin this Jurisdiction . . . Vnles they shall be licenced by such psons as are or shall bee appoynted by this cort for y^t end." The governor replied simply that he saw no need for such a system.

In 1660, however, monarchial rule returned to the mother country. Charles II reestablished licensing in 1662,

and Massachusetts—acting in harmony with what was taking place in England—passed a licensing act of its own.
Controversial, the act was repealed the next year but rein-
stated in 1664. Licensing, even if it was patterned after
Charles's legislation, seemed superfluous in America—until
Marmaduke Johnson brought a second, independent press
to Massachusetts in 1665. Not only did Johnson intend to
publish outside the oversight of Harvard's president, he
wanted to set up his press in Boston, not Cambridge. In England, press shops were limited to London, Cambridge, and
Oxford. It was easier to oversee their output that way, and
the rationale for publication in the university towns was obvious. Massachusetts authorities balked at the move to
Boston and emphasized that nothing would be printed on
either press in Massachusetts without prior approval. The
order stated: "For the preventing of irregularityes & abuse
to the authority of this country by the printing presse, It is
ordered by this Court & the Authority thereof, that there
shall be no printing presse allowed in any toune w^{th}in this
juridiciton but in Cambridge, nor shall any person or persons presume to print any copie but by the allowance first
had & obteyned vnder the hands of such as this Court shall
from tjme to tjme impower." In 1674, the General Court
relented and allowed Johnson to move his print shop to
Boston. It did not, however, remove its licensing decree.

　　Before 1682, no other colony had to worry about what
might be printed because there were no other presses in
British colonial America. That did not mean that governments were not concerned with the potential danger that
printing possessed. They were, especially governors appointed by the crown. Each year, they were required to

report on the state of affairs within their respective colonies, and not a single person in any position of political or ecclesiastical power in any portion of England's domains had advocated an unrestrained press. Even Oliver Cromwell shut down printing as much as possible, even for those who supported him during the Civil War. In 1671, Virginia's William Berkeley, in what has become an oft-quoted testimonial, reported on the state of his colony. "I thank God, there are no free schools nor printing; and I hope we shall not have these hundred years," the governor wrote, "for learning has brought disobedience, and heresy, and sects into the world, and printing has divulged them, and libels against the government. God keep us from both." Berkeley's sentiments were no doubt shared by most of his fellow colonial executives.

The problem that existed for governors and assemblies was that growth in their respective colonies meant they needed printed matter. Without a printing press, all official documents had to be sent to England, printed there, and returned. While ships regularly made the transatlantic voyage, the amount of time required to get legislated material back to America in print form could run from about fifteen weeks, under ideal conditions, to more than a year. For that reason, among others, London ordered all provincial governors to acquire a printing press in order to print the official business of their colonies. From 1686 to 1730, the instructions given to royal governors included this statement: "And forasmuch as great inconvenience may arise by the liberty of printing within our said territory under your government you are to provide by all necessary orders that no person keep any printing-press for printing, nor that any book pamphlet or other matters whatsoever be printed without your especial leave and license first obtained." Colonies needed a press, but all that they printed was to be published only with governmental approval. The licensing that Massachusetts had initiated in 1662 was now official colonial policy, even though England let licensing expire when it was up for renewal in 1694, and, at least in Massachusetts, printers would have to pay surety even to print licensed material. The colony ruled "that no Papers, Bookes Pamphlets &c should be printed in New England untill Licensed according to Law, and that no printer have Liberty to print till he hath given five hundred pound security."

Virginia applied the new licensing act almost immediately after the colony obtained a press in 1682 when printer William Nuthead took it upon himself to set the proceedings of the assembly without approval. Nuthead had only run proof sheets when officials uncovered his actions. The shop was immediately shut down, and the colony awaited word from England for what to do, since it was between governors. When the new executive, Francis Howard, arrived, he brought with him an order that in Virginia, "no person be permitted to use any press for printing upon any occasion whatsoever." Though London had required each colony to obtain a press, it appeared that in Virginia, at least, having a press and printer was too risky. Nuthead moved to Maryland and stirred up that colony by printing tracts attacking the Catholic government. He was not charged with seditious libel, however, because the colony's Protestant majority was looking for any reason to have the Catholics removed from power. Ignoring the tract was in the government's best interests.

In 1685, a fifth printing press joined the three operating in Massachusetts and the fourth in Maryland. William Bradford landed in Philadelphia, a settlement that the Quaker William Penn had helped found, with a press and training from his grandfather, a printer in Leicestershire, and from his father-in-law, Andrew Sowle, one of London's best-known printers. The Quakers were one of seventeenth-century England's most radical nonconformist groups and were persecuted heavily in both England and America. In New England, the Quakers, like the Baptists, were banished, and their teachings were said to be "full of blasphemies." Anyone found owning Quaker literature was to be fined up to £10 on the first two offenses and jailed on the third. All Quaker writings were also ordered to be burned by the executioners. Bradford was a Quaker, and he came to Philadelphia with Penn's blessing and a personal letter of recommendation from George Fox, founder of the Society of Friends. The Society promised Bradford printing work and an annual salary. It is ironic that he became the first printer in America to be jailed for what he published, considering the persecution that Quakers faced and their long-standing support of liberty of conscience and a free press to espouse those ideas.

In 1659, Quaker Richard Hubberthorne said that there must be "a free Hearing among all People that so it may be a free Nation." His views were the same as most nonconformists in terms of liberty of conscience. But as we have seen, first in England and then in Massachusetts Bay, whenever dissenters attained majority status, they quelled divergent ideas. That is to be expected, considering the nature of seventeenth-century religion, but Quakers, with their belief in an "Inner Light" that guided all individually, truly seemed to believe in individual autonomy. George Fox advocated that all people be allowed to debate "freely without any end, or reward, or bribery," which would produce "a free nation, a free people." But this concept quickly faded in Philadelphia after George Keith, the surveyor-general of New Jersey and the head of Philadelphia's Friends' School, asked Bradford to print a series of pamphlets and a broadside for him. Keith, in those publications, attacked Pennsylvania's Society of Friends. The Quaker government called the writings seditious and arrested both Keith and Bradford. Bradford was charged with printing seditious material and violating the Licensing Act of 1662. Authorities seized Bradford's press and type. In 1693, the printer was released. He took his press and moved to New York and set up shop there, where he would be involved indirectly in two important libel trials, those of Thomas Maule and John Peter Zenger.

In New York, Bradford worked as official printer to the colony, just as he had done in Pennsylvania, and he produced another work for a Quaker, Thomas Maule. Unlike Keith's writings, Maule's pamphlet, *Truth held forth and maintained,* was approved for publication in New York. It was not, however, approved for reading or discussion in Massachusetts, where authorities called its contents "wicked Lyes and Slanders . . . upon Government, and . . . utterly subversive of the true Christian religion and professed faith." Maule spent nearly a year in jail before going to trial. In a preview of what would happen with Zenger nearly forty years later, the Massachusetts Quaker appeared in front of a jury, rather than judges, to determine his guilt. As Leonard Levy has noted, Maule did not base his defense on freedom of the press but in the lack of evidence presented by the prosecution. The jury returned a not-guilty verdict, saying that since Maule had libeled the church, not the state, the wrong venue heard the trial. The fact that the jury saw a distinction between church and state in Massachusetts in 1696 reveals something about the changing nature of the colony, not the least being changes in attitudes due to the revolt against the newly instituted royal governor a decade earlier. With the emphasis on reading in New England, there can be little doubt that the writings of men such as Thomas Hobbes and John Locke could be found on the shelves at Harvard as well as in bookcases in the homes of the more affluent citizens. Ideas about the nature of government were changing, but officials were not yet ready to open the presses of the colony to everyone to print anything. Again, as Levy has said, the idea of free expression in printed form barely existed in seventeenth-century America. That was something that another printer had discovered when he printed America's first newspaper six years earlier.

NEWSPAPERS, NEWSLETTERS, AND SERMONS

What was read, printed, and discussed in America during the seventeenth century followed patterns similar to those in England during the sixteenth and seventeenth centuries. Issues dealing with liberty of conscience appeared first in print and were debated more frequently within the public sphere because of the significance people placed on their relationship with God. This does not mean that other types of information were not important to them. They were. In England as early as the 1620s, ministers formulated their sermons along the lines of newssheets, as Thomas Lushington did in a sermon preached at Oxford. To think that British colonials in New England would be interested solely in their immortal welfare gives more credit to Puritans than may be deserved, but we need to remember, too, that the Puritans were joined together in covenantal communities. What affected one member of the body had implications for all. So news of what happened in the world was of importance. English publications were readily available in America, even newspapers, and colonists, who, we sometimes forget, were British citizens, copied what their countrymen did—again, following behind by one to several decades, depending on the form of communication.

The means of sharing news information that colonials most quickly adopted was the sermon containing news. According to Harry S. Stout, "the sermon stood alone in local New England contexts as the only regular (at least weekly) medium of public communication. As a channel of information, it combined religious, educational, and journalistic functions." News of events, as presented in sermons and then in newssheets, reflected the nature of seventeenth-century life. In America—just as in England—it was believed that God's providence was behind all that happened, which is the exact reason Benjamin Harris gave for beginning *Publick Occurrences* in 1690. In the paper's only printing, Harris explained precisely why he was publishing a newssheet. "That which is herein proposed," he said in the prospectus, "is, First, That Memorable Occurents of Divine Providence may not be neglected or forgotten, as they too often are."

As the first means of sharing basic news of events in

America in a public way, sermons would have followed along the lines of the English coffeehouse in terms of oral transmission. In coffeehouses in the last half of the seventeenth century, however, discussion was usually initiated through some form of writing. Sermons did not allow for debate and discussion while being given, and most of what might have been discussed after a service would have been more theological than anything else. Still, sermons were often printed for public distribution, and the kind that were printed most often, and were therefore delivered most frequently from the pulpits, were the "fast-day" sermons. According to David Nord, these sermons were a "journalistic tool" that allowed for the introduction of current events to the people. God's hand in the event would, naturally, be a part of the sermon, but the message would be based in something that today we would call news. An example would be a 1675 sermon delivered by Increase Mather that was published. The opening phrase of Mather's title for the sermon reflected God's providence: "The Times of men are in the hand of God." The end of the lengthy title introduced the news event that initiated the sermon: "which hapned in Boston in New England, the 4th Day of the 3d Moneth 1675 (when part of a Vessel was blown up in the Harbour, and nine men hurt." Sermons, then, at least in New England, were a natural way to pass on news.

Newssheets were really not feasible in America even when Harris published *Publick Occurrences.* He proposed a monthly printing schedule, no doubt realizing that printing more often would be prohibitive financially because of the lack of concentrated population, even in Boston, which had a population of around five thousand at the time. Also, the small number of printing presses, the power that local governments wielded over them, and the royal pronouncement that all items printed in America had to be licensed limited the possibility that something as informative as a newspaper would be permitted.

All of this, however, did not deter Benjamin Harris. He may not have been a student of English journalistic history, but if he had been, he would have realized that when newsbooks appeared during the 1590s and even earlier, they were rarely censored by government because they dealt only with information that had no direct implications for England. Harris, of course, believed in journalism in more modern terms, despite the fact that he started his paper to reveal acts of God's providence. Harris believed that people would be more interested in news that directly affected them. It had proximity, and it would be as timely as possible for a monthly publication. He even provided an empty page for people to add their own news, expecting that people would share their newssheets, which was customary in England.

Harris, who had been forced to flee London after being jailed twice for what he published, applied the same principles to his American newspaper that he had to his newspaper efforts in England. He was a Baptist and strongly opposed to the government of Charles II, and when licensing expired in 1679, he had produced the first of the nonlicensed London papers. Its title explained everything one needed to know about his journalistic emphasis: *The Domestick Intelligence; Or, News both from City and Country.* Foreign news, at least if it had no application to events that affected the people, would not be found in Harris's newssheet.

When Harris faced arrest a third time after Charles re-instituted licensing, the printer fled to the Netherlands and then to America. Even though he was a Baptist and strongly religious, he settled in Boston because it was the only American city of any size and the only one that offered the possibility of working in the only trade he knew, printing. Harris's religious affections were of no matter because at about the same time that Harris arrived in Boston, Charles revoked the Puritan charter and made Massachusetts a royal colony. This produced unrest, something previously unknown in the Bay colony. Civil disturbances ensued, and the royal governor, Edmund Andros, was removed from office and thrown into jail. Despite decades of Puritan guidance, Massachusetts was, for a short time, without strong leadership. This is when Harris decided to publish a newspaper.

Not only was the colony in a state of anarchy, but England and France were at war in the first of four conflicts that played out on the European and American stage prior to the American Revolution. King William's War, as Americans called it, was like all the other English-French confrontations in North America to follow; Native Americans were actively involved, especially in the French effort. Harris believed that accurate information about New England's situation was vital, so on September 25, 1690, his paper appeared on the streets of Boston. Harris told of a ship seized by the French and Indians, who "Butchered the Master, and several of the men." He reported on the colony's military plans against the French, complaining that officials "have too much confided" in Indians from the Five Nations. He related information of how colonial forces had "cut the faces, and ript the bellies of two Indians, and threw a third Over board in the sight of the

French." He explained how the devil had caused a Water-Town man to commit suicide and that a smallpox outbreak in Boston was subsiding. Moreover, he said that King Louis of France was having sexual relations with his son's wife. Even though the colony's government was barely functioning, the Governor's Council still existed. On September 29, it ordered Harris never to publish *Publick Occurrences* or any other newssheet again in Massachusetts. Their decree stated: "that therein is contained Reflections of a very high nature: As also sundry doubtful and uncertain Reports, do hereby manifest and declare their high Resentment and Disallowance of said Pamphlet, and Order that the same be Suppressed and called in; strickly forbidding any person or persons for the future to Set forth any thing in Print without License first obtained from those that are or shall be appointed by the Government to grant the same."

The council's ban was not specific, but it called into question the accuracy of what Harris reported. The paper also embarrassed officials because it revealed what was happening in the northern part of the colony—Maine. The government appeared powerless to stop French and Indian encroachments there, and dependence upon Indians to stop Indians seemed foolhardy. It was an open criticism of the government, and Samuel Sewall, a council member, wrote in his diary that this comment and Harris's inferences about Louis XIV were reason enough to ban the paper. "A printed sheet entitled public Occurrences comes out, which gives much distaste because not Licensed," Sewall wrote, "and because of the passage referring to the French King and the Maquas [Mohawks]." Despite the fact that England and France were at war, references to royalty and sexual indiscretion were too much for the Puritan council members. Harris, as a result of the council's order, did not publish another newspaper in America. He returned to England in 1695 and began printing papers again in license-free London.

The absence of a paper in New England or in any other part of America in the 1690s and into the eighteenth century did not mean that information was not being shared. It was. As Francis Bacon wrote in 1597, "Knowledge itself is power," and a system of information sharing existed in America that ensured that those in power stayed in power. Most of the people who immigrated to America during the seventeenth century had to pay their way. That means they were not destitute. We know that they were literate, and we know that, at least in New England, education was a vital component of societal structure. According to Richard Brown, those in positions of power and importance in the colonies—clergy, lawyers, politicians, and anyone else whose economic standing allowed them a class position above the everyday workers—created information circles to provide them with the knowledge they needed to maintain their positions in society. Family, clergy, and those of similar status created overlapping information networks to provide a large base that disseminated information to those within it. The hierarchical nature of seventeenth-century society would have kept those in the upper elements of society from regular conversation with those considered to be lower class, but members of the lower class would have created their own sources of information, too. Although they would not have been privy to the information that allowed society's elite to retain power, they would have had information to share. All would have been able to share in the basic news presented in sermons and anything printed.

The information circles were not solely oral and not confined to geographic locations among America's elite. The news was also shared via letters, which were passed among people within the circles. Again, following a pattern established across the Atlantic, individual letter writing and the desire for information produced a new type of letter, one filled with as much information as possible and then hand copied so that multiple letters could be mailed to several people at once. In this way, identical information could be shared with people in a variety of locations quite efficiently. Boston's new postmaster, John Campbell, began to write letters in this fashion when he obtained his new job in 1700. Campbell's newsletters would not have replaced personal correspondence, but they nevertheless added a new layer of information. Campbell sent his letters to colonial governors and merchants throughout British colonial America. Operating in a manner that was certainly journalistic, Campbell gleaned information from ships arriving in Boston, and from letters he was able to obtain from people on ships and through his post office, pulled out what he believed would be of most value to people, and added these bits of information to his newsletters. His letters were shared, and demand for them rose rapidly.

Campbell's unique position allowed him access to information that crossed social boundaries. He also had ready access to the newspapers of London. Even with assistance, Campbell was not able to produce enough letters to meet the demand, so in April 1704, he asked printer Bartholomew Green to set his newsletter in type. Cognizant of what had happened when Benjamin Harris attempted to publish a newspaper, Campbell approached public officials with his plan. In 1690, the Governor's Council issued a decree "strickly forbidding any person or person for the future to Set fort any thing in Print without License first obtained from those that are or shall be appointed by the Government to grant the same." Campbell obtained approval to print the newsletter because he agreed to allow its contents to be approved by the governor's licenser. The information contained in Campbell's *Boston News-Letter,* he guaranteed, would not offend or injure government, and the hand of the licenser could censor items if there was any possibility of such offense. In the nameplate of Campbell's paper were the words "Published by Authority." As Sidney Kobre observed, America finally had a newspaper to share information, but it was decades behind those in England, where newssheets sold thousands of copies daily, some weeklies had circulations of ten thousand copies, writers had honed reporting skills, and licensing no longer existed. Moreover, Campbell's newspaper was just as limited in what it could say as anything else that had been published in America up to that time, perhaps even more so because the postmaster agreed to oversight by the licenser.

Political control of newspaper content would continue in Boston for at least another fifteen years, probably longer, according to Isaiah Thomas. A printer in colonial America and then of the early United States, Thomas believed that colonial governments influenced newspaper content well into the eighteenth century and noted that Virginia's printing "was thought to be too much under the control of the governor" until around 1766. In seventeenth-century America, the paucity of printing presses, and the scattered and small population, curtailed the rise of a print culture in terms of production. Colonists in America were not, however, isolated from the society from which they emigrated. The emigration explosion of the 1630s and 1640s meant that a constant stream of people and information from England arrived continuously in America. British colonists may have been more concerned about their survival in the "wilderness" of New Jerusalem than they were about civil war in the mother country, but what happened in England mattered to them.

In America, the dissemination of news occurred orally via information circles and sermons. Anything that was printed was closely monitored, and officials were wary of what might be printed. This did not mean that all types of dissent were banned. Colonials adopted the notion of the right to petition government for valid complaints. Unfortunately, as people in Virginia and North Carolina discovered, what they believed to be a valid complaint might be considered seditious speech by those in power. This would not change as long as government controlled printing presses and as long as a critical mass of people were not present to effect change. Ultimately, the attempt to protect government from any form of harm limited free speech in America. In a culture attuned to its religious origins, according to Larry Eldridge, authorities regulated speech in order to maintain a moral society as well as society's hierarchical structure, the public peace, and, of course, any institution that government created.

Americans of the seventeenth century analyzed the information they received through a religious lens. Sermons were a form of weekly newsletter long before any other type of information dispersal tool existed. Even Benjamin Harris said that the principal reason for the existence of *Publick Occurrences* was to help people realize God's hand in everyday events. Harris was a devoutly religious person and faced persecution in England because he published works by nonconformists who were considered scandalous and blasphemous by the authorities. Some of the stories in *Publick Occurrences* portray the hand of the divine upon the actions of man. But most of what was in the paper, viewed from a twenty-first-century perspective, was just news. Yes, the people who read it no doubt could give the rationale for what happened religious perspective, but it was nevertheless news that did not have the wrappings of a sermon. When John Campbell began publishing the *Boston News-Letter* in 1704, the same was true of the information that he presented. It could be interpreted through a religious lens, or it could be viewed as pure news. Campbell's first story in the April 24 edition dealt with a popish plot to take over England, and by inference, America. It was very much a story about people acting in the name of their religion, not God acting through people.

The information that people debated in America during the seventeenth century followed the same patterns of development that they did in England. In America, as in England, liberty of conscience became an important issue. Baptists, Quakers, and others did as they had in England: They shared their nonconformist beliefs and were suppressed. The Puritans, who had produced the largest amount of literature related to freedom of conscience in England, had no reason to do so in America. Instead, they became the censors. News as information also existed, but it focused not on foreign affairs, but rather on local events. Even the news in sermons was local in nature most of the time. Had Benjamin Harris produced a newspaper similar to the *London Gazette,* for example, it would probably have resulted in a reprimand for Harris for printing without official approval, but it would have no doubt been allowed. American news, in other words, very much approximated that of the English at the same time. That is because Americans were not starting from scratch; Harris, Bradford, and assorted intellectuals in the colonies had the practical experiences from England going back generations on which to base what they did.

Still, as Americans entered the eighteenth century, they lagged far behind England in terms of the availability of printed information. It would take nearly a century even to approximate the numbers and availability of newspapers in America that existed in England at the beginning of the eighteenth century, but as we have seen, America would profit from all that had gone on in England in terms of political philosophy and journalism. Efforts at suppression would naturally continue, but once competition for readers began and issues that tended to divide communities erupted, control of the press would be hard to maintain. The efforts of the seventeenth century to create order would take an unruly turn as the printed word became the impetus for the people's dialogue and debate. The rationale of why the printed word should be restricted that nearly all officials accepted in the seventeenth century would come under attack, as well. In eighteenth-century America, debate through the printed word was set to begin full force, and issues surrounding a free press were about to be debated on the streets and in the courts.

SIX

———————◇———————

TURNING POINTS FOR
EXPRESSION

In 1718, John Campbell lost his job. Since 1700, he had
served as postmaster in Boston. The franking privileges that
came with the position allowed him to send his creation, the
Boston News-Letter, to patrons in New England and down to
Philadelphia free of charge. As postmaster, he had access to
any information that traveled via the post. When Governor
Samuel Shute replaced Campbell with William Brooker, the
new postmaster assumed that the publication of the *News-
Letter* would be transferred to him. Since 1704, the *News-
Letter* had served as the official organ of the government,
which Campbell verified with the words "Published by Authority" in the paper's nameplate. Brooker was wrong, however, when he assumed the paper went with the office. The
sixty-five-year-old Campbell had no intention of retiring,
nor did he want to relinquish control of something that was
so much a part of his life. He continued printing the *News-
Letter,* and Brooker and the colony of Massachusetts were
forced to begin another paper to provide the colony with a

printed voice. On December 21, 1719, the first issue of the *Boston Gazette* appeared on the streets. Boston now had two newspapers, and more important, people now had two different options to choose from in acquiring written information. Competition now fueled the colony's newssheets.

When Campbell first began publishing the *News-Letter* as postmaster, Massachusetts officials had insisted that whatever was published in the paper meet with the approval of the licenser. A decade before that, the Governor's Council had shut down Benjamin Harris' *Publick Occurrences* for unlicensed printing and ordered that no other paper be published without governmental approval. Shute still operated under the oath that required that no "book pamphlet or other matters whatsoever be printed" without his "especial leave and license first obtained." Now, Campbell was publishing his newspaper sans the "Published by Authority" licensure in what was a direct violation of British colonial law. How was that possible? Was it because, for the past sixteen years, the *Boston News-Letter* had operated as an innocuous sheet, which approached news as history, and where Campbell attempted to present most information chronologically rather than as timely news? Was it because Campbell had never printed anything that attacked the colony's government? Or, had something else changed?

According to Clyde Duniway, the first two decades of the eighteenth century witnessed a change in the way government approached printing. Shute and his predecessors kept a close eye on publications that addressed political and religious themes, but in terms of newspapers, they adopted a stance more in keeping with English practice. In Britain at this time, the number and circulation of newspapers grew at a phenomenal rate. This growth went relatively unchecked, except by stamp taxes and an occasional seditious libel charge. The circulation figures of many London newspapers reached into the thousands per printing, perhaps as high as ten thousand copies per issue. Campbell's meager effort, which published at the most three hundred issues per week, posed no threat to the standing order of the colony and was apparently not seen as a revenue maker worthy of a stamp tax.

At the same time that the *Boston Gazette*'s start gave the town two papers, the colony faced economic crisis. Like their countrymen in England, the people of Massachusetts turned to the press as a means of airing their thoughts on the problem. As in England decades before, pamphlets were the front line in the public debate about proposed taxes on imported goods, but two public prints meant that new options were available for the conveyance of news, not just for readers but for the use of competing sides within Massachusetts government—the governor and the assembly. As a byproduct, the controversy led to an end of licensing in Massachusetts and paved the way for vicious newspaper debate.

The *Boston Gazette* and *Boston News-Letter* became vehicles for the controversy, perhaps because of animosity between the printers. Brooker believed he should have been given the *News-Letter* as part of his new job as postmaster. Campbell resented losing his job and blamed his successor. As the controversy grew, Brooker and the next postmaster, Philip Musgrave, naturally supported the position of Governor Shute, since each held the postmaster's position through royal appointment. Campbell's *News-Letter* became the voice of the assembly. The printers might not have been drawn into the turmoil and a free press might not have become an issue had not the assembly acquiesced to Shute's demands to drop taxes. In doing so, the assembly decided to publish its proceedings, and it included a lengthy preamble that attacked the governor and council for usurping the legislature's power. Both Brooker and Campbell adopted the practice of "paid advertisements," which were really editorial or essay insertions that dealt with the controversy.

Shute, as a result, decided to impose the power of his office and the governor's oath that he had taken, which required the licensing of printing, to stop opposition viewpoints from appearing in public. He threatened printers with arrest for seditious libel and then proposed a new law on printing for the province. "I therefore make no doubt but whoever is a Lover of the priviledges peace and Good order of this province, will be very desirous to have a law made to prevent this pernicious and dangerous practice," Shute said in a speech published in the *Boston Gazette* on March 20, 1721. "Especially since it is the King my masters positive Commands that no Book or paper, shall be printed without my Licence first obtained, which you have lately acquainted with." He also asked the Governor's Council about his legal standing to do this. The council pointed out that licensing had died out in England more than twenty-five years earlier, and despite any royal prerogative given in a royal governor's oath, he had little legal standing to stop the printing of anything in the colony. The assembly responded, too. In the April 3, 1721, *Boston News-Letter,* the assembly declared, "Should an Act be made to prevent the Printing any Book or paper, without Licence first obtained from the Governour," the people of the colony would be under "innumerable inconveniences and dangerous Circumstances." In Massachusetts, though not in other places in America for a while longer, the press was free of licensing. Just as political factions had discovered in England in the 1640s, in the 1680s, and in the post–Licensing Act era in the 1690s, the press was the ideal instrument to effect change in areas of importance to society—religion, politics, and economics. In England, printers of newssheets needed nearly a century to obtain such freedom for their prints. In Massachusetts, the removal of licensing had taken only thirty years.

The introduction of multiple news sources in America provided a new way for people to offer their ideas to the public for debate. Over the next thirty-plus years, as other government officials in America attempted to do the same things that Governor Shute had tried to do in Massachusetts to silence opposing voices, Americans, ever aware of what was taking place in Britain and elsewhere in the Western world, used the powerful arguments of Cato's Letters and the writings of other rationalists to advocate a free press. Printers, especially, turned to Cato's free press arguments whenever they came under attack for printing something, and increasingly, any printer who started a paper would glorify freedom of the press in his paper's first issue, based either on Cato's letter on free speech or some variation of it. Sometimes, the words of Milton from *Areopagitica* were used or adapted.

Pamphlets remained important to debate in America. As David Shields has pointed out, "manuscripts and fugitive pamphlet issues of the press" were the catalysts for the strongest expression of political dissent that occurred in

America to about 1750. But increasingly, newspapers were the chief means of sharing information and discussing public affairs. In 1750, printer James Parker commented that the desire of the people for information was something people of other nationalities did not seem to understand. "This taste," Parker said, "we Englishmen, have for News, is a very odd one; yet it must be fed." Six years later, Parker, now printing the *Connecticut Gazette,* expounded on a statement he had made while in New York. "The PRESS is not so much considered, as the Property of the Men who carry on the Trade of Printing, as of the Publick."

Americans were beginning the process that would lead to the unruly idea of a free press. Just how press debate would work needed little time to develop, however. In Boston, people would find out how it would work—just three months after the assembly declared licensing dead—with the introduction of yet another newspaper and the emergence of an issue that immediately divided a frightened community. The public dialogue included all the elements that draw people to news—public safety, community leaders and politicians accusing each other of malfeasance, religious divisions, and radical ideas. The news consumed people for weeks.

NEWSPAPERS AND PUBLIC DEBATE

The arguments in Boston over licensing may have seemed more of a political ploy on April 21, 1721, than it did later in August. By then, smallpox was raging through the city in the seventh major outbreak of the deadly disease in Boston since the beginning of the eighteenth century. Before the epidemic ended, nearly 60 percent of the town's 10,500 inhabitants would contract the diseases, with 15 percent of those who became ill dying. James Franklin, who had printed the *Boston Gazette* when it first appeared, introduced a third newspaper to Boston, the *New-England Courant,* at about the same time the outbreak occurred. In the fashion of twentieth-century muckrakers, Franklin announced that his paper would "expose the Vices and Follies of persons of all Ranks and Degrees." What would transpire during the next weeks was a hot and frantic public debate about inoculating people to prevent them from contracting the dreaded disease. The back-and-forth dialogue between pro- and anti-inoculators demonstrated the great value of a free press, but it also proved all the horrors of an unchecked press for those who believed it would be a danger to society.

The debate allowed the introduction of a controversial idea. Puritan minister Cotton Mather advocated a radical procedure. He suggested that people not afflicted with the disease be given it through inoculation. The concept of inoculation—the administration of a weakened form of a disease to someone who had not had it so that the body can build resistance to the illness—was not accepted by most European physicians and had never been practiced in America. Mather had learned of inoculation from his readings and from his African slave. Inoculating people as a preventative had been practiced in the Middle and Far East for a number of years, and Mather, who had lived through a case of smallpox in 1702 and had studied medicine before entering the ministry, believed the practice could stop the suffering and death the disease caused.

Mather began his crusade for inoculation by contacting Zabdiel Boylston, a Boston doctor, who agreed to inoculate individuals who were willing to try it. In the early eighteenth century, few of the physicians in America were educated in medicine. Rather, they were well-read individuals who dabbled in folk remedies and improvised with potions and drug mixtures, and they often experienced some success. Mather's plan for inoculation, however, was immediately opposed by Dr. William Douglass, Boston's only university-trained physician. He called inoculation "a Wicked and Criminal Practice" and the uneducated Boylston a "quack." The controversy was not solely about inoculating, however, even though John Checkley, the leading Boston Anglican who had arranged for Franklin to begin the *Courant,* stated explicitly that the initial purpose of the *Courant* was to stop inoculation. In reality, Checkley saw the paper as a means of ensuring that Anglicans could rid the colony of the power of Mather and other Puritans. Checkley and Mather had been at odds for years. Now that the Anglican's adversary had proposed a radical and controversial idea—smallpox inoculation—Checkley believed he could use public debate to shame Mather and eliminate him.

The Boston newspaper battle concerning inoculation lasted for months. The anti-inoculation writers often belittled their opponents in print but rarely used complete names in their attacks. The pro-inoculation forces generally avoided name-calling but did refute disparaging comments about Boylston. One of the practices employed, especially by the anti-inoculation writers, was the use of pseudonyms. Writers rarely used their own names in the papers of the eighteenth century for a variety of reasons, but an important one was that a writer might more easily avoid libel charges if no name was present. In the trial of John Peter Zenger, the printers of controversial material faced violation of sedition laws because their names almost always appeared on their publications, whereas the actual author's name was generally absent. Any seditious libel charges were therefore leveled at the person who produced the seditious material instead of the one who had written it.

Checkley and Douglass called Mather's inoculation idea "far fetched." They said Mather and the Puritan ministers who supported him were "profoundly ignorant" and referred to Mather as "the Town Lyar." The Puritans were certain that the *Courant*'s sole purpose was not just to stop inoculation but to "Vilify and abuse the best Men we have, and especially the principal Ministers of Religion in the Country." By current standards, the language of the 1721 inoculation controversy was mild, but at the time it would have been considered high slander. Those attacked, however, had nothing to do with government, and Governor Shute, an Anglican, probably did not care that Puritans, whom he considered a thorn in his side, bore the brunt of the *Courant*'s attacks. Ultimately, Mather, Boylston, and the others who supported inoculation were vindicated when the numbers of people dying from smallpox decreased greatly among the inoculated. These numbers were published, but the *Courant* continued to publish assorted attacks on various elements of Massachusetts society for another five years, causing run-ins for Franklin with the Massachusetts government.

What the inoculation controversy and the *New-England Courant* did for the developing ideas of free press in America, however, was to demonstrate that a voice unafraid of tackling major issues could provide society with stimulating essays and ideas for debate, even if its essays attacked "men in office, the clergy, and the prevailing religious opinions of the day." According to Wm. David Sloan, the *New-England Courant* ultimately failed to live up to these expectations, but it did pave the way for similar publications in Boston and in other colonies that could do more than print old news that, while of value, did not greatly enhance society.

EFFORTS TO SUPPRESS DEBATE

James Franklin's *New-England Courant,* while a stimulator of debate, revealed that despite all that had transpired in England and America in relation to the press during the past century, free and open debate on all subjects was neither assumed nor allowed legally. Protecting government was still a prime concern. While debate on smallpox inoculation was acceptable, questioning government actions was not. Pirate activity in the Atlantic had been affecting New England shipping, and now a ship flying the Jolly Roger was actively working off the Massachusetts coast. Many people, Franklin included, believed the government needed to act quickly to remove this menace to trade. On June 11, 1722, Franklin remarked that the government would take care of the ship "sometime this month."

The General Court construed Franklin's comment as a "high affront" to the government of Governor Shute and ordered Franklin arrested. The printer spent a month in jail. When he was freed in July, the Governor's Council released a statement saying that because the *Courant* contained "Paragraphs that tend to fill the Readers minds with vanity to the Dishonor of God, and disservice of Good Men," that "no such Weekly Paper be hereafter Printed or Published with-

out the same be first perused and allowed by the Secretary."
The notice also ordered Franklin to pay £100 as a surety
bond that he would comply with the council's orders. The
Massachusetts government was, in effect, reinstituting
licensing selectively on Franklin, with the secretary of the
council to act as the licenser. Franklin agreed to the terms of
his release, but he simply ignored the part about allowing the
secretary to peruse his paper before it was published. Rather
than arrest him again, though, Massachusetts officials allowed
the *New-England Courant* to continue its business as usual.

From July 1722 to January 1723, Franklin's paper published cutting satire, adding several essays on freedom of the
press by its cadre of writers known as the Hell-Fire Club.
Franklin also ran Cato's essay on libels on November 11 and
18. In January, however, Franklin ran into more legal trou-
bles as he returned to bashing the Puritan clergy of the
colony. An Anglican whose paper business started with the
strong support of John Checkley and other influential Anglicans in dealing with inoculation, Franklin had no use for
Cotton Mather or any other Puritan divine. At the same
time, the *Courant* suggested that Governor Shute, who was
sailing to England, was going there not to promote Massachusetts but to work against it. Immediately, the council issued a statement saying that Franklin's paper had a tendency
"to mock Religion" and had "injuriously reflected on, His
Majesty's Government." The council order said "That *James
Franklin,* the Printer and Publisher thereof, be strictly forbidden by this Court, to Print or Publish the New England
Courant, or any Pamphlet or Paper of the like Nature, except it be first supervised by the Secretary of the Province."
Again, Franklin ignored the order and published his paper on

schedule the next week. At that point, he faced an arrest order. As a way to get around this, he posted a £100 bond and, at least on the face of it, gave up publishing the *Courant*. The paper still appeared on schedule. Now, however, James Franklin was no longer listed as publisher: Benjamin Franklin's name appeared in its place. James's younger brother, as the well-known story goes, used this time to unburden himself as his oppressive brother's apprentice and prepare to enter the printing trade.

Despite James Franklin's ploys, arrest orders were issued for him. This time, however, he was to face a jury. Juries did not always render a verdict that government officials wanted. Thomas Maule, for example, had been released on a technicality in his jury trial in 1696, and William Bradford in 1692 had been released without penalty for agreeing not to publish anything else offensive. To ensure that he would not do so, the printer promptly left Pennsylvania. Similarly, Franklin received a not-guilty verdict when he appeared in court. He was charged with failing to have his paper licensed, and the jury simply rejected the notion that the Massachusetts licensing requirement was legal. Since the colony had no power to license publications, the jury said, Franklin had broken no law. According to Robert W. T. Martin, the growing tendency in America to use juries in trials involving the press helped to expand the notion of a free press, helped to promote America's newspaper culture, and even helped to change political culture. Juries were "the great jewel of liberty," according to a British publication that Franklin reprinted in the *New-England Courant*. What papers had to say about the importance of newspapers and the value of a free press may have influenced jurors as much as anything else.

At almost the same time that the Massachusetts assembly began its efforts to curtail James Franklin's "seditious" printing, the government of Pennsylvania called printer Andrew Bradford, William's son, before it to testify about a statement he had printed. Currency, not pirates, was the problem in Philadelphia, and Bradford, whose father had been the first American printer to be arrested for what he printed, simply stated that he hoped that the assembly would "find some effectual Remedy, to revive the dying Credit of this Province, and restore us to our former happy Circumstances." This printing, though, came after he had published, without his name, a pamphlet on the same subject. In Bradford's case, no trial was conducted, but the assembly still sought to impose a limited form of licensing on him. Bradford was told that "He must not for the future presume to publish any thing relating to or concerning the Affairs of this Government, or the Government of any other of his Majestys Colonies, without the permission of the Governour or Secretary of this province."

Like Franklin, who had ignored the Massachusetts licensing order, Bradford did the same in Philadelphia. Though he'd been told not to comment on any other colonial government, following Franklin's second run-in with authorities in 1723 he wrote that "the Assembly of the province of the Massachusetts Bay are made up of Oppressors and Bigots." No repercussions of any kind were leveled at Bradford, though he was arrested and jailed in 1729 for what Governor Patrick Gordon called "a wicked & seditious Libell." According to Anna Janney DeArmond, Bradford simply went quietly to jail and, when released, "went quietly back to work again." He seems never to have considered the required licensing standard anything other than idle words, despite his two convictions. Consistently in the 1730s, Bradford's paper made derogatory remarks about government actions throughout the colonies without repercussion. Licensing in Pennsylvania, in reality, was as much of an idle threat as it was in Massachusetts. Perhaps the most telling statement on the ability of either government to control comments in print came from Boston's Increase Mather. In reference to the *New-England Courant,* he said, "I can well remember when the Civil Government could have taken an effectual Course to suppress such a *Cursed Libel!*"

Of course, Mather was correct. There was little left of the repressive nature of sixteenth- and seventeenth-century law in relation to the control of printing that still existed in 1721, and the apologists for freedom of the press were at the height of their creativity. The Star Chamber and licensing vanished with the Long Parliament and with King William's refusal to renew the Licensing Act in 1641 and 1694, respectively. The law of seditious libel remained valid law, but by the beginning of the eighteenth century in England, judges were starting to place increased weight on the intent of statements rather than what they said at face value. Vicious intentions, falsity, maliciousness, and factiousness now weighed upon decisions. These details would have made no difference to the Star Chamber, but it was now sixty years deceased. As in libel actions brought against William Bradford, Thomas Maule, and James Franklin, juries increasingly played the deciding role in the verdicts of libel trials. This development may well have been due to increased attention among Britons to the Magna Carta, which said that "none shall be condemned without a Lawful Tryal by his Peers." Franklin ran this and other excerpts from the 1215 document, which was the basis of all English law, in the July 30, 1722, *New-England Courant*. But, according to Frederick Siebert, government officials found ways around runaway juries by charging them to determine guilt or innocence solely in matters of fact. Did the defendant, for example, actually publish the offending words? It was following these developments and under these jury guidelines that America's most famous eighteenth-century libel trial took place.

THE ZENGER TRIAL

In 1733, John Peter Zenger was a struggling printer in New York. He had learned his profession as an apprentice in the print shop of the colony's official printer, William Bradford. Zenger opened his own print shop in 1726, but he was no rival to his former master. Bradford received all of the colonial government's printing business and published the colony's only newspaper, the *New-York Gazette,* which he began to print the year before Zenger left his shop. Zenger published whatever he could, mainly stationery and some pamphlets and books.

The Zenger trial actually had more to do with political control and partisanship in New York than with freedom of the press in colonial America. Freedom of the press served as the means to an end for the political adversaries involved. Philadelphia lawyer Andrew Hamilton, however, made the case about the press, about jury trials, and about the importance of truth whenever charges of seditious libel were leveled at someone. The case established no legal precedents, but it did refocus thinking and stimulate discussion of seditious libel throughout the British colonies in the New World as well as in Britain itself. The anonymous "Z" in the *Pennsylvania Gazette* said Hamilton was "THE DEFENDER OF THE LIBERTY OF THE PRESS, by the Strength of his own Genius," and that he had "erected to himself a Monument, which will transmit his Memory *with Honour,* to latest Posterity."

The roots of the controversy that sent Zenger to jail for libel were buried deep in the partisan politics of New York, which gained new intensity when Governor John Montgomerie died in 1731. Naming a new governor was the crown's responsibility, and it often took more than a year for news of a governor's death to reach England and for a new governor to be named and to assume office. In the interim, the senior member of the colony's council served as governor. In New York, that was Rip Van Dam, a seventy-two-year-old Anglo-Dutch merchant. Van Dam had been a member of the council for nearly thirty years. Interim governors received the governor's pay until the governor arrived from England, and often, the interim would set aside half of this pay to give to the newly appointed governor when he arrived. But in Van Dam's case, the council decided that the whole salary should be Van Dam's, probably out of deference to his age, council seniority, and service to the colony.

When William Cosby arrived in New York and assumed the governorship, he demanded a pay raise and half of Van Dam's salary. The colony gave the new governor the pay increase, but Van Dam did not surrender half of the interim's pay. Governor Cosby brought suit and arranged for the colony's Supreme Court to sit in judgment of the case.

The move pitted the colony's two political factions

against each other. On one side was Governor Cosby and those who supported him—the "Court party." On the other side was Chief Justice Lewis Morris and a number of influential people, including lawyers James Alexander and William Smith, who opposed the governor—the "Popular party." The two Popular party lawyers argued that the court should not hear Cosby's petition. Justice Morris, Cosby's political opponent, naturally agreed. As a result, Governor Cosby removed Justice Morris from the court, which elevated the controversy to a new level.

The Popular party looked for a way to sway public opinion against Governor Cosby. Pamphlets and broadsides were possibilities, but letters and essays in a regularly published newspaper, they knew, would be better. The Popular party knew that Bradford would never print criticism of Governor Cosby in his *Gazette* because it would endanger his status as the colony's official printer, which amounted to a government subsidy. The Popular party needed its own newspaper. When party members contacted Zenger and offered to finance a newspaper for him, he agreed. Zenger became the mechanic, the printer, of the *New-York Weekly Journal,* and lawyers Alexander and Smith served as the editors and chief opinion writers. Immediately, the lawyers set the tone of the paper with free-speech essays and other items related to free expression. Then they began their newspaper assault on Cosby. They called the governor a French sympathizer for allowing a ship, the *Le Cæsar,* into New York harbor, and they called him a "Traytor" and boldly proclaimed, "Only the wicked Governours of Men dread what is said of them."

Governor Cosby immediately ordered Zenger's arrest

for seditious libel. The paper missed its next publication because its printer was in jail. At his hearing, the court set Zenger's bail at £600. Zenger could not afford the excessive bail, but the wealthy Popular party could. It chose, however, to leave Zenger behind bars; he was worth more as a martyr to the harsh practices of a tyrannical governor than as a printer. Zenger remained in jail until his August 1735 trial, but the paper continued to publish, with Zenger's wife, Anna, and apprentices doing the work.

Although the Popular party would not bail Zenger out of jail, it did intend to provide him with legal counsel—Alexander and Smith—in court. Cosby, however, had the pair disbarred and appointed a government official, John Chambers, to defend the printer. Nevertheless, when it came time for Zenger's defense, it was not Chambers who rose in the courtroom, but Andrew Hamilton. Hamilton was considered by most to be the best trial lawyer in the colonies. When Alexander and Smith were disbarred, they contacted Hamilton about assuming the role of counsel for Zenger when the printer went to court. The fifty-nine-year-old Hamilton admitted that Zenger printed the tracts in question, but he added that the charges the paper had leveled against the governor were "notoriously known to be true." The jury found Zenger not guilty after deliberating for only minutes.

The significance of the Zenger trial in the development of the concept of freedom of the press is threefold. First, jury trials became the norm in libel cases brought by government officials. As seen in Boston with James Franklin, juries had minds of their own, and Hamilton played to this point in Zenger's defense. "I must insist that where matter of law is complicated with matter of fact, the jury have a right to determine both," he said. "I hope it is sufficient to prove that jurymen are to see with their own eyes, to hear with their own ears and to make use of their own consciences and understandings in judging of the lives liberties or estates of their fellow subjects." Government officials in England and America tried to circumvent the unexpected verdicts that juries sometimes returned with specific instructions that required the jury to determine only whether the accused had made or printed the libel—which is exactly the direction given to the Zenger jury. Freeholder juries, however, were often as eager to interpret law themselves as to follow it. And, as in the case of Franklin in Boston, knowledgeable Britons returned to the Magna Carta as a means of demanding a trial by jury instead of in front of the magistrate only. "I only intend," Hamilton said in reference to the founding document of English law, "to show that the people of England saw clearly the danger of trusting their liberties and properties to be tried, even by the greatest men in the kingdom, without the judgment of a jury of their equals."

Second, the Zenger trial proposed that truth should be given public voice and not punished. In many ways, this was just an enlargement of the idea found in the English Bill of Rights that people were guaranteed the right to petition government for grievances, and it had been an element of determining intent by the bench in England for three decades. John Winthrop acknowledged this right in Massachusetts Bay in 1645, as did other Puritans from Elizabeth's reign forward as well as the Levellers during the English Civil War. But there was a difference. Petitioning government was not identical to making public statements against government, especially in the public prints. Seditious libel's entire purpose was the protection of government, and truth could be construed to make the libel even worse. Zenger's paper, echoing the ideas of the Levellers, Milton, Locke, and Cato's Letters, affirmed the power of truth when it declared, "Truth will always prevail over Falshood." Hamilton combined the idea of petitioning government with truth in his trial exposition. "I beg leave to insist that the right of complaining or remonstrating is natural," he stated. "*Truth* ought to govern the whole affair of libels." Even though Hamilton's defense did not change the law, it did become, according to one colonist writing in the *Pennsylvania Gazette* in 1738, "better than the law, it ought to be law, and will always be law wherever justice prevails," because the jury recognized its own power and the power of the truth.

Third, Zenger's defense elevated the role of the press in criticizing government. In keeping with Enlightenment thought, the attacks in the *New-York Weekly Journal* on the administration of Governor William Cosby were well within the rights of the citizenry. "I cannot think it proper for me," Hamilton said, "to deny the publication of a complaint which I think is the right of every free-born subject to make." Governing, Locke said in his 1690 treatises on government, was by the consent of the governed. People had the right to question and discuss public issues. Questioning and discussing individuals was a different matter, but gradually, people came to see public officials as an extension of government. They could be a part of the discussion, too. In fact, the *Weekly Journal's* articles often attacked Governor Cosby personally, and personal attacks became a regular feature of the revolutionary 1770s. In any case, questioning and debating issues quickly became the norm in America. A review of subject matter in post-Zenger newspapers reveals lively public debate on taxes, publicly funded education, currency, colonial trade policy, and any number of other legislative issues, including Indian policy. Though some printers did run afoul of the government in some instances, the majority of printers continued to publish debate on controversial governmental issues without any repercussions whatsoever.

In making his final summation to the jury, Hamilton wrapped his entire argument in Lockean thought. Taken out of context, one might think the words came from a fiery revolutionary rhetorician like Samuel Adams or Thomas Paine. Hamilton placed Zenger's cause into a larger one whose outcome would have repercussions for all Americans. "Men who injure and oppress the people under their administration provoke them to cry out and complain," Hamilton pointed out. "[T]he question before the Court and you gentlemen of the jury is not of small nor private concern. . . . It may in its consequence affect every freeman that lives under a British government on the main of America. It is the best cause. It is the cause of liberty . . . every man who prefers freedom to a life of slavery will bless and honor you as men who have baffled the attempt of tyranny; and by an impartial and uncorrupt verdict, have ourselves, our posterity, and our neighbors that to which nature and the laws of our country have given us a right—the liberty—both of exposing and opposing arbitrary power . . . by speaking and writing truth."

By the time of the writing of the Constitution, Thomas Jefferson could make this statement: "The people are the only censors of their governors, and even their errors will tend to keep these to the true principles of their institution. To punish these errors too severely would be to suppress the only safeguard of the public liberty." Though Jefferson's quotations on the press run from unrestricted support to total disgust, in 1787, at least, he advocated a press that served as the center of public debate, that could discuss all issues freely—even politicians—and that could even make errors in discussions that dealt with the people's government. Even though Jefferson never mentioned Zenger or his trial, he and most of his contemporaries—at least at this point, when they were hammering out a unique, new type of government and discussing the need for a bill of rights—fully concurred in the idea that the press was a proper place for any discussion of government. This is an idea that provided one of the subtexts of Zenger's defense and that brought about a vital concession in the development of freedom of the press.

Jefferson and other founders may have come to their conclusions about freedom of the press through Cato, Locke, and others, but the Zenger trial certainly acted as a catalyst in America on the significance of trial by jury and a free and open press. Little was said in contemporary papers about the case in 1735, but James Alexander set out to rectify that by publishing *A Brief Narrative of the Case of John Peter Zenger* in 1736. Benjamin Franklin, for one, printed the volume, and in 1737 a brief newspaper debate on the trial took place. The *Barbados Gazette* ran a series of articles opposing the verdict, as did Philadelphia printer Andrew Bradford. Bradford, it should be noted, had a long-standing dislike of and feud with Andrew Hamilton. The Zenger trial had also belittled Bradford's father, William, the government printer of New York. Alexander countered the anti-Zenger columns with those of his own, which Franklin printed in the *Pennsylvania Gazette.* Alexander said that free speech was "the *principal pillar* in a free Government." He added that countries "derive their strength and vigor from a *popular examination* into the actions of the Magistrates" and that "a Free Constitution and Freedom of Speech have such a reciprocal dependence on each other that they cannot subsist without consisting together."

Though an unknown writer to the *Pennsylvania Gazette* in 1738 was correct when he said that Zenger's trial produced no law to protect speech, the debate around the trial in 1737 and 1738 no doubt stimulated thought about truth, papers, and jury trials. Several printers faced libel charges in the twenty years following the trial, and the results of those trials reflected the Zenger decision. In 1742, the Council of Massachusetts charged Boston printer Thomas Fleet with libel. Wanting a quick and decisive prosecution, the council circumvented the jury process, but Fleet produced witnesses who verified his stories. All charges were dropped. In 1747, a South Carolina grand jury declined to bring charges against printer Peter Timothy even though two stories in his *South-Carolina Gazette* leveled attacks at Governor James Glen. The grand jury said that taking any action would be "*destructive* of THE LIBERTY OF THE PRESS." The same year, New York Governor George Clinton ordered printer James Parker not to print a statement by the colony's assembly that denounced the governor's financing of defenses against the French and Indians. Parker ignored the governor and printed the complaint. Clinton did nothing.

Despite these and other examples, the press still faced restrictions during this period. In 1741, South Carolina authorities locked up the *South-Carolina Gazette*'s printer for publishing a letter that attacked the colony's Anglican clergy. New York printer Hugh Gaine either had to apologize to the assembly for what he printed or face jail time. The Massachusetts assembly ordered a pamphlet printed by Daniel Fowle burned in 1754 and the printer jailed for six days and fined. Finally, the assembly dropped the charges, and Fowle moved to New Hampshire. Others faced similar litigation, but newspapers, pamphlets, and broadsides—especially as the century progressed—often took on a much more vituperative tone than anything that Timothy, Gaine, or Fowle ever printed, and government officials were much more likely to ignore these criticisms than to take exception to them.

In all of this discussion, however, it ought not be forgotten that printers were often hired "mechanics" who simply published whatever they received or what people paid them to insert. John Campbell hired Bartholomew Green to print the *Boston News-Letter*. William Brooker paid James Franklin to run the *Boston Gazette*. Zenger was in many ways the "fall guy" for Alexander and Smith in their attacks on Governor Cosby. Other printers, such as Benjamin Franklin, Andrew Bradford, and James Parker, were mechanics of the press but also essayists. Even James Franklin wrote essays for the *New-England Courant*. The dialogue surrounding a free press was not one produced by printers solely; it encompassed much more than that. In fact, people not associated with the printing trade produced more of the writings in the period from 1720 forward than printers did because of the nature of submissions to papers—they were almost always anonymous, either via the practice of using pseudonyms or with no name attached at all. Printers may well have known the true names of submitters, and some readers may have, too, but most of these names have been lost. For whatever reasons people chose to have their submissions remain anonymous; that decision allowed them to make more powerful statements about the inherent rights for expression and a free press than they might have been able to do otherwise.

TALKING ABOUT A FREE PRESS

Literally thousands of lines of type addressed free-expression rights in colonial America. While the rhetoric was sometimes used as a preface to justify an impending attack on some issue, that should not detract from what was said. After all, seditious libel was valid law in America throughout the colonial period, and despite public opinion that truth was a defense against libels, no law said so until Pennsylvania incorporated truth into its laws concerning libel in 1790. Another fifteen years passed before another state, New York, incorporated truth into its legal language. But truth in language eventually gained near universal acceptance in America. The repressive 1798 Alien and Sedition Act could be applied only if a statement was malicious and false. Truth was considered a defense if one was charged under the act. Truth, however, was only a reason for not punishing people for what they said. The notion of why people needed a free press encompassed more, and that is why people wrote of it so often.

People also needed a free press to express their ideas, especially when they ran counter to current practice, belief, or policy. As in England, freedom of the press early on was a means to an end, not the end itself. In America, the same would have been true. According to Larry Eldridge, more than 1,200 seditious speech prosecutions took place in the British American colonies in the seventeenth century. Few of these dealt with the printed word, because being able to print was so difficult, but the massive number tells us that people had things to say that government and church officials did not like. By the 1680s, five presses operated in America, and it was at this time that Philadelphia's William Bradford experienced a rash of run-ins with the Quaker government over what he printed. In 1685, 1687, and 1689, he received warnings from the government, and he was arrested in 1692. In 1689, he explained to the council the realities of being a printer. His initial words made it sound as if he was very much a mechanic; he simply printed the page without having any investment in what was said. But his comment also explained why a press was needed and why it had to be open to all. "I get my living, to print; and if I may not print such things as come to my hand which are innocent, I cannot live," he said. "If I print one thing to-day, and the contrary party bring me another to-morrow, to contradict it, I cannot say that I shall not print it. Printing is a manufacture of the nation, and therefore ought rather to be encouraged than suppressed."

During the first two decades of the eighteenth century, the colonies' only newspaper, the *Boston News-Letter,* had no need to publish statements on liberty of the press since post-master Campbell agreed to have his paper approved by the colony's licenser. Since colonies had state-supported churches, dissenters produced pamphlets arguing for liberty of conscience, but these were almost exclusively printed in

England and imported. Nonconformists in South Carolina, for example, hired Daniel Defoe to write a pamphlet pleading their cause in 1705. Defoe did not need to argue for liberty of the press in *Party-Tyranny,* though, as publishing it in England was not a violation. Dissemination with the hope of changing South Carolina policy was the aim of those who employed Defoe, and liberty of conscience was their goal; printed matter was the means to obtain it.

Newspapers were the place where free-speech and free-press advocacy appeared, no doubt because the regular publication of papers provided the easiest and best way to share ideas. Promoting free press paved the way for much of the controversial subject matter in papers, especially the early newssheets. The same rationale for free-press rhetoric later in the eighteenth century was also valid, but increasingly, printers and those who inserted essays in papers saw a free press as a vital element in governance, a point that Locke and others drove home in their writings.

James Franklin's *New-England Courant* began the newspaper dialogue on free expression by quoting from the ultimate source, Cato. Many people believed Franklin's paper had slandered important people of the Bay colony in the inoculation debate. He, in turn, found the perfect answer, an essay printed in the *London Journal,* the newspaper of John Trenchard and Thomas Gordon, the men behind the "Cato" pseudonym. Franklin published their essay on libels in response to those who condemned him for the caustic words in his paper. "The exposing . . . of publick Wickedness, as it is a Duty which every Man Owes to Truth and his Country, can never be a Libel in the Nature of Things," Cato had said, and Franklin presented the same words in support of his paper's commentary in September 1721. Perhaps more important, however, for the fact that he was an American espousing free-expression ideas, was what the printer wrote for his paper later in the year. The accusations in the inoculation controversy continued to escalate, and Franklin admitted that sometimes, in the heat of debate, "unjust and groundless Charges" are leveled. For Franklin, that was no reason for bringing a lawsuit or suppressing the press. On the contrary, it was reason number one for having an open press, for "the Law of Nature, not only *allows,* but *obliges* every Man to defend himself against his Enemies, how great and good soever they may appear." Two weeks earlier, Franklin said, "Even Errors made publick and afterwards publickly expos'd, less endanger the Constitution of Church or State, than when they are (without Opposition) industriously propagated in private Conversation." In other words, the right of reply in a public setting such as a newspaper was the best deterrent to any comment, be the comment truth or falsehood.

Printers regularly promoted a free press whenever they began papers or assumed control of existing ones. Thomas Whitmarsh couched his ideas in poetry. Though he did not use the phrase "freedom of the press," he equated printing with religion, saying it "clear'd the Head," "reform'd the Heart," and "purg'd the Relicks of barbaric Rage." In Boston, Gamaliel Rogers and Daniel Fowle produced the short-lived *Independent Advertiser.* In their prospectus, the pair promised to be impartial in what they printed. Impartiality was code for printing whatever the printers could obtain that would allow them to make a living by printing a paper. Impartiality, by its very nature, advocated a free and open press. "For ourselves, we declare we are of no Party, neither shall we promote the narrow and private Designs of any such. We are ourselves free, and our Paper shall be free . . . yet we will thankfully receive every Thing from every quarter conducing to the Good of the Publick and our general Design," they promised. The *Independent Advertiser* was also the first mouthpiece of the revolutionary spokesman Samuel Adams. He used the paper, which stopped printing in 1749, to attack the government of William Shirley, who brought no libel charges against the paper. Adams suggested that the people had the right to know what government was doing, and that supplying them with that information was the purpose of the press. The only reason information and the press might be curtailed, he supposed, would be in time of war.

Benjamin Franklin produced the most famous of the statements concerning the role of printers and what they produced. He first ran his article, entitled "An Apology for Printers," on June 10, 1731, after he was chided for running an advertisement that criticized Philadelphia's Anglican clergy. He promised to rerun it yearly, and he did reproduce the piece, or some variation of it addressing free discussion and debate, in papers for years. The original contained twelve points and included these statements:

1. That the Opinions of Men are almost as various as their Faces. . . .
2. That the Business of Printing has chiefly to do with Mens Opinions; most things that are printed tending to promote some, or oppose others. . . .
4. That it is unreasonable in any one Man or Set of Men to expect to be pleas'd with every thing that is printed. . . .

5. Printers are educated in the Belief, that when Men differ in Opinion, both Sides ought equally to have the Advantage of being heard by the Publick; and that when Truth and Error have fair Play, the former is always an over-match for the latter: Hence they chearfully serve all contending Writers that pay them well, without regarding on which side they are of the Question in Dispute. . . .

7. That it is unreasonable to imagine Printers approve of every thing they print, and to censure them on any particular thing accordingly; since in the way of the Business they print such a great variety of things opposite and contradictory. It is likewise as unreasonable what some assert, *That Printers ought not to print any Thing but what they approve*; since if all of that Business should make such a Resolution, and abide by it, an End would thereby be put to Free Writing, and the World would afterwards have nothing to read but what happen'd to be the Opinions of Writers.

8. That if all Printers were determin'd not to print any thing till they were sure it would offend no body, there would be very little printed. . . .

In some ways, Franklin was attempting to remove responsibility for what was printed from the printer and place it with the writers, since the printer was only relaying to the public what people gave him or paid him to insert. That is exactly what William Bradford had said forty years earlier and what Rogers and Fowle implied in 1748. But like his fellow printers, Franklin reminded readers of the concepts of the marketplace, and he seems to have believed that truth would always be discerned if ideas were debated in public.

Other printers and papers were more direct in their language concerning freedom of the press. As we have seen, the *New-York Weekly Journal* of John Peter Zenger framed its existence in the notion of a free press. Using the Cato moniker, attorneys Alexander and Smith outlined the importance of a free press, using Milton as well as Trenchard and Gordon as their guide. "The Liberty of the Press is a Subject of greatest importance, and in which every Individual is as much concern'd as he is in any other part of Liberty," the essay announced. The lawyers then explained that freedom of expression was synonymous with liberty. "No Nation Antient or Modern ever lost the Liberty of freely Speaking, Writing, or Publishing their Sentiments, but forthwith lost their Liberty in general and became Slaves. *LIBEERTY* [*sic*] and *SLAVERY!* how amiable is one! how odious and abominable the other! . . . I believe every honest Britton, of whatever Denomination, who love his Country, if left to his own free and unbyassed Judgment, is a Friend to the Liberty of the Press, and an Enemy to any Restraint upon it." In subsequent weeks, before beginning the attack on William Cosby's administration, the *Weekly Journal* ran articles on the freedoms provided by the Magna Carta as well as Cato's Letters on the role that people had in a free government. Even after the attacks began, Alexander and Smith inserted items related to free expression and free government in the paper.

Alexander was probably the most passionate apologist for free expression in prerevolutionary America. In 1737, the New York lawyer wrote a series of essays on the subject that was based, in part, on the original essays produced in the *New-York Weekly Journal.* His series was also a reaction to attacks in the *Barbados Gazette* and the *American Weekly Mercury* on the way that Andrew Hamilton had used freedom of the press as the basis to obtain a not-guilty verdict for Zenger. "THE FREEDOM OF SPEECH is a *principal Pillar* in a free Government: when this support is taken away the Constitution is dissolved, and Tyranny is erected on its Ruins. Republics and limited Manarchies derive their Strength and Vigor from a *popular Examination* into the Actions of the Magistrates," Alexander said. "To suppress Enquiries into the Administration is good Policy in an arbitrary Government: But a free Constitution and freedom of Speech have such a reciprocal Dependence on each other that they cannot subsist without consisting together." He boldly stated that "WHOEVER ATTEMPTS TO SUPPRESS" either freedom of speech or the press, what Alexander called "OUR NATURAL RIGHTS," "OUGHT TO BE REGARDED AS AN ENEMY TO LIBERTY AND THE CONSTITUTION."

In 1755, Benjamin Edes and John Gill assumed the dual editorship of the *Boston Gazette.* They began their paper with essays on freedom of the press that stretched over three months. On April 21, they published Cato's Letter No. 15, "Of Freedom of Speech." It appeared in its entirety. More of Cato's letters on personal freedom and press rights followed. On May 26, the printers republished a lengthy essay entitled "*An Apology for the* LIBERTY *of the* PRESS," taken from an April issue of a London paper. The writer acknowledged that freedom of the press was not a right given by England's constitution, but he said it was nonetheless a right that was essential. The essay opened with this paragraph: "THE Fredoom [*sic*] of the Press, by which I mean the Freedom which every Subject has to communicate his Sentiments to the Publick, in that Manner, which may make them most universally known, is a Freedom which does not proceed from any Peculiarity in the Frame of the English Constitution, but is essential to and coeval with all free Governments, into which it is not adopted, but born."

Interestingly, the essay ended with a paragraph that attacked virtual representation, the principle asserting that members of Parliament represented all Englishmen even if all Englishmen did not vote, and that the House of Commons, by its nature, served to represent the interests of all Englishmen. Freedom of the press, the essay said, was the way to compensate for virtual representation by giving everyone a chance to put ideas into the public sphere for discussion. This is exactly the same argument that Americans would use a decade later, once England began adding taxes to the colonies as a means of replenishing its treasury following the Seven Years' War, specifically the part of it fought in America and called the French and Indian War. The writer said that "this priviledge, which we call the *Liberty of the PRESS,* becomes much more necessary for preserving the liberties of the people under a government, where they are restricted from the power of deciding, and from carrying their opinions into judgment and execution which is the case in *England.*"

In nearly every one of these examples, however, the writers offered an exemption clause declaring that there may be times when the press should not print something.

"Printers do continually discourage the Printing of great Numbers of bad things, and stifle them in the Birth," Franklin said in his "Apology for Printers." Even Alexander said that "To infuse the Minds of the People an ill Opinion of a just Administration is a Crime that deserves no Mercy." From the 1720s through the 1750s, most people who wrote in support of a free press also believed that malicious and false attacks were not deserving of a place in a public print, but again, what was false and malicious was dependent upon personal views. The exception clause in essays may have been simply a way for the printer to protect himself, because the same apologists consistently supported the marketplace of ideas concept where true and false statements were able to vie for support in the arena of public debate and acceptance. Printing statements that were not true was part of the nature of an open press. According to Jeffery Smith, as the eighteenth century progressed, printers believed that the infusion of falsity into the public debate only made the truth all the more obvious to readers. In the 1740s, however, Americans entered into an argument in print about the ultimate truth as a religious revival known as the Great Awakening engulfed the colonies. Even though the argument centered on the divine, it tells something about the growing concept of a free press in America.

THE GREAT AWAKENING AND PUBLIC DEBATE

Liberty of conscience, the belief that people have the right to interpret scripture and worship God according to the dictates of their own understanding, was the catalyst for calls for freedom of the press from the beginning of the Protestant Reformation through the English Civil War of the 1640s and Glorious Revolution in 1688. Even if factions did not always want to grant the same freedoms to those who held varying interpretations of the church, religious writings were at the forefront of calls for a press open to all, especially in the seventeenth century. America experienced a revolution in the 1740s that touched on issues of religious freedom. The Great Awakening reinvigorated many Americans' enthusiasm for the divine, but it also created splits in denominations and changes in the religious order of the colonies. According to Robert Martin, the Great Awakening provided Americans with the chance to sift through a voluminous amount of literature reflecting the various facets of religious debate. This literature, just as that produced on other subjects of importance to society, including politics and economics, expanded American appreciation for the right of an open press.

The Great Awakening was a series of revivals that spread throughout colonial America. It pitted, according to Henry May, those who accepted, explained, and worshipped God through the rational and natural lens of the Enlightenment against those who believed that God guides humans through revelation, tradition, and spiritual illumination. Though the Great Awakening may have begun as early as the 1720s, it was not until the 1740s that the revivalists and those who opposed them turned to the press in massive numbers as a means of spreading their ideas and attacking what they considered to be the blasphemous concepts of others. This phenomenon occurred when, in late 1739 and through 1740, an English itinerant preacher named George

Whitefield preached a series of revivals from Massachusetts to Georgia. People turned to Whitefield as they had turned to no other person in colonial history—largely because of the printing press.

The polemicists of the Great Awakening used newspapers and pamphlets to spread their ideas. Pamphlets, as they had been in England a century earlier, were an important medium. Printers, no doubt, enjoyed increased income during this time because the number of pamphlets printed skyrocketed. In 1738, for example, only about 133 pamphlets of any kind were published in America. The subject matter of 56 of them was religious. Three years later, after the initial explosion of revival preaching, printers produced more religious pamphlets than they had on all subjects in 1738. Apologists sent 146 religious tracts to printers in 1741, which made up more than 60 percent of all pamphlets published.

Newspapers, however, truly reflected the intense debate concerning religion. During Whitefield's first preaching tour of the colonies, newspapers in Philadelphia, New York, and Charleston devoted between 14 and 18 percent of their total news content to religious issues, compared with a maximum of only 2 percent five years earlier. New England newspapers also increased their religious news but continued the dialogue much longer, with more than 20 percent of total news content devoted to the issues that the Great Awakening created five years later.

Whitefield, according to Harry Stout, pioneered the use of the press among all strata of American society. He essentially developed a new form of communication, Stout said, "in which people were encouraged—even commanded—to speak out concerning the great work of grace in their souls." He became, according to Isaiah Thomas, "the common topic of conversation from Georgia to New Hampshire. All the newspapers were filled with paragraphs of information respecting him, or with pieces of animated disputation pro or con."

What made Whitefield different from other preachers in terms of public debate, besides the controversial nature of his preaching and the fact that he urged people to speak out, was the fact that he employed perhaps the first public relations specialist in American history. Traveling with Whitefield was William Seward, who wrote up announcements about the itinerant and sent them to papers along the path of his revival tour. After Whitefield arrived in Philadelphia in 1739, for example, and started his tour, he headed south toward Savannah, Georgia, where he had promised to build an orphanage. People along the way in Annapolis, Williamsburg, Charleston, and the surrounding countryside, however, knew of his impending arrival well before he entered their towns because Seward prepared press releases and sent them ahead to the local print shops. Once Whitefield preached in a place, Seward prepared another release that told of the people in attendance at Whitefield's sermon, a number that always reached into the thousands, and other divine glories that had transpired with the preaching. Even though Whitefield was moving south on the initial leg of the tour, people from Philadelphia north to Boston knew of what was happening with him because the public prints from the southern towns traveled by ship to the northern ports. Before Whitefield ever arrived in Boston in the fall of 1740, the Boston papers had published extensive news of him. This, naturally, heightened interest in him and his preaching.

In eighteenth-century America, just as in England, people often called for the suppression of religious ideas they believed to be in error. So naturally, people in Boston, Philadelphia, and Charleston worked to ban Whitefield's use of existing churches to preach and tried (almost always unsuccessfully) to keep news about Whitefield out of the papers. Boston newspapers, as in the inoculation controversy, took sides. The *Boston Evening-Post,* for example, strongly denounced Whitefield, while the *Boston Gazette* supported him. The religious nature of Massachusetts from its founding to 1745, and its multiplicity of papers, provided the perfect scene for newspaper debate.

With the Great Awakening and Whitefield, people did not find it necessary to preface their debate in the rhetoric of free speech, though they still did when government officials and colonial law were the subject of debate. Instead, there was open debate, something that would never have occurred in seventeenth-century America or England. Despite state-supported churches in most colonies, Enlightenment thought, even for those of the Great Awakening who trusted revelation, had already created the foundation for separation of church and state. Quakers, who were hanged in Massachusetts a century earlier, were granted the use of Faneuil Hall in 1740, while Jews were granted religious liberty in Pennsylvania in 1755. The same year, a *New-York Mercury* column called "The Watchtower" declared, "IT is evident that Religion of whatever kind, can have no other Connection with the affairs of civil Society, than as it has a natural Tendency to refine, and improve the Morals of its Members."

By the 1740s and 1750s, something had changed drastically in relation to religious debate. While people still called for the suppression of religious groups, especially newly founded ones like Methodists, other people were writing about religious toleration. The Great Awakening caused divisions and splits in the standing order of America's religious denominations, but these and other elements of the religious upheaval of the times were as much a result of the openness of the press and the resulting dissemination of information and debate surrounding it as any preaching. The fact that George Whitefield did not leave the spread of his message to the Holy Spirit and his preaching tour solely, but instead turned to America's newspapers via a public relations practitioner to make sure the message was dispersed to as large a number of people as possible, says much about the state of debate in the press in the middle of the eighteenth century.

From 1720 forward, the press in America, in general, could be said to have made great strides toward a free press. On a colony-by-colony review, America still had few printing shops and newspapers, and, in some places, powerful royal governors could still control the press. This could be done in single-newspaper towns more effectively than in cities with multiple print shops and newspapers. The experience of England again eased the way for colonials. While religious toleration was still a problem in places because of government-supported state churches, and some persecution occurred at certain times and in certain places, in general people could worship as they pleased. For that reason, there was less need for an active press campaign in America dealing with liberty of conscience, though one still existed.

The fact that a well-reasoned body of literature existed that supported freedom of the press accelerated its acceptance and application in America. Cato's letter on libels appeared in the *New-England Courant* only three months after Trenchard and Gordon published it in the *London Journal*. The speed with which American printers and citizens alike adopted libertarian thought on the rights and necessity of a free and open press highlights how quickly these ideas were becoming engrained into American thought.

The fact that assemblies and royal governors were not as willing to allow the press to print without imposing restrictions was not a surprise, either. After all, it had taken Parliament and the monarchy in the mother country more than two centuries of printing for its laws to evolve to the point where licensing was no longer needed. As an extension of England, the American colonies, naturally, followed that path. Life in America was not like life in England's large cities, however, even though Philadelphia and Boston had five-digit populations by the 1720s. If one traveled west, sometimes only a few miles, one entered a wilderness incomprehensible to most Britons of the early eighteenth century. This issue, as well as other problems in the colonies, including trade and monetary ones, meant that government officials often felt they needed to keep tighter control on what transpired in their jurisdictions than might be necessary in England.

The American people had already developed a certain level of independence, however, and used the examples of their English brethren to voice their complaints in the press. English newspapers had existed, at least in newsbook form, from the mid-1500s on. By the end of the seventeenth century, printers were relatively free to print papers. The early newsbooks and first newssheets dealt solely with foreign news, so they never were a threat to government and were not censored. By the time of the Puritan Revolution in the late 1630s, newssheets were beginning to discuss domestic issues. From that time until the Glorious Revolution of 1688 and the end of licensing in the 1690s, government limited newspapers as much as possible to those published by authority. By the time that the *Boston Gazette,* the *American Weekly Mercury,* and the *New-England Courant* joined the *Boston News-Letter* in America, British citizens, especially in London, were accustomed to dozens of newspapers with huge circulations that had few government restraints. Those papers regularly crossed the Atlantic, so people in America knew that information was readily shared in England. Doing so in America seemed natural. As a result, people no doubt felt freer to discuss issues than would have been the case had the American press developed in a vacuum.

The growth of the use of the press for public debate, and public officials' desire to stop some discussion, ran head-on in the 1720s and 1730s. Though a few printers were jailed and fined, not much happened to deter the expansion of freedom of the press. The trial of John Peter Zenger turned from a political power struggle into an apology for a free press, truth, and jury trials. All three were part of the Enlightenment ideals for what was needed to create a country that operated on the consent of the governed. That the Zenger decision had no implications of law is important, but it may be more significant that so many people in America believed that what happened in the case *should* have become law. Even though a few other printers would face seditious libel charges after the Zenger trial, government officials could never really regain control of what appeared in print.

The fact that James Franklin in Boston, Andrew Bradford in Philadelphia, and Peter Timothy in Charleston basically ignored orders to cease printing controversial material supports this observation. Also, when the *Independent Advertiser* of Boston waged a public attack on Governor William Shirley in 1748, the governor did nothing. Even when printers were taken up on libel charges, none in post-Zenger colonial America were ever convicted.

Most apologists for freedom of the press provided an exception clause within their arguments to acknowledge that false and malicious accusations against governments ought to be punishable. But even here, the rhetoric was conflicting. While allowing for the exemption, writers also promoted the marketplace of ideas notion, saying that even false statements should be allowed into public debate because they would always ultimately lose in a logical argument waged against truthful statements. Even as early as William Bradford's experience in seventeenth-century Philadelphia, this aspect of the rationale for a free press was expounded. Bradford used the exception clause but also said that both factions in a debate had the right to print their ideas. Could both sides be right? Printers continued to support both ideas because the exemption clause seemed to remove some of the responsibility from them and place it squarely on the shoulders of the writers. As "meer Mechanics," as Stephen Botein referred to colonial printers, they were simply printing what people paid them to print.

Printers tended to have opinions, however, when it came to the biggest story of the first half of the eighteenth century, religious revival and George Whitefield. Whitefield's first preaching tour, from 1739 to 1741, energized

America's newspapers. News content quickly focused upon Whitefield's preaching. The conflict surrounding the Great Awakening and its effects on the religious standing of America created a new level of newspaper discussion and debate in the colonies. People in Boston earlier had debated inoculation, and some papers in 1737 and 1738 had debated the merits of Zenger's libel defense, but every American newspaper ran stories about Whitefield and the issues concerning religion that the Great Awakening created. What happened in Charleston concerning Whitefield appeared in Boston papers. When Whitefield preached in New York, people in Annapolis could read about it. By using a press agent, William Seward, Whitefield forged a new way of stimulating conversation. From the beginning of his first preaching tour until he returned for his second in 1745, people throughout the colonies used newspapers to debate the issues Whitefield stirred up. More people than ever used the press to voice opinions. Even though denominational divisions threatened the standing order of religion in some colonies, this religious debate did not directly affect colonial governments. So, except in a few rare instances, such as in South Carolina, where the printer was briefly jailed for printing religious material at odds with the Anglican state church and associated with Whitefield, public officials stayed out of the fray. Once the people were let loose to discuss things, however, reining them in would be impossible.

The press in America through the middle of the 1750s surely encountered limits on what was considered suitable for print. Printers and essayists remarked on these limits, but when one looks at what the papers actually discussed, it is hard to say there was more control than there was freedom

to print and discuss issues of controversy. The issues surrounding the Great Awakening were divisive. They were
seriously intense, and the outcome, many believed, had eternal implications. What would happen to the press when it
had to handle an issue that affected nearly everyone in America to a similar degree? The French and Indian War was such
an event, and coverage of it, and discussion about it in public places, would affect the press in ways that had not yet been
imagined.

SEVEN

DEBATE AND THE PUBLIC SPHERE

The uniquely American dialogue that took place in America throughout the eighteenth century, spanning the introduction of multiple newspapers in 1719, the French and Indian War of 1754 to 1763, and the Stamp Act crisis of 1765, led citizens of the British colonies in North America to begin to think of themselves as a community separate from Britain. This occurred even though many Americans—perhaps as many as one-third—strongly opposed independence from the mother country. At the center of the discussion that transformed America from thirteen British colonies into an independent nation was what printers produced—books, pamphlets, broadsides, and newspapers. Increasingly, though, newspapers assumed a central role in debate because they were produced on a regular basis with updated information and were easily shared and read aloud in public places and homes. According to Michael Schudson, newspapers created a space that had to be filled. Printers, increasingly, packed that space with reports on current affairs that stimulated both writers and readers. As printer John Holt, who began working in a newspaper shop in 1754, said, speaking of America's efforts to be free of British tyranny, "It was by means of News papers that we receiv'd and spread the Notice."

Freedom from Great Britain is not a main focus of this book. But just as the Act of Toleration would not have occurred in England as quickly as it did without dissenter publications that called for religious liberty in conjunction with the right to discuss it via a free press, Patriots of the revolutionary era would have faced a much more difficult time coordinating their efforts against Britain had the press not obtained by the 1760s a level of freedom that was void of almost any type of censure. Explaining how America arrived at that point, and why the people insisted that free speech and press clauses be added to the Constitution, is this work's aim.

Americans from the 1720s on used the printed word for a multitude of purposes, and one of them was to engage in debate. Public officials repeatedly tried to silence any words they believed were a threat, but their efforts failed because the people, increasingly, became a part of the process. Jury trials gave people an active role in government, and jurors tended to ignore instructions given to them. Printers also tended to disregard government sanctions, with few repercussions. All of this happened because people realized the power of the printed word. Virginia Governor William Berkeley, like most other royal governors and political officials, feared printing that was not restrained. In 1671, Berkeley thanked God that his colony had no printing press because it had brought heresy and libels into the world. In the eighteenth century, individuals learned that the printed word had a power that, once released to the public, could effect dramatic changes and assume a life of its own. Benjamin Franklin, even as an apprentice in his brother James's Boston shop, knew that a cleverly turned phrase in a well-constructed letter could set a community to talking. This is why he produced the anonymous "Silence Dogood" letters. Later, in Philadelphia, he used well-crafted essays in the *American Weekly Mercury* to ensure that the town's other newspaper would lose advertising revenue and circulation, so that he could buy it for a pittance. Samuel Adams, the fiery orator of the American Revolution, was really no orator at all. He rarely spoke in public, opting instead to use the printed word to communicate his ideas. Adams utilized more than twenty-five pseudonyms and did not sign his name to what he wrote.

John Adams believed that the struggle to obtain liberty of conscience and the evolving notion of a government of consent ultimately and logically brought America to the edge of rebellion during the Stamp Act crisis of 1765. In the August 12 *Boston Gazette,* he wrote, "From the time of the reformation, to the first settlement of *America,* knowledge gradually spread in Europe, but especially in *England*; and in proportion as *that* increased and spread among the people, *ecclesiastical* and *civil* tyranny . . . seem to have lost their strength and weight." The idea of being free from tyranny, Adams said, crossed the Atlantic with the colonists. It became engrained in them, and it was shared. Later, when Adams reflected on all that had happened in the turbulent decades of the 1760s and 1770s, he said that the fighting of 1775 on was not the revolution. The revolution was found in the hearts and minds of the people. Anyone who wanted to find out what they thought, he suggested, need only consult the pamphlets and newspapers, "by which the public opinion was enlightened and informed." The press, just as it had been for religious dissenters in seventeenth-century England, was the means to an end. In order to obtain freedom, people needed a press that would allow them to discuss and debate matters of importance. Adams, when looking back on the end of America's colonial era, would have said that nothing was more important than freedom from tyranny, and the chief catalyst in obtaining it was the press.

The idea that newspapers were "necessary & important Alarms," as printer William Goddard said, referred not to everything that appeared in newspapers but to those items that affected the welfare of people closely. Although the public used the printed word in any form to discuss a myriad of subjects they believed affected them, the topics on which they ultimately found themselves mired in controversy generally revolved around political issues. Printing and newspapers, according to German sociologist Jürgen Habermas, created what he called "the public sphere." This new realm came into existence, according to Habermas, in the late seventeenth century in England. As we have seen, by the end of the 1600s the English people had already gone through a century of struggles to achieve freedom of conscience. There had been a Puritan Revolution and a civil war. The chief tool in formulating events had been the printing press; the 1640s—the time of the English Civil War—produced an estimated twenty thousand publications related to the state of affairs in the country. These publications no doubt fueled the justification for rebellion. In a foreshadowing of what happened in America that led Adams to state that the American Revolution consisted not in the fighting itself but in what occurred in the hearts and minds of the people, it could be said that the English Civil War was fought not by means of arms but on the pages of these publications. The give and take of power that occurred from that point through the early 1690s ultimately put an end to nearly all government control of the press in England. As a result, newspapers grew in number because they no longer had to be licensed. People from all strata of life who were able turned to the press as a source of discussion and commentary.

Within the public sphere, Habermas said, a "reasoning public" found a way to be critical of those in power as a means of affecting politics. The venue that people used was the printed word, which was used to stimulate debate and discussion in coffeehouses, taverns, and other public gathering spots. In America, especially in terms of the reaction to the Stamp Act, it even spurred people to action. Habermas said that the public sphere was open to anyone with access to print. Though this could be interpreted as access to the printing process itself, it should not necessarily be construed that way. Access to print could mean writing something and then having it published. It could also mean simply having the ability to read an item. It could even mean hearing about these items, perhaps when they were read aloud, and then pondering them or offering opinions on them. Habermas stressed the significance of reading within the public sphere, however.

The great advantage of the public sphere, if one accepts that hearing, not just reading, allowed people access to it, is that the public sphere then becomes truly democratic, something Habermas claimed that it was. The most democratic of publications was the newspaper. Relatively cheap, readily available, easily shared, in America newspapers were considered "the gen'ral source throughout the nation, of ev'ry modern conversation." By the middle of the 1750s, people of all strata of life were using it to take part in discussion in the public sphere. "How common is it to see a Shoemaker, Taylor, or Barber, haranguing with a great deal of Warmth on the publick Affairs?" a New Yorker observed in 1756. "He will condemn a General, Governor, or Province with as much Assurance as if he were of the Privy Council, and knew exactly wherein they had been faulty:—He gets his Knowledge from the News-Papers, and looks upon it undoubtedly true because it is printed." What newspapers were able to produce over time was a common rhetoric, and in America, it was increasingly based in Enlightenment thought as the gulf between colonists and mother country widened. What was printed in papers was shared and gave the impression of a unified front—presenting the Sons of Liberty and other Patriots from 1765 on as *the* voice of the people even though not all Americans agreed with their position, for example.

For the public sphere to exist successfully, people had to be relatively free of any constrictions on what was said. From the time of James Franklin on, printers generally felt free to print at will whatever came to them. Franklin, Andrew Bradford, Peter Zenger, Thomas Fleet, and James Parker, among others, faced public criticism and legal prosecution for what they printed. Neither form of scrutiny seemed to deter the producers of the public prints from printing what appeared in their newssheets. What the public sphere offered people was the opportunity to put the idea of open debate into practice in a realm where, as Milton said, truth and falsehood may grapple. Here, any ideas could be presented. This and other libertarian concepts, such as the consent of the governed, brought colonial America to the point where, as John Adams said, printing "should be encouraged, and that it should be easy and cheap and safe for any person to communicate his thought to the public." At the same time, he praised printers for their "readiness and freedom in publishing the speculations of the curious." Adams did not say it, but a free and open press was absolutely vital when matters of fundamental importance worthy of public discussion and debate existed.

In the 1750s, Americans found plenty of issues worth debating in the public sphere. In New York, for example, William Livingston and others harangued the colony's government over plans to establish public schools with religious ties, while people in New England debated the merits of paper currency after Parliament passed the Currency Act of 1751, which allowed colonial governments to print money and create spiraling inflation. But when war broke out in the backcountry of the Ohio Valley in 1754, newspapers took on a responsibility that shaped them and the public sphere for the serious debate of the 1760s and 1770s. The French and Indian War created news that was truly unmatched in colonial America. In many ways, how print shops covered the war was not dependent upon any notion of freedom of the press. Coverage was necessary for survival as Americans knew it. In the process of meeting the challenges of providing this information, printers and others learned firsthand why a free and open press was absolutely necessary.

"THE MAIN SUBJECT OF THE PUBLICK ATTENTION"

In 1757, after three years of fighting between British colonists and the French, Boston printer Thomas Fleet described the war as "The Main Subject of the Publick Attention." He was correct. The French and Indian War, the American segment of a worldwide conflict between Britain and France called the Seven Years' War, was, according to historian Fred Anderson, "the most important event to occur in eighteenth-century America." This claim puts the war's role in American history above some truly significant occurrences that took place after the war's end in 1763, including the signing of the Declaration of Independence, the Revolutionary War, and development and ratification of the Constitution and the Bill of Rights. But all of these pivotal points in American history to a certain extent owe a debt to the French and Indian War. The French and Indian War gave Great Britain sole control of the eastern part of North America, eliminating the French. It created a massive British war debt that Parliament decided the Americans should help repay through a series of taxes. These taxes led to protests and rebellions and eventually revolution. According to Anderson, the Seven Years' War also rearranged the politics of Europe and Latin America because it changed the political power of Europe. In light of all that the French and Indian War set in motion, it is no wonder that media historian Frank Luther Mott called it "the great running story" of the colonial era.

As the "great running story" of the era, the French and Indian War, naturally, had repercussions for America's press. From the beginning, the war was viewed by most as a threat to the survival of all American colonies. "We cannot forbear to express our just Indignation at the unwarrantable Encroachments, and hostile Proceedings of the French . . . in what we agree to be the common Cause of all the *British* Colonies upon this Continent," newspaper stories from Maryland and Virginia reported. Newspaper printers approached coverage of the conflict with a sense of urgency and as a common cause. America's newspapers published every bit of information that could be obtained about the conflict with the French and Indians. News of attacks in the backcountry of Virginia appeared in New England papers. Trouble in northern New York played out in Charleston, South Carolina. Any news about Indian activity or meetings between colonial officials and tribal sachems received coverage and was reprinted from one newspaper to another up and down the Atlantic seaboard. French aggression on the seas received the same treatment.

For printers and many other Americans, unity in opposition to aggression was America's only hope. Benjamin Franklin, in fact, developed the greatest image of unity of the early American era when he published an editorial cartoon depicting a disjointed snake with the words "JOIN, or DIE" under it, as a direct response to French incursions into the colonies. The fact that Americans reused the cartoon's image and implications to oppose British taxes in the 1760s and to promote separation from Great Britain in the 1770s is testament to the image's power. In 1754, American printers quickly created their own versions of the cartoon and joined together—though not always intentionally—to provide colonists with the most complete, up-to-date, factual accounts possible of the events that were rapidly encompassing all facets of life. At the height of the war in 1758, Parliament's appointed deputy postmasters—Benjamin Franklin and Williamsburg, Virginia, printer William Hunter—authorized postage-free exchange of newspapers among all printers. The result was an easier and more cost-effective means of sharing and exchanging war information, especially for cities within a few days' ride of each other such as Philadelphia, New York, and Boston.

American printers in 1740 had covered a story that interested almost all colonists when they had covered George Whitefield's first preaching tour. "You will see all about him in the Papers" was the way Deborah Franklin, Ben's wife, described Whitefield news years later. Even though the press had covered a story of intense interest to colonials, it was unaccustomed to having to cover a story of such massive significance and implications for readers. "Countrymen!" the *Virginia Centinel* declared in a 1756 letter to newspapers. "I need only repeat, YOUR COUNTRY IS IN DANGER . . . certainly, you must be alarmed, when YOUR COUNTRY IS IN DANGER." Printers had already taken the *Centinel*'s message to heart. As a result, they sought ways to make sure that as much information as possible reached people. They added supplements, or "extraordinaries," whenever they received news that would be of value to people between the days of normal publication of their weekly papers. Some printers reduced the amount of space reserved for advertisements so that more war news could be published. Americans quite naturally wanted all the news possible about the war, which "increased the demand for public journals," according to Isaiah Thomas, who became a print-shop apprentice in 1756 and wrote the first history of printing in America in 1810.

In fact, newspapers grew at twice the rate of the colonial population during the 1750s, and this growth is attributable directly to the French and Indian War. Papers were, according to a printer who started one during the war period, "so necessary at this Juncture." When the war started, eleven English-language papers were printed regularly in America. By 1760, and the capitulation of Canada to the British, the number of papers had grown to nineteen. By the time news of the war's official end reached the colonies in 1763, another five papers had joined them, and every colony except for New Jersey, whose population was served by papers in New York and Philadelphia, now had at least one. In a decade, the number of English papers in America grew by about 110 percent.

During the French and Indian War, the columns of newspapers were open to any and all who wanted to contribute information relating to the fighting. It is impossible to find anything in the papers of the times that justified French activity or placed the blame for the war on British or American shoulders, because colonials were united in the effort to stop the French and their Indian allies. All elements of the war, however, did not meet with such a unified front. This was especially evident in calls for a union of colonies that grew out of the Albany Congress held near the beginning of the war. At that meeting, set for late June and early July 1754 in New York with the leaders of the Six Nations, colonial representatives adopted Franklin's Albany Plan of Union. The plan called for all colonies from Massachusetts southward to unite for mutual defense and security and to extend British settlements in North America. A government of the united colonies, comprising a president, a grand council, and a house of representatives based on population, would assume control of trade and treaties with Native Americans and maintain soldiers for America's defenses. Any monies needed would be raised through taxes. Tax levies would be based on the abilities of the colonies to pay, presumably on population and economic feasibility.

Despite representative approval by those at Albany and general support by most colonial governors, the assemblies of the colonies voted against the proposal, principally because representatives believed the unified government would usurp some of the power of individual colonies and assemblies. Legislatures did, however, follow the spirit of the plan by sending militiamen and funds to the colonies most in harm's way from French and Indian attacks. As news arrived from the backcountry of Virginia, Pennsylvania, and New York concerning increasing attacks by the French and Indians, newspapers debated the validity of the Albany Plan of Union. Printers, especially, seemed to support the plan. "*I hope, and pray the Almighty, That the British Colonies on this continent, may cease impolitically and ungenerously to consider themselves as distinct States . . . and secure to themselves and their Posterity, to the Ends of Time, the inestimable Blessings of Civil and Religious Liberty, and the Possession and Settlement of a great Country,*" printer Hugh Gaine appended to an article on the state of British colonial America.

In Boston, Congregational minister Jonathan Mayhew urged union from the pulpit, and papers subsequently printed his sermon. "Ye cannot be saved from the Storm you are now threatened with, yea, which is already begun, except ye are at UNION AMONGST YOURSELVES," Mayhew declared. The farther people were from the fighting, however, the more they spoke out against the union. James Glen of South Carolina suggested that if his colony helped others and joined a union of colonies, soon "we shall gradually consume ourselves in vain, and waste our Strength." Yet even many people in colonies under invasion believed union was wrong. An anonymous New York writer suggested that instead of worrying about other colonies, New York should be "more concern'd" with "its own Defence."

Debates concerning the Albany Plan of Union were not ones that might elicit suppression from government officials, though, since the plan was only a proposal, not governmental action. It was simply an issue that directly affected the welfare and direction of British America. With or without the union, the colonies remained in a fight for existence. Other elements of the war made for news items that might have incurred punishment upon printers had not the colonies progressed in terms of freedom of the press to the point that they had by 1754.

In July 1755, the British suffered a debilitating loss along the Monongahela River when General Edward Braddock's British regulars and American militiamen were routed. Braddock, a professional soldier with more than forty years experience, had sailed to Virginia early in the year along with two regiments of seasoned Irish troops. The general then met with governors from the major colonies and devised a plan to roust the French from the continent. Word of Braddock's plan soon spread, "to the great Satisfaction of People of all Ranks," the *Boston News-Letter* reported. Braddock was so sure that he and his troops would crush the French that he turned down help from Native Americans. But Braddock and his men were not prepared for warfare in

the American wilderness. The French and Indians sur-
rounded them, firing from the forests at Braddock's redcoats,
who were lined up shoulder to shoulder in European fighting style. Before the massacre ended, Braddock lay mortally
wounded, and the French Indians swooped in upon the
wounded, scalping and killing them. Americans could not
believe that such a massacre could occur.

The defeat was so devastating to colonial morale that
New York Governor James De Lancey enjoined the colony's
printers from even mentioning it. Printer Hugh Gaine, however, ignored the governor's decree. On August 4, he printed
"the melancholly Accounts of the Defeat of the Forces
under the immediate Command of General Braddock." A
month later, in the editorial essay entitled "The Watch-
Tower," Gaine's paper blasted New York's war effort. "We
have already felt the fatal Consequences of a careless Security, in a Defeat, which ignominious as it was, should still be
remembered, to excite us by Vigilance and Assiduity, to
avoid a great and more dangerous Disgrace," the paper said.
It wasn't Gaine's first swipe at New York defenses, either. In
January, he had charged that De Lancey's administration
lacked proper attention to the colony's safety. "Such is our
Situation, that we have an extensive Frontier, and a great
Variety of Ports to defend, which nothing but good Fortifi-
cations can secure," "The Watch-Tower" explained, going
on to say that unless the colony shored up its defenses, New
York would "be given up a Prey to our designing Enemies."

Gaine faced no repercussions for his attacks on the
government, but other printers in the town, James Parker
and William Weyman, were arraigned the next year for
making similar charges about lax defenses by the colonial

government. They apologized, and Parker continued to publish on the issue, much as he had done in 1747 when Governor George Clinton had ordered him to stop discussing colonial defenses during King George's War. In 1756, though, Parker added an essay on freedom of the press that quoted from Cato's Letters.

Because printers tended to support the war effort, they chided government officials for not responding with adequate support, be it monetary or physical. The New York printers advocated funding for a proper defense of the colony because any kind of indecision on the part of royal governors or assemblies could put people at risk. In Philadelphia, printers did the same. With the governor and the assembly at odds over funding, Pennsylvania's backcountry was under siege after Braddock's failure to capture the French forces at Fort Duquesne. The stalemate left whites living west of the Susquehanna River in a tenuous position. They faced an uncertain future as Indian war parties moved eastward. When Indians overran the Moravian settlement at Gnadenhutten in late November 1755, they massacred every person they could find and left no buildings standing. Finally, in April 1756, the colony reacted, declaring war on the Delaware nation. Before reaching that point, Governor Robert Morris ordered *Pennsylvania Gazette* printers Benjamin Franklin and David Hall not to publish anything the assembly said about the controversy. Franklin sidestepped the governor, saying he was obliged to print the legislature's proceedings and votes. No further constraints were placed on war printing.

Printers and citizens complained about other governmental actions during the war, but nothing foreshadowed the future more than complaints about taxes. One Connecticut man bemoaned escalating taxes in his colony being used to pay for the war, calling them "needless public Expences" because he believed the colony's officials were squandering funds already at hand to aid in the war effort and burdening people excessively in the process. Printers in New York and Massachusetts faced a type of tax not used before in America but a staple of Britain since the beginning of the century—a tax on paper. In Britain, the stamp tax was a means of raising revenue, but it also may have been used to limit freedom of the press. The stamp tax had never been implemented in America, probably because the number of papers that each printer produced was so small in comparison with those produced in London that a tax would have raised little money. Still, a paper tax could have helped William Cosby in New York and other governors to silence troublesome papers, like the *New-York Weekly Journal*.

When Massachusetts levied a tax on paper, printer Thomas Fleet, especially, complained about it. Just as other printers would in 1765, Fleet referred to the stamp required on paper to prove the tax had been paid as "the fatal *Stamp.*" Other Boston printers, such as Benjamin Edes and John Gill of the *Boston Gazette,* simply raised the price of their paper until the tax expired in 1757. In New York, printers did the same. That move rarely helped printers, since Americans were notorious for not paying their newspaper subscriptions, something the printers noted. Because of the war and the need for as much capital as possible, Americans did not complain about the stamp tax, and printers had little recourse but to accept it. Hugh Gaine, however, used the tax to remind readers of the importance of a free press. Even in a time of war, the press needed to be able to address important issues without worry of interference. "THE *Liberty* of the *Press* has very justly been esteem'd *one* of the main Pillars of the Liberty of the People. While *this* is maintain'd the *first* Steps to Oppression are detected, and the Attention of the People *seasonably* awaken'd," Gaine's *New-York Mercury* stated. "It is the Privilege of *Britons* to speak Truth with Impunity, and *even* to fear no Danger from *Speculative Error* whether in *Religion* or *Poltiscks*. . . . 'Tis to be hop'd the Guardians of our Liberties and Laws in whose Custody we have deposited every Thing dear and valuable to us, will preserve the minutest Part of this sacred Trust inviolable." The paper tax expired, but printers, especially in Massachusetts and New York, no doubt remembered it when the British imposed a colony-wide stamp tax in 1765. George Grenville, lord of the treasury, assumed another paper tax in 1765 would be accepted by the American colonies partly because of the ease with which it had become law during the war.

Grenville, of course, was wrong in his estimation, thanks largely to the overall experience of printers during the French and Indian War. The overall collective consciousness that the press had helped to create during the war had changed the way news was presented and the way that colonists viewed their own welfare. The way that information was shared throughout the colonies—for example, the manner in which news from South Carolina became important in New England—made it imperative that the press have the ability to print anything of value to the people. The need to know was now essential. Consequently, the public sphere increased in importance. Even during war, printers were able to criticize government actions. While some officials took action against printers, even those who were arraigned returned to business as usual as soon as possible. Printers even reminded readers during the war of the importance of freedom of the press. All of this combined to reinforce the vital importance of the press to the populace and to confirm the ideas of British writers who had been espousing its virtues for decades. Grenville's new taxes led Americans to use the press and press freedom as never before, based in great measure on its application in the 1750s with the French and Indian War.

THE PRESS REVOLTS

Philip Davidson, in his book *Propaganda and the American Revolution,* observed that propagandists of revolution reached Americans through newspapers. Andrew Eliot, the pastor of Boston's New North Church, commented shortly after the repeal of the Stamp Act that newspapers could and did "awaken and rouse" the people. In the immediate aftermath of the Treaty of Paris in 1763, however, there was little need to rouse the American colonists. With the war over and the treaty signed, France no longer owned territory in North America. Americans rejoiced; Britons wondered what the massive sacrifice to secure the American colonies would mean for them. After all, the loss of life and the amount of money spent to save them had been astronomical.

As news of impending peace reached America in late 1762 and early 1763, newspaper stories celebrated the prospects for the future. Printer Jonas Green of the *Maryland Gazette* fashioned a headline—unusual on stories of the era—that informed his readers that the peace treaty would soon be ratified: "A GOOD PIECE OF NEWS. NEWS OF A GOOD PEACE!" In New York, a writer rejoiced that "we shall complete our Empire in North-America, and fix its security on a firm basis." The empire referred to Britain, not an independent America. A year after the end of the war, however, the American situation was different. Newspaper articles spouted contemptuous words for England and threatened public officials in the colonies, leading Massachusetts Governor Francis Bernard to inform London officials, "To send you all the incendiary papers which are published upon this Occasion would be endless."

What had changed American attitudes of euphoria at the close of the war to inflammatory rhetoric a year later? In 1764, Britain established a series of taxes on the colonies. The Sugar Act was the first of the assessments that Grenville intended to institute in an effort to recoup war debts. In America, however, colonists saw the taxes as a double burden. Colonial legislatures had spent thousands of pounds on the war already. That money had to be repaid. Many Americans believed that paying taxes to their respective colonies and to Britain represented double taxation; they were paying for the war twice. As word of Grenville's assorted taxes reached America, people turned to the printed page to complain. The American press of the French and Indian War era, which had given printers the opportunity to share information quickly, widely, and freely, was ready to spread news of Britain's new tax schemes.

What turned Grenville's tax proposals into an outright press revolt, however, were reports that he planned to place a universal tax on paper products. In 1764 and early 1765, the lord of the treasury could not have imagined that a paper tax would cause such an uproar in America. After all, printers in England had used stamped paper for decades, and Massachusetts and New York had levied paper taxes during the French and Indian War. Grenville had even written to a Boston official to find out how people had reacted to the paper tax during the war, asking, "What difficulties have occurr'd in executing it? What objections may be made to it, and what additional provision must be made to those in force here?" Few printers had complained at that point. Instead, they had simply passed the tax on to subscribers via increased prices. Grenville therefore believed that a stamp tax on paper would cause few problems. He was wrong.

On March 22, 1765, the British Parliament passed the Stamp Act. It placed a tax "upon every paper, commonly called a pamphlet, and upon every newspaper." It also taxed "every advertisement to be contained in any gazette, news paper, or other paper," and it taxed almanacs based on their size and the number of pages they contained. Nothing that a printer produced would escape the stamp tax, which would take effect on November 1, 1765. As the people who controlled the flow of information, most printers quickly realized that, although their livelihoods were in jeopardy, they had at their disposal a means to address the issue.

Printers used every publication imaginable to complain about the stamp tax, and the people joined them. Civic leaders spoke out against the tax. Ministers preached against the immorality of it. Merchants organized boycotts of British goods. Ordinary citizens, spurred to action by what they read and heard, discussed the tax in public places and hanged effigies of stamp sellers on the streets. Legislatures called the act an affront to liberty. In Boston, riots erupted in the streets. Almanacs, the one periodical publication that could be found in nearly every colonial home, served to foment opposition to the stamp tax. Produced by printers everywhere, almanacs adopted anti-tax rhetoric. One Boston almanac boasted sixty thousand subscribers in 1764, and its compiler, Nathaniel Ames, added politics and public awareness to his poetry as England levied taxes. "The sole end of government is the happiness of the people," he reminded readers. "Ignorance among the common people is the very basis and foundation of tyranny and repression." Anywhere that a barb could be placed and directed at the stamp tax, it was. Thomas and John Fleet, reporting on the execution of one Henry Halbert, appended this comment to the story: "*He will never pay any of the taxes unjustly laid on these once happy lands.*"

Papers everywhere contained lines that were truly seditious. A New York writer called all colonial political officials responsible for the Stamp Act "Ye ruthless crew! Ye infernal corrupted, detested incendiaries! . . . Think not, whoever you are, that have been instrumental in ruining your country, that you will escape with impunity." In Boston, another equated Grenville with Satan. "'Tis G———le calls, and sink or swim. You'd go to H———l to follow him." In Virginia, the House of Burgesses went so far as to declare that Parliament had no authority to tax the colonies. The assembly, according to resolves printed in newspapers, "HAVE the Sole Rights and Authority to lay Taxes and Impositions upon It's [*sic*] Inhabitants . . . to lay or impose any Tax whatever on the Inhabitants thereof, shall be Deemed, AN ENEMY TO THIS HIS MAJESTY'S COLONY."

In New York, Lieutenant Governor Cadwallader

Colden charged that newspapers used "every falshood that malice could invent to serve their purpose of exciting the People to disobedience of the Laws & to Sedition." Colden concluded that "considering the present temper of the People, this is not a proper time to prosecute the Printers & Publishers." In Boston, Chief Justice Thomas Hutchinson repeatedly attempted to have grand juries indict printers for seditious libel in the wake of the commentary surrounding the Stamp Act. Each time, however, the grand juries refused to charge anyone, leading Hutchinson to complain that the people of Massachusetts believed freedom of the press meant that printers could "print every Thing that is Libelous and Slanderous." Hutchinson concluded by saying that this was "truly astonishing, and of the most dangerous Tendency." In Virginia, Governor Francis Fauquier was helpless to stop the actions of the assembly. He asked that the body reverse some of its statements when it reconvened. The assemblymen, however, ignored the governor's request.

The united front of Americans in opposition to the stamp tax made punishing anyone for their printing activities impossible. Shortly, though, divisions would occur among the people and among the press that would make it possible for colonial officials under attack in the press at least to arrest someone on charges of sedition. In 1770, New York locked up Alexander MacDougall for something that he had written in 1769. James Parker had printed the piece. Parker died before the trial could take place, however, leaving the state without its incriminating evidence against MacDougall, who was then set free.

It is easy to see why printers were so riled at the tax imposed by the Stamp Act, but why did the colonies unite in opposition to the tax and advocate freedom of the press so vehemently at the same time? The answer may be found in the papers. By 1765, Enlightenment thought was so pervasive that it was incorporated into most of what was printed about the stamp tax. Without doubt, the *Boston Gazette* of Edes and Gill was the most radical of papers at the time. The paper printed commentary from a host of people opposed to British tax proposals and, later, supporting independence. Samuel Adams was a regular in the paper's print shop. John Adams said that the partnership between the two printers and Samuel Adams for the next decade was "a curious employment," where the trio spent its time "cooking up paragraphs, articles, occurrences, &c., working the political engine." The Enlightenment thought found in the paper in 1765 and 1766, however, needed no cooking. It was simply an American interpretation of Locke, Milton, Cato's Letters, and other writings.

In a letter "To the Inhabitants of the Province of the *Massachusetts-Bay,*" the anonymous B. W., who was probably Samuel Adams, reminded the people that it was their duty to speak freely. B. W. said people needed to "declare your Thoughts freely, nor scruple to deliver your Sentiments in a Affair of such unspeakable Consequences." He also said, "Truth is omnipotent, and Reason must be finally victorious." As we have repeatedly seen, though, a free press was needed in order to voice opposition or support of beliefs. By 1765, it appears as if a free press was not just a means to an end but proof that a government of consent, as proposed by Locke in his treatises on government, existed. "Man, in a state of nature, has undoubtedly a right to speak and act without controul," the *Gazette* stated. "That society whose laws least restrain the words and actions of its members, is most free. . . . For should it ever be dangerous to exercise this privilege, it is easy to see, without the spirit of prophecy, slavery and bondage would soon be the portion."

B. W. also reminded his readers, "It is a standing Maxim of *English Liberty* 'That no Man shall be taxed but with his own consent,' and you very well know we were not." The next week, in an unsigned letter, the *Gazette* reminded readers, "We have always understood it to be a grand and fundamental Principle of the Constitution, that no Freeman should be subject to any Tax, to which he has not given his own Consent." Lack of consent meant that actions such as the stamp tax were unauthorized and that people had given up their basic fundamental rights to life, liberty, and property, the bases of Locke's *Second Treatise on Government.* Without the consent of the governed, which the paper tax ignored, the people were reduced to "RANK Slavery—For if their Superior sees fit, they may be deprived of their whole Property. . . . And a People, without Property, or in the precarious Possession of it, are in no better State than Slaves; for Liberty, or even Life itself, without the Enjoyment of them flowing from Property, are of no Value." On November 18, 1765, the *Gazette* dropped the paraphrases of Locke's second treatise and quoted it directly: "NO government can have a RIGHT to obedience from a people, who have not *freely consented* to it; which they can never be supposed to do til either they are put in a full state of *liberty* to chuse their government and governors or at least, till they have such standing laws to which they have by *themselves* or their *representatives given their consent.*"

By 1768, Adams, Edes, and Gill synthesized all that had

happened in terms of the importance of the press—from the free and complete dissemination of information during the French and Indian War period to the press's protests of the Stamp Act—with the ideas of the libertarian thinkers— Milton, Locke, Cato, and others—into a statement of purpose for the press. The press, they said, protects the liberties of the people. It keeps government in check. As the voice of the people, the press assures that officials will follow the consent of the governed. The *Gazette* declared, under the pseudonym Populus:

> THERE is nothing so *fretting* and *vexatious*; nothing so justly TERRIBLE to tyrants, and their tools and abettors, as a FREE PRESS. The reason is obvious; namely, Because it is, as it has been very justly observ'd . . . "the *bulwark of the People's Liberties.*" For this reason, it is ever watched by those who are forming plans for the destruction of the people's liberties, with an *envious* and *malignant* eye. . . . *Your* Press has spoken to us the words of truth: It has pointed to this people, their danger and their remedy: It has set before them Liberty and Slavery; and with the most perswasive and pungent Language, conjur'd them, in the name of GOD, and the King, and for the sake of all posterity, to chuse Liberty and refuse Chains.

In essence, according to Leonard Levy, the battle surrounding the Stamp Act created an atmosphere where the press no longer worried about censure or arrest through charges of seditious libel. Alexander MacDougall's detention was an anomaly in this atmosphere. Government would not be able, in John Adams's words, to silence the voices "by loading the press . . . with restraints and duties."

Unfortunately, at least in terms of complete and open freedom of the press at the time, the rancor surrounding the Stamp Act crisis evolved into a struggle for independence from Britain. Most American printers were not as committed to a cause as Edes and Gill. Despite their united opposition to the Stamp Act, most still professed a certain loyalty to Britain and to printing impartially on matters of importance. They had to decide quickly on what side they would stand, Patriot or Tory. Most American printers would support the Patriot cause, partly because of economic pressures, partly because the cause was worthwhile, and partly because of the activities of the Sons of Liberty, societies that formed in 1765 to protest the Stamp Act and continued to work to usurp British tyranny in the colonies. During the Stamp Act crisis, the opposition to the tax was so complete that newspaper correspondence attempting to justify the tax was almost nonexistent. There were people who opposed separation from Britain; however, it would also have been difficult to find a paper expressing those ideas. From 1768 through the beginning of the American Revolution in 1775, printers who were considered Loyalists were threatened, beaten, and burned in effigy. They had their shops ransacked. Angry mobs destroyed presses. Boston printer John Mein, who, to his misfortune, referred to the Boston Massacre of March 5, 1770, as "a most unfortunate affair," rather than as an act of barbarism by redcoats, wrote to Thomas Hutchinson, asking him "what protection the Law can afford to a person in my Situation."

The most famous of Tory printers, James Rivington, was arrested after his *New-York Gazetteer* reported on the Battles of Lexington and Concord in its May 25, 1775, issue.

The paper contained four columns on the front page. The first two were filled with affidavits of American Patriots present at Lexington who attested to the fact that the British fired first and initiated the confrontation. The other two columns were filled with a speech by New Jersey Governor William Franklin. Franklin's speech was a reaction to Lexington and Concord and talked about why America should remain a part of Britain. It discussed proposed changes in the taxing scheme for America that would make it more in line with the thinking of Locke and others. Rivington was arrested not for providing a balanced look at the crisis at hand and for printing what Patriots considered traitorous speech.

Partisanship became the norm for the press. Samuel Adams formulated the *Journal of Occurrences,* a news package created in Boston and sent throughout the colonies, to publicize British atrocities in an occupied city. Governor Bernard said, "there could not have been got together a greater Collection of impudent virulent and seditious Lies, perversions of truth and misrepresentations than are to be found in this publication." Many Patriot printers, however, believed that Britain's violations of American rights had so radically suppressed the libertarian concept of the consent of the governed that it was morally wrong to give opposition voices a place in their publications. John Holt declared his paper open "to the cause of truth and justice," yet he also said that the lies of Tories were too great. "I would endeavor to find a place and give a fair hearing to such a performance,—but when I see every thing on that side to be no better than barefaced attempts to deceive and impose upon the ignorant, and imprudently overbear and brazen them out of their reason, their liberty and their property—I disdain such publication." By the time of the Revolution, some Americans appeared to be reneging on elements of their Enlightenment ideals. Holt believed, as Richard Baxter had said more than a century earlier, "If ten mens voyces be louder then one, then would the noyse of Errour drown the voyce of Truth." Patriot printers, it seems, were intent on making sure that America's presses were free not so that truth and error could grapple, but so that the speech of freedom solely might be heard.

The transformation of America's press in the twenty years beginning with the French and Indian War in 1754 was remarkable. In ten years, the number of papers more than doubled. In twenty years, the number of papers grew by more than 260 percent. During this time, printers never stopped producing other publications, so that within the public sphere Americans were continually provided with material to spark debate and shape public opinion. During the French and Indian War, printers learned and honed effective means of information dispersal. They realized that connectedness was vital. People realized they needed newspapers to stay abreast of events. Even though news of an event taking place in South Carolina might not reach New England for weeks, people came to realize that what happened in one colony hundreds of miles away could have repercussions for them. During the war, printers united in a cause, something they would do again during the Stamp Act crisis of 1765.

During the French and Indian War, the press criticized the government as printers or correspondents deemed that criticism was warranted. Though officials sometimes cited them for their comments, printers tended to ignore any reprimands and to continue the denigration in subsequent papers, a tendency that had developed in the colonies since the 1720s. By the time of the Stamp Act crisis, America's press had informed the colonies of a war that affected the very existence of British colonial America and of the fighting that took place around the globe between Britain and France. When taxes threatened printers' financial livelihood, they were prepared to react.

The Stamp Act crisis produced a new round of apologies for freedom of the press, and more than ever, the rhetoric revolved around Enlightenment ideals. A free press was essential to ensuring that public officials were aware of the feelings of the governed. The crisis also produced a new sentiment in America, the idea that perhaps the colonies should be free and independent from Britain. "Let these *truths* be indelibly impressed on our minds—*that we cannot be* HAPPY, *without being* FREE—that we cannot be secure in our property, *if, without our consent, others may, as by right take it away,*" John Dickinson said in the last of his "Letters from a Farmer in Pennsylvania." In the process of espousing their rationale for separation, Patriots developed a sense that the press should be free for their ideas solely. Anything that advocated support of and allegiance to Britain was so blatantly opposed to the concepts of libertarian government in the form presented by Locke that they believed it needed to be silenced. Or, as Stephen Botein has said, "printers in America began to discard their neutral trade rhetoric, in order to behave aggressively and unapologetically as partisans." They and numerous other Americans believed that the only way truly to be free was to silence those who would destroy the libertarian dream. Calls for freedom of the press now were calls for a press of freedom. If printers were perceived at all to favor the Tory line, they were harassed, attacked, arrested, and ultimately forced from business. Nearly 100,000 Americans left all that they owned in America when the Revolution began never to return because they felt they could never function in a society of such contradictions.

In this environment, printers who favored impartiality or the Tory line advocated free press rights using rhetoric that assumed a tone akin to that proposed in England and America for more than a century: "Can they be friends to liberty, who will not allow any to think or speak differently from themselves, without danger? Will they compel the society to act according to their arbitrary decisions, and yet tell us we are free?" Rivington's paper asked. Even though Tories—whether they were printers or ordinary citizens—were threatened in the 1770s, opposing ideas did make it into print. Daniel Leonard, the solicitor general of the Boston customs board, wrote extensively under the penname Massachusettenis in an effort to undermine the work of Sam Adams and others, calling Adams's work the "seed of sedition." In Philadelphia, William Smith, provost of the College of Philadelphia, adopted the pseudonym "Cato" (like Trenchard and Gordon) in a series of polemical jousts with Thomas Paine on why the colonies did not need to declare independence from England and exacerbate hostilities. Despite efforts to curtail all publications to the Patriot line, the activities and role of the press for fifty years could not be usurped completely.

As America entered the period of revolution, mixed signals on freedom of the press emerged. According to Leonard Levy, Patriots accepted nothing less than submission to their cause; the Continental Congress nevertheless offered a free press as the prime reason that the Province of Quebec should join the colonies below the lakes in revolt. "The last right we shall mention regards the freedom of the press . . . and its consequential promotion of union among them, whereby oppressive officials are shamed or intimidated into more honorable and just modes of conducting affairs." In New York, however, angry Patriots warned printers that "if you print, or suffer to be printed in your press anything against the rights and liberties of America, or in favor of our inveterate foes, the King, Ministry, and Parliament of Great Britain, death and destruction, ruin and perdition, shall be your portion."

During the Revolution, Congress refused to punish printers, instead opting for repercussions, if they were to transpire, to take place on the state level, though not much occurred there, either. What happened to printers such as John Mein and James Rivington was purely a means to an end, just as freedom of the press had been for Britons for two centuries. Richard Buell Jr., suggesting that this suppression should be understood in terms of the times, offered New York lawyer William Livingston's writings in the *Independent Reflector* as the lens through which to view this interpretation. Livingston, in an essay entitled "*Of the Use, Abuse, and* LIBERTY OF THE PRESS," said, "All those who oppose the Freedom I have contended for,—a Liberty of promoting the common Good of Society, and of publishing any Thing else not repugnant thereto,—are Enemies to the Common Wealth; and many will fall under this Character, who are as ready to cry out for the *Liberty of the Press* as the warmest Patriot." Even though Livingston was writing more than thirty years before the American Revolution, he was steeped in Enlightenment thought. He understood that a free press had to operate within a sphere that ensured the success of the commonwealth as he and other rational libertarians understood it. This helps to explain how some could propose in one sentence the absolute right of free speech for their ideology yet advocate complete suppression for views contrary to their own. The contradiction is evident in Livingston's *Independent Reflector* columns. In 1753, Livingston also said, "But how great is the Absurdity to suppose, that Government was ever designed to *enslave* the *Consciences of Men!*"

Using this frame of reference, Buell proposed that the hostilities exhibited toward Tory printing in the 1770s was not really a suppression of speech, but a way of putting into practice the ideals of Cato, Locke, and other Enlightenment thinkers, which required a break with Britain. The only way that America could be successful in obtaining independence was to allow no dissension from its policies adopted to end British taxes and other acts considered oppressive to a people who believed they should govern themselves. Once the ties that bound colonies and mother country had been broken by around 1780, there was no reason to silence opposing views. Printers were no longer the object of libel charges, according to Buell, though authors were. Now it was time truly to put into practice the libertarian concept of a free press that printers and others had advocated for decades, the Enlightenment's unruly legacy.

EIGHT

CONCLUSION

The amazing evolution of the right of expression and, consequently, the liberty of the press from the 1500s through the American Revolution might be characterized as God-given right tempered with reason. But the path from the Star Chamber, Stationers' Company, and licensing to the words of the First Amendment is also one of continued resistance, gains, losses, and nonconsensus. It is a right whose exact meaning is argued today as much as it was during the period of this study. Dwight Teeter has said that if we knew what freedom of the press meant to the Founding Fathers then we would know what it means today. Therein lies the problem. "Few of us, I believe," Benjamin Franklin said, "have distinct Ideas of Its Nature and Extent." Alexander Hamilton, in his push for ratification of the Constitution, asked, "What is the liberty of the press? Who can give it any definition which would not leave the utmost latitude for evasion? I hold it to be impracticable; and from this I infer, that its security, whatever fine declarations may be inserted in any constitution respecting it, must altogether depend on public opinion, and on the general spirit of the people and of the government."

Did the people at the end of the Revolution believe as Eleazer Oswald did, when he explained in his Philadelphia paper that "considerable Lattitude must be allowed in the Discussion of Public Affairs, or the Liberty of the Press will be of no Benefit to Society"? Did they share Isaiah Thomas's hope in 1788 when he wrote, "Heaven grant that the FREEDOM of the PRESS, on which depends the FREE-DOM of the PEOPLE, may, in the United States, be ever guarded with a watchful eye, and defended from *Shackles,* of every form and shape, until the trump of the celestial Messenger shall announce the final dissolution of all things"?

Or did the people believe that restraints needed to be placed on expression? At the same time that America's press was completing its concerted effort to repeal the Stamp Act, jurists were beginning to provide legal definitions of what freedom of the press meant. William Blackstone, in his *Commentaries on the Laws of England,* concluded in 1769, "The liberty of the press is indeed essential to the nature of a free state: but this consists in laying no previous restraints upon publications, and not in freedom from censure from criminal matter when published." In America, Thomas Hutchinson, chief justice in Massachusetts, concurred. "The Liberty of the Press is doubtless a very great Blessing; but this Liberty means no more than a Freedom for every Thing to pass from the Press without a Licence." Blackstone and Hutchinson firmly believed that although people could say what they wanted, they had to be prepared for repercussions, because seditious libel remained valid law in the British Empire.

By 1778, all of the states had adopted some statement

regarding free expression. As Leonard Levy has pointed out, one cannot assume that all of the states sought to protect speech only in the restricted way suggested by Blackstone's understanding. The press had become an invaluable component in the actions and activities of the people. Although Levy placed this development in the 1760s and beyond, such a late starting point for the increase in the value and the use of the press in society overlooks all that happened with the press during the French and Indian War and as other issues and events played out and became subjects of debate even before the war in colonial America. Levy also explained that most people understood press freedom as a guarantee to continue existing press practices. This meant that the press was partisan and could be quite abusive in its remarks. This is confirmed by what Hutchinson said of the press in the tumultuous post–Stamp Act era. People, Hutchinson lamented, understood freedom of the press as the right to "print every Thing that is Libelous and Slanderous."

Of course, Hutchinson's opponents would never have qualified their writings as anything so malicious. They felt, instead, that their writings expressed truth. These ideas, men such as Samuel Adams would have said, *must* be heard so that the people could shake off tyranny and oppression. The common saying, adapted from Cato's Letters, became, "the Freedom of the Press is one of the greatest Bulwarks of Liberty." Americans applied it to almost every issue from the 1770s on, and in some cases much earlier, but dissenters had practiced liberty of conscience since the 1500s and had used the printed word to express it. During the reign of the Tudors and early Stuarts, a divine right given to a ruler provided absolute authority to the monarchy. When the divine right of kings was questioned, people died. As time progressed, however, religious dissenters came to understand authority as possessing at least two elements: the divine and the secular. The king ruled not by divine right but by the consent of the governed. Writers, harkening back to the humanists of the Middle Ages, introduced a new and enlightened way of understanding the relationship between God and humankind as well as between God and rulers. The idea that scripture alone was enough to save a person and that each believer could accomplish her or his salvation through personal connections with God, called the "priesthood of the believer," was the first step. "'Tis common freedome every man ought to aime at, which is every mans peculiar right," the Leveller William Walwyn wrote in 1644 in support of religious liberty. And how should that right be shared? Walwyn was explicit on this point, advocating "That the Presse may be free for any man" to share his views.

But depending upon one's perspective, nearly all expression from the time of Luther's Ninety-Five Theses through the American Revolution could be characterized as "Libelous and Slanderous," as Thomas Hutchinson did in 1767, or as the "most damnable Heresies," as Henry VIII did in 1529, by someone, especially those who held political and ecclesiastical power. Initially, expression that questioned the pillars of the country often resulted in execution for the violator. As power changed hands—from Catholicism to Anglicanism to Puritanism in the religious realm and from monarchy to commonwealth and back again in the political realm—people in England sought avenues of expression to voice their discontent. Being discontent, at least in the religious realm, meant that some were absolutely wrong in their beliefs and understanding according to those who held differing views. For those of the standing order, any understanding of religion other than that prescribed by the state was heretical. Heretics had to be silenced. It was the rare individual or group that acknowledged that the right to express ideas must be open to any group or interpretation, but that is what the first Baptists did, followed by the Levellers in the 1640s.

From its earliest use, the press provided a means to an end. Henry VIII printed *Defense of the Seven Sacraments* as a response to what he and Rome considered the heretical designs of the Protestant reformers, and the Tudor king received the blessings of the pope and was named Defender of the Faith. By the time of Elizabeth's reign, a new group of dissenters, called Puritans, turned to the press in an effort to reform the Anglican Church. Because the government continually silenced them, they claimed that in a country with a representative government the ideas of the "noble or other, tag and rag, learned and unlearned, of the basest sorte of people" were "freely receaved." During the last years of the reign of Charles I, tens of thousands of publications turned up on the streets of London and the rest of England addressing the political and ecclesiastical issues that brought England to civil war. Even when the standing order changed, those with newfound power were ready to clamp down on the opposition.

A problem, however, arose. Those in power in the 1640s and 1650s had bitterly protested the denial of their own rights. In an effort to be heard, they had equated their own liberty of conscience with the right to be heard, to have what they believed printed and disseminated to the public, leading one writer in the turbulent England of the 1640s to say that "the art of Printing will so spread knowledge, that the common people, knowing their own rights and liberties will not be governed by way of oppression." Oppression continued, of course, but something else happened during this time. The thinking that denied rule by divine right also advocated new thinking in religion and in the rights of the people. The Levellers, with their democratic ideas of government, society, and expression, may have been too radical even for civil-war England, but others who were less radical either adopted their proposals or came to the same conclusions. They believed that man was God's crowning creation. Would the divine master create a world that was not understandable by his chief creation? Would public discussion of beliefs damage God? The proponents of these ideas, whom we call Enlightenment thinkers, emphatically answered no to these questions. Humankind, they said, had the ability to understand divine actions, and public debate would not harm God and would not harm the state, either, so long as the people understood their relationship with the divine.

It is important to remember that what the Levellers, John Milton, John Locke, and others proposed in relation to government and free expression rested upon a religious foundation. Even in the last half of the eighteenth century in America, writers and most other people never forgot how religion underpinned everything. Even when writings were not overtly religious in their phrasing, people understood what they read through a lens tinted by their spiritual beliefs. Most Americans of the twenty-first century might find it unfathomable that the American Revolution could have been as much about stopping the establishment of Anglicanism as the state church in America as it was about throwing off the shackles of tyranny and oppression. And yet that is just what has been proposed by Patricia U. Bonomi, who suggested that modern interpretations of the revolution have overlooked the importance of religion to the society of the revolutionaries.

By the end of the seventeenth century, England adopted laws guaranteeing religious toleration and ending licensing of published items. The 1689 Bill of Rights gave people the right to petition government and speak freely, but it did not provide a clause guaranteeing freedom of the press. That omission was inconsequential, for the most part. During the first decades of the eighteenth century, newspapers were commonplace throughout Britain, and bookshops thrived, meaning the people had ready outlets for their views and opinions through various printed forms. Despite the miles of ocean between the mother country and America, regular contact between the two meant that colonials were cognizant of what was taking place in England. Newspapers, pamphlets, and books from England traveled to America, something that had taken place throughout the seventeenth century, as well. Because American colonists were British, what took place in the advancement of free-expression rights, religion, and Enlightenment thought in England became a part of the American experience. Colonials, of course, faced experiences in settlement and survival that their counterparts in the Isles did not face, but the experiences of England meant that Americans were able to speed through many of the conflicts that their brethren in England had faced before them. Nowhere was this more true than with printing.

Though American newspaper growth and expansion, along with the print trade in general, lagged behind that of England by decades, owing to lack of population density, print and expression nonetheless benefited from all that had transpired in the mother country. Expression in seventeenth-century America was almost exclusively oral, since no more than five presses operated during the century in the colonies, and three of them were in Massachusetts. Government officials were able to keep much better overall control of what was considered religious and political subversive expression than their English counterparts, but even in America, complete control was impossible. "Heretics" such as Roger Williams and Anne Hutchinson, and political "revolutionaries" such as Nathaniel Bacon and George Durant, could never be silenced completely. Press control was easier than control over oral expression, though. Both Benjamin Harris and William Bradford discovered that printing and politics created tenuous relations when religious dissenters who had been suppressed in England—Puritans in Harris's case and Quakers in Bradford's—used the same censorship tactics against them that the dissenters themselves had suffered in England. What was different, however, was the speed with which American colonists moved through this period of excessively tight political control of the press. By 1721, voices of opposition arose in Boston's printing environment. Government sanctions and arrests followed, but by the time of the trial of John Peter Zenger in 1735, printers were regularly ignoring sanctions against them not to publish certain types of information and opinions.

How was this possible? The English experience of two centuries, religious toleration, Enlightenment thought, and the letters of John Trenchard and Thomas Gordon all combined to provide a religious and rational foundation for speaking freely. People took all to heart and used the printed word as the foundation for public discussion and debate. At the same time, Americans incorporated into their publications and discussions another element of British expression that existed alongside writings advocating liberty of conscience and a government that responded more to the will of the people. That other element was news. People want to know what's going on and how it affects them, and this is a desire that is as old as human interaction itself. They want to be entertained, and they want access to information that can guide them socially and economically, not just politically. English newsbooks had been filling these needs since the sixteenth century, and they continued to do so through the seventeenth and into the eighteenth. In America, newspapers simply patterned themselves after their British counterparts, incorporating news with the other elements of publishing that addressed political and ecclesiastical issues.

By the time of the French and Indian War, America's printing network was able to share information, update people on events, and provide a mouthpiece for discussion on a level that included all the colonies and to a certain extent events from around the globe. This press was prepared for all that took place from the end of the war in 1763 forward. Even during the war period, printers regularly published essays advocating a free press. The call would become a rallying point from 1765 on. But during the next fifteen to twenty years, the press seemed to regress in this regard. By about 1770, many of the American Patriots accepted the ideas of Locke and other Enlightenment thinkers so completely that, ironically, they believed that it had become necessary to silence any voice that would keep the people suppressed. People threatened and attacked printers in the effort to keep Tory ideas from being published and, in some cases, destroyed print shops. When it became obvious, however, that the Revolution would be successful and that oppression would be thwarted, Americans reinstituted their libertarian concepts of free expression. States adopted free speech and press provisions, and in order to ensure ratification of the Constitution, the federal government had to create a series of ten constraints—the Bill of Rights—the first guaranteeing the right to petition government and protection of speech and press rights along with protection of religious belief and practice.

Americans, by the middle of the eighteenth century, had developed a good understanding of the significance of free expression, especially via the printed word. Perhaps no one statement encapsulated that awareness better than this one from a New York paper:

> THE *Liberty* of the *Press* has very justly been esteem'd *one* of the main Pillars of the Liberty of the People. While *this* is maintain'd the *first* Steps to Oppression are detected, and the Attention of the People *seasonably* awaken'd. When *this* is suppress'd the Suspicions of the People, and their Ruin, may admit to so *sudden* a Transition, as renders the Success of the *first* impracticable, and the Miseries attending the *latter* unavoidable. So dangerous is this Blessing to lawless Power, that the *farthest* Approaches to it are resolutely oppos'd or rigorously punish'd. So essential is this to Freedom, Property and Happiness, that the most plausible Attempts to

curtail it *even* in the smallest Degree, have always been strenuously oppos'd by; the virtuous, free and unbiass'd Patriot. It is the Privilege of *Britons* to speak Truth with Impunity, and *even* to fear no Danger from *speculative Error* whether in *Religion* or *Politicks*. . . .

   [T]he Deprivation of our whole Liberty may be justified on the *same* Principles as the *Liberty of the Press* undoubtedly is, 'Tis therefore humbly to be hoped, that the old American Spirit so exemplary free in former and better Times, will never submit to *new* and unwarrantable Restrictions. 'Tis to be hop'd the Guardians of our Liberties and Laws in whose Custody we have deposited every Thing dear and valuable to us, will preserve the minutest Part of this sacred Trust inviolable, and while there remains no *just* doubt of this we have Reason to acquiesce in their Tenderness, Watchfulness and Fidelity.

One can see the value of a free press in any era when religion, politics, social differences, and economic disparity affect a nation. That is what the writer of the above words understood, and the same may be applied to our times. The urge to suppress and censor is always elevated in times that are perceived to be dangerous for a country or a people. Opposing voices to the majority are always both threatening and threatened in times of alarm. As in Benjamin Franklin's day in the 1780s, today it is not certain exactly what freedom of speech and the press permit. Many truly believe that allowing extremist points of view to be expressed will destroy the foundation of a nation. Of course, in some ways they are correct. The Protestant Reformation and the English Civil War changed England forever. Those in power resisted both and did all that was politically and physically possible to silence dissent. The American Revolution produced an armed revolt that overthrew the supervising government of the colonies and replaced it with an experimental one.

But how many Americans would say that the Reformation was a bad thing or that it was wrong to fight for America's independence? The meaning of a free press has changed with the times and will continue to do so as long as the people have a voice in their governance. The legacy surrounding it will never change: People want and need a voice in the things that affect their lives. That the people were able to obtain that voice in the eighteenth century is the Enlightenment's gift. Governments and religions may find a way to silence the people, but whenever the slightest break in oppression occurs, people will speak. The Enlightenment's unruly legacy is that one bold group of people as they formed a nation insisted that their government would protect the right of expression so that the people could have a voice in what transpired relating to their own welfare. The ebb and flow in terms of the consent of the governed will continue so long as, in the language of Cato, "A free people will be shewing that they are so, by their freedom of speech."

CHAPTER ONE

1 *I know you:* T. D., *A True Discourse of the most happy victories obtayned by the French King, against the Rebels and enemies of his Majesty. With a particuler declaration of all that hath beene done betweene the two Armies, during the monthes of September and October, and part of November. 1589. Also of teh [sic] taking of the Subburbes of Paris by the King. Faithfully translated out of French into English, according to the Coppy imprinted at Tours.* (London: J. Wolfe and E. White, 1589), quoted in Paul J. Voss, *Elizabethan News Pamphlets: Shakespeare, Spenser, Marlowe & the Birth of Journalism* (Pittsburgh, Pa.: Duquesne University Press, 2001), 34.

45,000: Voss, *Elizabethan News Pamphlets,* 1.

2 *This Taste, we Englishmen: New-York Gazette,* January 22, 1750.

3 *If God gave:* Fredrick Seaton Siebert, *Freedom of the Press in England, 1476–1776: The Rise and Decline of Government Control* (Urbana: University of Illinois Press, 1965), 7.

But how great: William Livingston, "The Absurdity of the civil Magistrate's interfering in Matters of Religion," *Independent Reflector* (New York), August 9, 1753, reprinted in Milton M. Klein, ed., *The Independent Reflector* (Cambridge, Mass.: Harvard University Press, 1963), 313.

Establish truths: Henry F. May, *The Enlightenment in America* (Oxford: Oxford University Press, 1976), xiv. May divided the Enlightenment into four categories. The first, the moderate Enlightenment, encompasses the time period of this study and was the basis of thought in England and

America through at least the middle of the eighteenth century.

4   *Caxton's publications:* See Nellie Slayton Aurner, *Caxton: Mirrour of Fifteenth-Century Letters* (New York: Russell and Russell, 1965); George D. Painter, *William Caxton: A Biography* (New York: G. P. Putnam's, 1977); and Freida Elaine Penninger, *William Caxton* (Boston: Twayne, 1979).

5   *Frith proposed:* Frith's ideas are outlined in John Frith, *A boke made by Iohn frith ansawering vnto Th Mores lettur whtch he wrote agenst the first litle tretyse that Iohn frith made* (Monster [Münster]: C. Willems, 1533).

        Frith's enlightened thought: William A. Clebsch, *England's Earliest Protestants, 1520–1535* (New Haven, Conn.: Yale University Press, 1964), 128.

6   *Henry VIII responded quickly:* Siebert, *Freedom of the Press in England,* 2.

7   *Personal correspondence:* M. A. Shaaber, *Some Forerunners of the Newspaper in England, 1476–1622* (Philadelphia: University of Pennsylvania Press, 1929; reprint, New York: Octagon Books, 1966), 2.

        The public sphere: The public sphere is a concept developed and presented in Jürgen Habermas, *The Structural Transformation of the Public Sphere: An Inquiry into a Category of Bourgeois Society,* trans. Thomas Burger (Cambridge, Mass.: Harvard University Press, 1989).

9   *Exposition of beliefs:* David Paul Nord, *Faith in Reading: Religious Publishing and the Birth of Mass Media in America* (New York: Oxford University Press, 2004).

        The long line of martyrs: John Foxe, *The Acts and Monuments of the Church* (London: 1563).

        It's evident the Freedom: Anonymous [Matthew Tindal], "A Letter to a Member of Parliament, Shewing That a Restraint on the Press Is Inconsistent with the Protestant Religion, and Dangerous to the Liberties of the Nation" (London, 1688), reprinted in George Orwell and Reginald

Reynolds, eds., *British Pamphleteers,* 10 vols. (London: Allan Wingate, 1948), 1:183.

10 *I can not in conscience:* John Frith, *The articles wherefore Johann Frith died which he wrote in newgatae the 23 daye of June the yere of oure Lorde 1533* (Monster: C. Willems, 1533), no numbered pages.

God made man righteous: William Walwyn, *The Power of Love* (London, 1643), 2–3, 48, in William Haller, ed., *Tracts on Liberty in the Puritan Revolution, 1638–1647,* 3 vols. (New York: Columbia University Press, 1934; reprint, New York: Octagon Books, 1965), 2:279–80, 302. The pamphlet was published anonymously.

11 *There are some things:* Benjamin Keach, *Tropologia: A Key to open Scripture Metaphors* (London, 1681), bk. iv, 40.

12 *Bonomi has pointed out:* Patricia U. Bonomi, *Under the Cope of Heaven: Religion, Society and Politics in Colonial America* (New York: Oxford University Press, 1986), 4–5.

13 *New-York Weekly Journal:* See, for example, *New-York Weekly Journal,* November 12, 1733.

The Devout Man: The Spectator, No. 245 (London), August 12, 1712, in Joseph Addison and Richard Steele, *Selections from* The Tatler *and* The Spectator, 2nd ed., with an introduction by Robert J. Allen (Fort Worth, Tex.: Holt, Rinehart and Winston, 1957), 423–24.

14 *Ultimately in the nineteenth century piety would become:* May, *The Enlightenment in America,* xv.

The old American Spirit: New-York Mercury, March 22, 1756.

Ye cannot be saved: Pennsylvania Gazette (Philadelphia), August 29, 1754.

15 *Every falsehood:* Quoted in Arthur M. Schlesinger, *Prelude to Independence: The Newspaper War in Britain, 1764–1776* (New York: Alfred A. Knopf, 1958), 72–73.

CHAPTER TWO

22 *Single Question:* Anonymous [Matthew Tindal], "A Letter to a Member of Parliament, Shewing That a Restraint on the

Press Is Inconsistent with the Protestant Religion, and Dangerous to the Liberties of the Nation" (London, 1688), reprinted in George Orwell and Reginald Reynolds, eds., *British Pamphleteers,* 10 vols. (London: Allan Wingate, 1948), 1:183.

22   *The religious motive:* William M. Clyde, *The Struggle for the Freedom of the Press from Caxton to Cromwell* (London: Oxford University Press, 1934; reprint, New York: Burt Franklin, 1970), 10.

Good rule of this realm: Star Chamber Act, 1487, in Paul L. Hughes and Robert F. Fries, eds., *Crown and Parliament in Tudor-Stuart England: A Documentary Constitutional History, 1485–1714* (New York: G. P. Putnam's Sons, 1959), 13.

Henry was responding: Fredrick Seaton Siebert, *Freedom of the Press in England, 1476–1776* (Urbana: University of Illinois Press, 1965), 24–25.

24   *Luther added:* James M. Kittelson, *Luther the Reformer: The Story of the Man and His Career* (Minneapolis: Augsburg, 1986), 112–13; Tim Dowley, ed., *The History of Christianity* (Grand Rapids, Mich.: Wm. B. Eerdmans, 1977), 360–61.

A total of thirty: A. G. Dickens, *Reformation and Society in Sixteenth-Century Europe* (London: Thames and Hudson, 1966), 51. Luther quoted in Elizabeth L. Eisenstein, *The Printing Press as an Agent of Change,* 2 vols. (Cambridge: Cambridge University Press, 1979), 1:304.

For the first time: Dickens, *Reformation and Society in Sixteenth-Century Europe,* 51. Many early publications included woodcut illustrations, no doubt a tradition continued from the ornate hand-produced books of the Middle Ages.

The king's book: David L. Edwards, *Christian England,* 3 vols. (Grand Rapids, Mich.: Wm. B. Eerdmans, 1980), 2:285, 315–17.

26   *More was the most important:* Jasper Ridley, *Statesman and Saint: Cardinal Wolsey, Sir Thomas More, and the Politics of Henry VIII* (New York: Viking, 1982), 239.

27   *Knowleg thy self:* John Frith, *A pistle to the Christian reader: the reuelation of antichrist* (Antwerp: H. Luft Hesse, 1529), ii.

Frith ronneth: Walter M. Gordon, "A Scholastic Problem in Thomas More's Controversy with John Frith," *Harvard Theological Review* 69 (January 1976): 134–35.

The cause of my death: John Frith, *The articles wherefore Johann Frith died which he wrote in newgatae the 23 daye of June the yere of oure Lorde 1533* (Monster [Münster]: C. Willems, 1533), no numbered pages.

28   *The king's subjects:* Quoted in Siebert, *Freedom of the Press in England,* 45.

Henry provided an addendum: Siebert, *Freedom of the Press in England,* 46.

29   *A two-edged sword:* Ridley, *Statesman and Saint,* 279.

As protector, Somerset: Marshall M. Knappen, *Tudor Puritanism* (Chicago: University of Chicago Press, 1939; reprint, Gloucester, Mass.: Peter Smith, 1963), 72–73.

30   *Concerning religion and opinion:* First Treasons Act, 1547, in Hughes and Fries, eds., *Crown and Parliament in Tudor-Stuart England,* 72–73.

No printer or other person: Proclamation of April 28, 1551, in Robert Steele, *Tudor and Stuart Proclamations, 1485–1714* (Oxford: Oxford University Press, 1910), no. 395.

31   *Foxe's* Acts and Monuments: Barrington R. White, ed., *The English Puritan Tradition* (Nashville, Tenn.: Broadman, 1980), 13–14; Edwards, *Christian England,* 3 vols., 2:70–72.

32   *For mens religion:* Thomas Helwys, *A Short Declaration of the mistery of iniquity* (1612; reprint, London: Kingsgate, 1935), 69.

Viewed the other: J. Sears McGee, *The Godly Man in Stuart England: Anglicans, and Puritans, and the Two Tables, 1620–1670* (New Haven, Conn.: Yale University Press, 1976), 2.

I abhor unlimited liberty: Richard Baxter, *Plain Scripture Proof* (London, 1651), 246.

33   *A series of publications:* Knappen, *Tudor Puritanism,* 235.

33 *Noble or other:* Anonymous, *An Admonition to the Parliament* (London, 1572), in White, *The English Puritan Tradition,* 31.

They claimed protection: Margaret A. Blanchard, "Turning Worlds Upside Down: Freedom of Expression through the Revolution," unpublished manuscript, 1992.

34 *Seditious and heretical books:* "Charter," the Stationers' Company, quoted in Clyde, *The Struggle for the Freedom of the Press,* 12.

Dyvers contentyous: Clyde, *The Struggle for the Freedom of the Press,* 20–21.

A series of anonymous pamphlets: Siebert, *Freedom of the Press in England,* 98–100.

35 *Faint stirrings of rebellion:* Ibid., 103–4.

36 *The new king:* Knappen, *Tudor Puritanism,* 317–18.

37 *From God through the king:* Siebert, *Freedom of the Press in England,* 110.

38 *In 1275:* Philip Hamburger, "The Development of the Law of Seditious Libel and the Control of the Press," *Stanford Law Review* 37 (1985): 661–765; William T. Mayton, "Seditious Libel and the Lost Guarantee of a Freedom of Expression," *Columbia Law Review* 84 (1984): 91–142; and Siebert, *Freedom of the Press in England,* 118–19.

39 *Freedome of speech:* Leonard W. Levy, *Emergence of a Free Press* (New York: Oxford University Press, 1985), 4; W. E. Lunt, *History of England,* 4th ed. (New York: Harper and Row, 1957), 398.

Laud decreed: Edwards, *Christian England,* 3 vols., 2:203.

40 *Everything published:* Clyde, *The Struggle for the Freedom of the Press,* 42–43; Siebert, *Freedom of the Press in England,* 142–43.

The revolt of the pamphleteers: William Haller, ed. *Tracts on Liberty in the Puritan Revolution, 1638–1647,* 3 vols. (New York: Columbia University Press, 1934; reprint, New York: Octagon Books, 1965), 1:1.

Writers continued to quote: Ibid., 1:4.

41 *'Tis common freedome:* Anonymous [William Walwyn], *The Compassionate Samaritane Vnbinding The Conscience, and powring Oyle into the wounds which have been made upon the Separation: recommending their future welfare to the serious thoughts, and carefull endeavours of all who love the peace and vnity of Commonwealths men, or desire the vnanimous prosecution for the Common Enemie, or who follow our Saviours rule, to doe unto others, what they would have other doe unto them* (London, 1644), 5–6, 78–79, in Haller, ed., *Tracts on Liberty in the Puritan Revolution,* 3 vols., 3:67, 103–4.

42 *To speake what I thinke:* F. R., "The Publisher to the Reader," in John Lilburne, *A Worke of the Beast or A Relation of a most vnchristian Censure, Executed upon IOHN LILBVRNE, (Now prisoner in the fleet) the 18 of Aprill 1638. With the heavenly speech vtterred by him at the time of his suffering* (1638), in Haller, ed., *Tracts on Liberty in the Puritan Revolution,* 3 vols., 2:4.

43 *Political and religious controversialists:* Siebert, *Freedom of the Press in England,* 173–74.

   Even Parliament was divided: Conrad Russell, *The Crisis of Parliaments: English History, 1509–1660* (Oxford: Oxford University Press, 1971), 356–61; Lunt, *History of England,* 434.

44 *That you will open the Press:* John Lilburne, *Englands New Chaines,* quoted in Clyde, *The Struggle for the Freedom of the Press,* 171.

   If Government be just: John Lilburne, *The Second Part of England's New Chaines Discovered* (1649), in Siebert, *Freedom of the Press in England,* 201.

45 *Instead, a new piece of legislation:* Siebert, *Freedom of the Press in England,* 201.

   They read Areopagetica: Douglas Bush, *John Milton: A Sketch of His Life and Writings* (New York: Macmillan, 1964), 98.

46 *Milton's tract:* Caroline Robbins, *The Eighteenth-Century Commonwealthman* (Cambridge, Mass.: Harvard University Press, 1959), 46; George F. Sensabaugh, *Milton in Early*

America (Princeton, N.J.: Princeton University Press, 1964); Jeffery A. Smith, *Printers and Press Freedom: The Ideology of Early American Journalism* (Oxford: Oxford University Press, 1988), 34–35.

46   *God gave him reason:* John Milton, *Areopagitica: A Speech of Mr. John Milton for the Liberty of Unlicens'd Printing, to the Parliament of England* (London, 1644), in *The Works of John Milton,* 20 vols. (New York: Columbia University Press, 1931), 4:319, 337, 346, 347.

47   *Baptist-turned-Seeker:* Roger Williams, *The Bloudy Tenent of Persecution for Cause of Conscience Discussed in a Conference between Peace and Truth* (London, 1644), 144.

48   *And because the passion: The Declaration of Breda,* April 1660, in Hughes and Fries, eds., *Crown and Parliament in Tudor-Stuart England,* 255.

49   *All such persons:* Iohn Sturgeon, *A Plea for Toleration of Opinions and Persuasions in Matters of Religion differing from the Church of England* (London, 1661), in Edward Bean Underhill, ed., *Tracts on Liberty of Conscience, 1614–1661* (London: Hanserd Knollys Society, 1846), 313.

   No person or persons: An Act for Preventing the Frequent Abuses in Printing Seditious, Treasonable and Unlicensed Books and Pamphlets, and for Regulating of Printing and Printing-Presses, in Andrew Browning, ed., *English Historical Documents, 1660–1714* (New York: Oxford University Press, 1953), 67.

   Enforcement of it: Siebert, *Freedom of the Press in England,* 257.

   Still, for books or pamphlets: Christopher Hill, *The Century of Revolution, 1603–1714* (Edinburgh: Thomas Nelson, 1961), 248.

   In 1664, he published: David A. Copeland, *Benjamin Keach and the Development of Baptist Traditions in Seventeenth-Century England* (Lewiston, N.Y.: Edward Mellen Press, 2001), 18–20.

50   *Other Baptists:* B. R. White, *The English Baptists of the Seven-teenth Century* (London: Baptist Historical Society, 1983), 111–12.

51   *That it is the right of the subjects:* An Act Declaring the Rights and Liberties of the Subjects and Settling the Succession of the Crown, in Hughes and Fries, eds., *Crown and Parliament in Tudor-Stuart England,* 310.

   The time had come: G. M. Trevelyan, *England under the Stuarts* (London: Methuen, 1904; reprint, New York: Routledge, 2002), 449.

   The entire purpose: Siebert, *Freedom of the Press in England,* 262–63.

CHAPTER THREE

53   *A thursty desyer:* The Bloudy booke, or the Tragicall and desperate end of Sir John Fites (London, 1548), quoted in Mitchell Stephens, *A History of News: From the Drum to the Satellite* (New York: Viking, 1988), 14.

54   *The end of a religious society:* John Locke, *A Letter Concerning Toleration* (1685, 1689) in *John Locke on Politics and Educa-tion,* introduction by Howard R. Penniman (Roslyn, N.Y.: Walter J. Black, 1947), 30.

   Newsbooks, broadsides, pamphlets: Joseph Frank, *The Beginnings of the English Newspaper, 1620–1660* (Cambridge, Mass.: Harvard University Press, 1961), 4.

55   *The first printed sources:* Frederick Seaton Siebert, *Freedom of the Press in England, 1476–1776* (Urbana: University of Illi-nois Press, 1965), 29.

   Placed relatively little: Sandra Clark, *The Elizabethan Pamphle-teers: Popular Moralistic Pamphlets, 1580–1640* (Rutherford, N.J.: Farleigh Dickinson University Press, 1985), 88–89.

56   *I am that one man:* Quoted in Clifford Chalmers Huffman, *Elizabethan Impressions: John Wolfe and His Press* (New York: AMS Press, 1988), 1.

   I had a prospect: Boston Evening-Post, March 27, 1741.

57   *Wolfe printed the majority:* M. A. Shaaber, *Some Forerunners of the Newspaper in England, 1476–1622* (Philadelphia: University of Pennsylvania Press, 1929; reprint, New York: Octagon Books, 1966), 284.

The fact that newsbooks were allowed: Thomas Nashe, *The Works of Thomas Nashe,* ed. Ronald B. McKerrow, 5 vols. (London: Sidgwick, 1910), 1:161, quoted in Paul J. Voss, *Elizabethan News Pamphlets: Shakespeare, Spenser, Marlowe & the Birth of Journalism* (Pittsburgh: Duquesne University Press, 2001), 12.

News revolution: Voss, *Elizabethan News Pamphlets,* 15.

The term "newspaper": Shaaber, *Some Forerunners of the Newspaper in England,* 3.

The lines in the Henry VI plays: Voss, *Elizabethan News Pamphlets,* 13.

58   *What's the best News:* Thomas Lushington, "A Repetition Sermon," in George Orwell and Reginald Reynolds, eds., *British Pamphleteers,* 10 vols. (London: Allan Wingate, 1948), 1:53.

59   *Discourse concerning the state:* Siebert, *Freedom of the Press in England,* 150–51.

60   *The Long Parliament was in the process:* William M. Clyde, *The Struggle for the Freedom of the Press from Caxton to Cromwell* (London: Oxford University Press, 1934; reprint, New York: Burt Franklin, 1970), 60–61.

61   *Nearly half of all literate:* Frank, *The Beginnings of the English Newspaper,* 57.

That the Presse: Anonymous [William Walwyn], *The Compassionate Samaritane Vnbinding The Conscience, and pouring Oyle into the wounds which have been made upon the Separation: recommending their future welfare to the serious thoughts, and carefull endeavours of all who love the peace and vnity of Commonwealths men, or desire the vnanimous prosecution for the Common Enemie, or who follow our Saviours rule, to doe unto others, what they would have other doe unto them* (London, 1644), 5–6, 78–79, in William Haller, ed., *Tracts on Liberty in the Puritan Revolution, 1638–1647,* 3 vols. (New York: Columbia University Press, 1934; reprint, New York: Octagon Books, 1965), 3:103–4.

61   *This combat:* Henry Robinson, *Liberty of Conscience: or the Sole means to obtaine Peace and Truth. Not onely reconciling His MAJESTY with His Subjects, but all Christian States and Princes to one another, with the freest passage for the GOSPEL. Very seasonable and necessary in these distracted times when most men are weary of War, and cannot find the way to Peace* (1643/1644), 17, in Haller, ed., *Tracts on Liberty in the Puritan Revolution,* 3 vols., 3:133.

62   *Two or Three Sheets: Lords Journals,* IX, 441, quoted in Frank, *The Beginnings of the English Newspaper,* 135.

63   *The number of individual issues:* Siebert, *Freedom of the Press in England,* 222–23, 203.

To speake what I thinke: F. R., "The Publisher to the Reader," in John Lilburne, *A Worke of the Beast or A Relation of a most vnchristian Censure, Executed upon IOHN LILBVRNE, (Now prisoner in the fleet) the 18 of Aprill 1638. With the heavenly speech vtterred by him at the time of his suffering* (1638), in Haller, ed., *Tracts on Liberty in the Puritan Revolution,* 3 vols., 2:4.

The most unlikely of champions: Frank, *The Beginnings of the English Newspaper,* 135–36.

64   *The laws and Government:* Gilbert Mabbott, *The Moderate,* November 7, 1648, quoted in Frank, *The Beginnings of the English Newspaper,* 157.

65   *Because that Imployment:* Quoted in Clyde, *The Struggle for the Freedom of the Press,* 174.

66   *A permanent social:* Siebert, *Freedom of the Press in England,* 220.

67   *Give me liberty to know:* John Milton, *Areopagetica: A Speech of Mr. John Milton for the Liberty of Unlicens'd Printing, to the Parliament of England* (London, 1644), in *The Works of John Milton,* 20 vols. (New York: Columbia University Press, 1931), 4:346, 349.

67   *People who broke:* Clyde, *The Struggle for the Freedom of the Press,* 240–41.

68   *Finally, Cromwell ordered:* Commons Journal, VII, 288, in Siebert, *Freedom of the Press in England,* 230–31.

   Newsbook after newsbook: Clyde, *The Struggle for the Freedom of the Press,* 251.

69   *L'Estrange's principal target:* James Sutherland, *The Restoration Newspaper and Its Development* (Cambridge: Cambridge University Press, 1986), 1–2.

   In 1663, L'Estrange held: Siebert, *Freedom of the Press in England,* 291–93.

   The first was the outbreak: Sutherland, *The Restoration Newspaper,* 7–12.

70   *A printer of Baptist tracts:* Christopher Hill, *The Century of Revolution, 1603–1714* (Edinburgh: Thomas Nelson, 1961), 249.

71   *Before Charles could curtail:* Sutherland, *The Restoration Newspaper,* vii–viii.

   The almost hysterical state: Siebert, *Freedom of the Press in England,* 297.

   The remarkable outburst: Sutherland, *The Restoration Newspaper,* 20.

   I think it not natural: The Debates in the House of Commons assembled at Oxford (1681), in Sutherland, *The Restoration Newspaper,* 21.

CHAPTER FOUR

75   *Fifty-nine master printers:* Frederick Seaton Siebert, *Freedom of the Press in England, 1476–1776* (Urbana: University of Illinois Press, 1965), 239.

76   *The two institutions:* Henry F. May, *The Enlightenment in America* (Oxford: Oxford University Press, 1976), 4–5.

77   *That every man ought to have:* Anonymous [William Walwyn], *The Compassionate Samaritane Vnbinding The Conscience, and powring Oyle into the wounds which have been made upon the Separation: recommending their future welfare to the serious* *thoughts, and carefull endeavours of all who love the peace and vnity of Commonwealths men, or desire the vnanimous prosecution for the Common Enemie, or who follow our Saviours rule, to doe unto others, what they would have other doe unto them* (London, 1644), 5, in William Haller, ed., *Tracts on Liberty in the Puritan Revolution, 1638–1647,* 3 vols. (New York: Columbia University Press, 1934; reprint, New York: Octagon Books, 1965), 3:67.

78   *God hath dealt abundantly:* Anonymous [William Walwyn], *The Power of Love* (London, 1643), 7, in Haller, ed., *Tracts on Liberty in the Puritan Revolution,* 3 vols., 2:282.

Heretical democracy: Christopher Hill, *The Century of Revolution, 1603–1714* (Edinburgh: Thomas Nelson, 1961), 130.

79   *This document said that:* A. L. Morton, *The World of the Ranters: Religious Radicalism in the English Revolution* (London: Lawrence and Wishart, 1970), 14–15.

For by natural birth: Richard Overton, *An arrow against all tyrants and tyranny, shot from the prison of Newgate into the prerogative bowels of the arbitrary House of Lords and all other usurpers and tyrants whatsoever* (London, 1646), in G. E. Aylmer, ed., *The Levellers in the English Revolution* (London: Thames and Hudson, 1975), 68.

80   *A natural and innate birthright:* John Lilburne, *Innocency And Truth Justified* (1645), in Theodore Calvin Pease, *The Leveller Movement: A Study in the History and Political Theory of the English Great Civil War* (Washington, D.C.: American Historical Association, 1916; reprint, Gloucester, Mass.: Peter Smith, 1965), 115–16.

Insufferable, unjust: Anonymous [John Lilburne], *Englands Birth-Right Justified Against all Arbitrary Usupation, whether REGALL or PARLIAMENTARY, or under what Vizor soever* (London, 1645), 10–11, 24, in Haller, ed., *Tracts on Liberty in the Puritan Revolution,* 3 vols., 2:268–69.

81   *Receive all Information:* Haller, ed., *Tracts on Liberty in the Puritan Revolution,* 3 vols., 3:282.

81   *In 1640s England, Lilburne's writings:* Howard Shaw, *The Levellers* (New York: Harper and Row, 1968), 28.

That you will open the Press: John Lilburne, *Englands New Chaines Discovered: Or the serious apprehensions of a part of the People, in behalf of the Commonwealth; (being Presenters, Promoters, and Approvers of the Large Petition of September 11, 1648* (London, 1648), in William Haller and Godfrey Davies, eds., *The Leveller Tracts, 1647–1653* (New York: Columbia University Press, 1944; reprint, Gloucester, Mass: Peter Smith, 1964), 156–70.

Let everyone freely speake: Anonymous [William Walwyn], "To the Reader," *The Power of Love* (London, 1643), A10, in Haller, ed., *Tracts on Liberty in the Puritan Revolution,* 3 vols., 2:278.

83   *Born in 1608:* There are many biographies of Milton. See, for example, Dustin H. Griffin, *Regaining Paradise: Milton and the Eighteenth Century* (Cambridge: Cambridge University Press, 1986); Christopher Hill, *Milton and the English Revolution* (New York: Penguin, 1979); Barbara Kiefer Lewalski, *The Life of John Milton: A Critical Biography* (Malden, Mass.: Blackwell, 2000); David Masson, *The Life of John Milton Narrated in Connexion With the Political, Ecclesiastical, and Literary History of His Time,* 7 vols. (1875; reprint, Gloucester, Mass.: Peter Smith, 1965); William Riley Parker, *Milton: A Biography,* 2nd ed. (Oxford: Oxford University Press, 1996); A. N. Wilson, *The Life of John Milton* (New York: Oxford University Press, 1983).

84   *The unlicensed booklet:* William Haller, ed. *Tracts on Liberty in the Puritan Revolution, 1638–1647,* 3 vols. (New York: Columbia University Press, 1934; reprint, New York: Octagon Books, 1965), 1:135.

85   *Tindal used Milton's 1644 analogy:* Anonymous [Matthew Tindal], "A Letter to a Member of Parliament, Shewing that a Restraint Press Is Inconsistent with the Protestant Religion, and Dangerous to the Liberties of the Nation" (London, 1698), reprinted in Jeffery A. Smith, *Printers and*

Press Freedom: The Ideology of Early American Journalism (New York: Oxford University Press, 1988), 34.

85 *American revolutionaries in the 1770s:* May, *The Enlightenment in America,* 156, 293; Siebert, *Freedom of the Press in England,* 383.

To Americans of the Framers' generation: Leonard W. Levy, *Emergence of a Free Press* (New York: Oxford University Press, 1985), 97.

Extirpats all religions: John Milton, *Areopagetica: A Speech of Mr. John Milton for the Liberty of Unlicens'd Printing, to the Parliament of England* (London, 1644), in *The Works of John Milton,* 20 vols. (New York: Columbia University Press, 1931), 4:349.

86 *Read any books:* Ibid., 4:308.

If we think to regulat: Ibid., 4:317, 319.

Give me the liberty to know: Ibid., 4:346–47.

87 *For Milton, conscience:* Susan Achinstein, *Literature and Dissent in Milton's England* (Cambridge: Cambridge University Press, 2003), 130.

It would not be improper: New-York Weekly Journal, November 12 and 19, 1733.

88 *My discourse of Commonwealth:* Thomas Hobbes, "To My Most Honor'd Friend Mr. Francis Godolphin, of Godolphin," "The Introduction," *Leviathan or the Matter, forme and Power of a Commonwealth Ecclesiasticall and Civil* (London, 1651), ix, in Edwin Curley, ed., *Leviathan, with Selected Variants from the Latin Edition of 1668,* (Indianapolis: Hackett, 1994), 1, 3.

89 *When a multitude of men:* Ibid., Chapter XVIII, "Of the Rights of Sovereigns by Institutions," 88–89, in Curley, ed., 110.

There can happen no breach: Ibid., Chapter XVIII, 160–61, in Curley, 111.

The ruler can do nothing to harm: Ibid., 165–68, in Curley, 115.

90 *I cannot imagine:* Ibid., Chapter XXIX, "Of Those Things that Weaken a Commonwealth," 313–15, in Curley, 215;

Chapter XLII, "Of Power Ecclesiastical," 285, in Curley, 354.

90 *Locke best represented all the theorists:* Thomas P. Peardon, "Introduction," in John Locke, *The Second Treatise of Government* (Indianapolis: Bobbs-Merrill, 1952), vii–xi.

91 *No one . . . can be . . . subjected:* Locke, *The Second Treatise of Government,* 54, 48.

92 *Consent of the majority:* Ibid., 120, 128.

Locke would have agreed: Siebert, *Freedom of the Press in England,* 261.

93 *Locke's ideas on government:* Gillian Brown, *The Consent of the Governed: The Lockean Legacy in Early American Culture* (Cambridge, Mass.: Harvard University Press, 2001), 6, 11.

Coffeehouses popped up: Hill, *The Century of Revolution,* 249.

94 *It was God's ordinance:* John Locke, *Two Treatises of Government,* ed. Thomas Hollis (London: A. Millar, 1764), Chapter II, Section 8.

95 *Newspapers superseded pamphlets:* Hannah Barker and Simon Burrows, eds., *Press, Politics and the Public Sphere in Europe and North America, 1760–1820* (Cambridge: Cambridge University Press, 2002), 4.

By 1712, London's daily papers: James Sutherland, *The Restoration Newspaper and Its Development* (Cambridge: Cambridge University Press, 1986), 228–29.

96 *By 1711, there were at least:* Richmond P. Bond, *New Letters to the* Tatler *and* Spectator (Austin: University of Texas Press, 1959), 4.

A natural Right in all matters: Matthew Tindal, *Reasons against Restraining the Press* (London, 1704), 9–10, quoted in Leonard W. Levy, *Emergence of a Free Press* (New York: Oxford University Press, 1985), 102–3.

97 *This is the Day:* Joseph Addison, "Tanti non es ais. Sapis, Luperce. Mart," *The Spectator,* No. 445, July 31, 1712, in Donald F. Bond, ed., *The Spectator,* 5 vols. (Oxford: Clarendon, 1965), 4:62.

97   *Subsidization, or political patronage:* Siebert, *Freedom of the Press in England,* 289–392.

Whilst all Opinions: Cato [John Trenchard and Thomas Gordon], "Discourse Upon Libels," *London Journal,* October 27, 1722, in *Cato's Letters, or Essays on Liberty, Civil and Religious, and Other Important Subjects,* ed. Ronald Hamowy, 4 vols. (Indianapolis: Liberty Fund, 1995), 3:151.

98   *That it is a right of the subject:* The Bill of Rights, in Paul L. Hughes and Robert F. Fries, eds., *Crown and Parliament in Tudor-Stuart England: A Documentary Constitutional History, 1485–1714* (New York: G. P. Putnam's Sons, 1959), 312.

Without freedom of thought: Cato, "Of Freedom of Speech: That the Same Is Inseparable from Public Liberty," *London Journal,* February 20, 1720/1721, in Hamowy, ed., *Cato's Letters,* 4 vols., 1:74–77.

99   *The exposing therefore:* Cato, "Reflections Upon Libeling," *London Journal,* June 10, 1721, in Hamowy, ed., *Cato's Letters,* 4 vols., 1:153, 156, 154.

100   *Their* London Journal*'s circulation reached:* Siebert, *Freedom of the Press in England,* 339.

If ten mens voyces: Richard Baxter, "To the Reader," *Aphorismes of Justification* (1649), in William Haller, ed., *Liberty and Reformation in the Puritan Revolution* (New York: Columbia University Press, 1955), 2.

Daniel Defoe supported: Robert W. T. Martin, *The Free and Open Press: The Founding of American Democratic Press Liberty, 1640–1800* (New York: New York University Press, 2001), 26–27.

A design to suppress printing: The Review (London), March 29, 1711, in William L. Payne, ed., *The Best of Defoe's Review: An Anthology* (New York: Columbia University Press, 1951), 77.

101   *Habermas labeled the "public sphere":* Jürgen Habermas, *The Structural Transformation of the Public Sphere: An Inquiry into* *a Category of Bourgeois Society,* trans. Thomas Burger (Cambridge, Mass.: Harvard University Press, 1989).

CHAPTER FIVE

103 *England suffered from economic depression:* David Hackett Fischer, *Albion's Seed: Four British Folkways in America* (New York: Oxford University Press, 1989), 16.

104 *By 1624:* George Brown Tindall, *America: A Narrative History* (New York: W. W. Norton, 1984), 54.

  And here are no hard Landlords: John Smith, *A Description of New England: or The Observations, and Discoveries, of Captain John Smith (Admiral of that Country), in the North of America, in the year of our Lord, 1614* (London, 1616), quoted in Julie Hedgepeth Williams, *The Significance of the Printed Word in Early America: Colonists' Thoughts on the Role of the Press* (Westport, Conn.: Greenwood, 1999), 36.

105 *Estimates put the number of titles:* Meiling Hazelton, "'Mony Choaks': The Quaker Critique of the Seventeenth-Century Public Sphere," *Modern Philology* 98 (2000): 253.

  Speake what I thinke: F. R., "The Publisher to the Reader," in John Lilburne, *A Worke of the Beast or A Relation of a most vnchristian Censure, Executed upon IOHN LILBVRNE, (Now prisoner in the fleet) the 18 of Aprill 1638. With the heavenly speech vtterred by him at the time of his suffering* (1638), in William Haller, ed. *Tracts on Liberty in the Puritan Revolution, 1638–1647,* 3 vols. (New York: Columbia University Press, 1934; reprint, New York: Octagon Books, 1965), 2:4.

106 *Puritans did not hope:* Fischer, *Albion's Seed,* 202–3.

  He that is willing to tolerate: Quoted in Douglas Hill, *The English to New England* (New York: Clarkson N. Potter, 1975), 34.

107 *Printer Stephen Daye:* John Winthrop, *History of New England, 1630–1649,* ed. James Kendall Hosmer, 2 vols. (New York: Charles Scribner's, 1908; reprint, New York: Barnes and Noble, 1946), 1:293; Isaiah Thomas, *The History of*

Printing in America (1810; reprint, New York: Weathervane, 1970), 43–49; Lawrence C. Wroth, *The Colonial Printer* (Portland, Maine.: Southworth-Anthoensen Press; reprint, New York: Dover, 1994), 16–17.

107 *London and the surrounding cities:* Christopher Chalklin, *The Rise of the English Town, 1650–1800* (Cambridge: Cambridge University Press, 2001), 1, 5.

108 *America's population: Historical Statistics of the United States: Colonial Times to 1970* (Washington, D.C.: U.S. Department of Commerce, 1975), 1:168.

Which reached 600,000: Historical Statistics of the United States, 1:168; "A Population History of London: The Demography of Urban Growth," *The Proceedings of the Old Bailey,* http://www.oldbaileyonline.org/history/london-life/Population%20History%20of%20London.html (accessed July 19, 2005).

109 *Theological writings, as might be expected:* Richard Beale Davis, *A Colonial Southern Bookshelf: Reading in the Eighteenth Century* (Athens: University of Georgia Press, 1979), 17–18.

By 1671, most New England colonies: Fischer, *Albion's Seed,* 132.

Knowledge of the scriptures: The Book of the General Lawes and Libertyes (Cambridge, 1660); Fischer, *Albion's Seed,* 132.

110 *The colony removed:* Larry D. Eldridge, *A Distant Heritage: The Growth of Free Speech in Early America* (New York: New York University Press, 1994), 36.

To eradicate: Williams, *The Significance of the Printed Word in Early America,* 57.

Hath broached: Henry Martyn Dexter, *As to Roger Williams, and his 'Banishment' from Massachusetts Plantation* (Boston: Congregational Publishing Society, 1876), 59.

111 *To obtain riches quickly:* T. H., preface to *A History of New-England From the English planting in the Yeere 1628 untill the Yeere 1652* (London, 1654), in Williams, *The Significance of the Printed Word in Early America,* 55.

111   *Nother knowe God:* John Rastell, *Interlude of the Four Elements* (London, 1519), quoted in David A. Copeland, *Colonial American Newspapers: Character and Content* (Newark: University of Delaware Press, 1997), 44.

He mastered Algonquin: Williams, *The Significance of the Printed Word in Early America,* 59.

112   *Be totally suppressed:* Clyde Augustus Duniway, *The Development of Freedom of the Press in Massachusetts* (Cambridge, Mass.: Harvard University Press, 1906; reprint, New York: Burt Franklin, 1969), 38–39.

Everything that the press produced: Ibid., 40.

114   *Full and free tollerance:* Thomas Hutchinson, *A Collection of Original Papers relative to the History of the Colony of Massachusets-Bay* (Boston, 1679), 154, quoted in Duniway, *The Development of Freedom of the Press in Massachusetts,* 30.

It is the same kind of liberty: John Winthrop, "Little Speech on Liberty" (1645), in John Winthrop, *The History of New England from 1630 to 1649,* ed. James Savage, 2 vols. (Boston: Little, Brown, 1853), 2:228–30.

116   *Scandalous and seditious papers:* Eldridge, *A Distant Heritage,* 16–17.

Culpeper's Rebellion: Thomas C. Parramore, *Carolina Quest* (Englewood Cliffs, N.J.: Prentice-Hall, 1978), 37–42.

117   *Nathanial Bacon, elected to:* Charles M. Andrews, ed., *Narratives of the Insurrections, 1657–1690* (New York: Charles Scribner's Sons, 1915), 11–14.

The covenantal arrangement: Harold M. Hyman, *To Try Men's Souls: Loyalty Tests in American History* (Berkeley: University of California Press, 1959), 15–22.

118   *Virginians were required:* Margaret A. Blanchard, "Turning Worlds Upside Down: Freedom of Expression through the Revolution," unpublished manuscript, 1992.

In 1651, three Rhode Island Baptists: Richard Hofstadter and Walter P. Metzger, *The Development of Academic Freedom in the United States* (New York: Columbia University Press,

1955), 78–113; Duniway, *The Development of Freedom of the Press in Massachusetts,* 34–35.

119   *Inevitably endangered:* Eldridge, *A Distant Heritage,* 19.

120   *For as much as Seuerall:* Quoted in Duniway, *The Development of Freedom of the Press in Massachusetts,* 25.

121   *For the preventing of irregularityes:* Quoted in Thomas, *The History of Printing,* 66.

122   *I thank God, there are no free schools:* Quoted in David A. Copeland, *Debating the Issues in Colonial Newspapers* (Westport, Conn.: Greenwood, 2000), 4.

   And forasmuch as great inconvenience: Quoted in A. C. Goodell, *Proceedings of the Massachusetts Historical Society* (June 1893), 173.

123   *That no Papers, Bookes Pamphlets &c:* Quoted in Duniway, *The Development of Freedom of the Press in Massachusetts,* 66.

   No person be permitted to use: Quoted in Wroth, *The Colonial Printer,* 39.

   He was not charged with seditious libel: Williams, *The Significance of the Printed Word in Early America,* 109–10.

124   *Anyone found owning Quaker literature:* Duniway, *The Development of Freedom of the Press in Massachusetts,* 36–37.

   The society promised: Anna Janney DeArmond, *Andrew Bradford: Colonial Journalist* (Newark: University of Delaware Press, 1949), 2–3. Information on Bradford comes from DeArmond unless otherwise noted.

   A free Hearing among all People: Richard Hubberthorne, *The Real Cause of the Nations Bondage and Slavery* (London, 1659), 3, quoted in Hazelton, "'Mony Choaks,'" 262.

125   *Freely without any end:* George Fox, *To the Parliament of the Common-wealth of England. Fifty Nine Particulars* (London, 1659), 5, quoted in Hazelton, "'Mony Choaks,'" 258.

   Wicked Lyes: Leonard W. Levy, *Emergence of a Free Press* (New York: Oxford University Press, 1985), 29.

126   *The idea of free expression:* Ibid., 28.

127   *Ministers formulated:* See Thomas Lushington, "A Repetition Sermon," in George Orwell and Reginald Reynolds, eds.,

British Pamphleteers, 10 vols. (London: Allan Wingate, 1948), 1:52–67.

127 *The sermon stood alone:* Harry S. Stout, *The New England Soul: Preaching and Religious Culture in Colonial New England* (New York: Oxford University Press, 1986), 3.

That which is herein proposed: Publick Occurrences Both Forreign and Domestick (Boston), September 25, 1690. For a detailed analysis of God's providence and news, see David Paul Nord, "Teleology and the News: The Religious Roots of American Journalism, 1630–1730," *Journal of American History* 77 (1990): 9–38.

128 *Journalistic tool:* Nord, "Teleology and the News," 18–21. On fast-day sermons, see Stout, *The New England Soul,* 74–76.

129 *The Domestick Intelligence:* Information about Harris comes from James Sutherland, *The Restoration Newspaper and Its Development* (Cambridge: Cambridge University Press, 1986), 13–25; and Wm. David Sloan and Julie Hedgepeth Williams, *The Early American Press, 1690–1783* (Westport, Conn.: Greenwood, 1994), 1–8.

131 *That therein is contained Reflections:* Quoted in Copeland, *Debating the Issues,* 5.

A printed sheet entituled: Samuel Sewall, *The Diary of Samuel Sewall, 1674–1729,* ed. M. Halsey Thomas (New York: Farrar, Straus and Giroux, 1973), 267, in Sloan and Williams, *The Early American Press,* 6.

132 *Those in positions of power:* Richard D. Brown, *Knowledge Is Power: The Diffusion of Information in Early America, 1700–1865* (New York: Oxford University Press, 1989), 21–25.

133 *Identical information:* Henry L. Snyder, "Newsletters in England, 1689–1715, with Special Reference to John Dyer—A Byway in the History of England," in Donovan H. Bond and W. Reynolds McLeod, eds., *Newsletters to Newspapers: Eighteenth-Century Journalism* (Morganton: West Virginia University, 1977), 4.

133 *Campbell gleaned information:* On Campbell's handwritten newsletters, see Sidney Kobre, *The Development of the Colonial Newspaper* (1944; reprint, Gloucester, Mass.: Peter Smith, 1960), 17–19.

134 *America finally had a newspaper:* Ibid., 18.

Thomas believed that colonial governments: Thomas, *The History of Printing in America,* 552.

135 *Authorities regulated speech:* Eldridge, *A Distant Heritage,* 9.

CHAPTER SIX

139 *Campbell lost his job:* Sources do not agree on whether Campbell lost his job or retired from the position. Sidney Kobre, the nation's preeminent expert on the colonial press for much of the twentieth century, wrote in *The Development of the Colonial Newspaper* (1944; reprint, Gloucester, Mass.: Peter Smith, 1960), 27, that Campbell lost the job. Of equal stature to Kobre, Frank Luther Mott, said, in *American Journalism, A History: 1690–1960,* 3rd ed. (New York: Macmillan, 1962), 14–15, that Campbell retired. Major media history sources support Kobre. These include Willard Grosvenor Bleyer, *Main Currents in the History of American Journalism* (Boston: Houghton Mifflin, 1927), 51; Michael Emery and Edwin Emery, *The Press and America: An Interpretive History of the Mass Media,* 6th ed. (Englewood Cliffs, N.J.: Prentice Hall, 1988), 26; Frederic Hudson, *Journalism in the United States, from 1690–1872* (New York: J. and J. Harper, 1873), 58; James Melvin Lee, *History of American Journalism* (Garden City, N.J.: Garden City Publishing, 1917), 281; George Henry Payne, *History of Journalism in the United States* (1920; reprint, Westport, Conn.: Greenwood, 1970), 28; Wm. David Sloan and Julie Hedgepeth Williams, *The Early American Press, 1690–1783* (Westport, Conn.: Greenwood, 1994), 21; Isaiah Thomas, *The History of Printing in America* (1810; reprint, New York: Weathervane, 1970), 220. Charles E. Clark, *The Public Prints: The Newspaper in Anglo-American Culture,*

1665–1740 (New York: Oxford University Press, 1994), 104, suggested that Campbell may have announced his retirement as a face-saving measure when in reality he had been replaced, first by the Massachusetts government and then by the British postmaster general, who did not know the action had already been taken in Boston. Philip Musgrave was London's choice for the postmaster, and he took over the job and the *Boston Gazette* in 1720.

140 *Book pamphlet or other matters:* Quoted in A. C. Goodell, *Proceedings of the Massachusetts Historical Society* (June 1893), 173.

 The first two decades of the eighteenth century: Clyde Augustus Duniway, *The Development of Freedom of the Press in Massachusetts* (Cambridge, Mass.: Harvard University Press, 1906; reprint, New York: Burt Franklin, 1969), 84–86.

141 *Circulation figures of many London newspapers:* James Sutherland, *The Restoration Newspaper and Its Development* (Cambridge: Cambridge University Press, 1986), 228–30.

 Vicious newspaper debate: A number of sources discuss the controversy and are used here. See Thomas Hutchinson, *The History of Massachusetts, from the first Settlement thereof in 1628, until the year 1750,* 3rd ed., 2 vols. (Boston, 1795; reprint, Cambridge, Mass.: Harvard University Press, 1936), 163–218; Duniway, *The Development of Freedom of the Press in Massachusetts,* 83–96; Kobre, *The Development of the Colonial Newspaper,* 29–30; Sloan and Williams, *The Early American Press,* 22–24.

143 *Manuscripts and fugitive pamphlet issues:* David S. Shields, *Oracles of Empire: Poetry, Politics, and Commerce in British America, 1690–1750* (Chicago: University of Chicago Press, 1990), 99.

144 *This Taste . . . we Englishmen: New-York Gazette,* January 22, 1750.

 The PRESS is not so much considered: Connecticut Gazette (New Haven), February 7, 1756.

144 *Nearly 60 percent:* John Duffy, *Epidemics in Colonial America* (Baton Rouge: Louisiana State University Press, 1953), 51.

145 *Expose the Vices and Follies: New-England Courant* (Boston), August 7, 1721.

Mather had learned of inoculation: Sloan and Williams, *The Early American Press,* 25.

146 *A Wicked and Criminal Practice: Boston News-Letter,* July 24, 1721, 3.

The initial purpose of the Courant: *New-England Courant* (Boston), August 21, 1721.

147 *The Town Lyar: Boston News-Letter,* July 24, 1721; *New-England Courant* (Boston), August 7 and 21, 1721.

Vilify and abuse the best Men: Boston Gazette, January 15, 1721/1722.

Men in office, the clergy: Thomas, *The History of Printing in America,* 235.

148 *The* New-England Courant *ultimately failed:* Sloan and Williams, *The Early American Press,* 30.

Paragraphs that tend to fill: Quoted in Thomas, *The History of Printing in America,* 237.

149 *That* James Franklin, *the Printer:* Quoted in Thomas, *The History of Printing in America,* 239. Numerous sources discuss Franklin's run-ins with Massachusetts authorities. See, for example, Duniway, *The Development of Freedom of the Press in Massachusetts,* 98–103; Jeffery A. Smith, *Printers and Press Freedom: The Ideology of Early American Journalism* (New York: Oxford University Press, 1988), 102–4.

150 *The growing tendency:* Robert W. T. Martin, *The Free and Open Press: The Founding of American Democratic Press Liberty, 1640–1800* (New York: New York University Press, 2001), 40–41.

151 *Find some effectual Remedy: American Weekly Mercury* (Philadelphia), January 2, 1721/1722.

He must not for the future presume: Quoted in Anna Janney DeArmond, *Andrew Bradford: Colonial Journalist* (Newark: University of Delaware Press, 1949), 14.

151   *The Assembly of the province: American Weekly Mercury*
(Philadelphia), February 21, 1722/1723.

Wicked & seditious Libell: Quoted in DeArmond, *Andrew Bradford,* 18.

152   *Licensing in Pennsylvania:* DeArmond, *Andrew Bradford,* 18–19, 72–75.

I can well remember: Boston News-Letter, August 28, 1721, quoted in Smith, *Printers and Press Freedom,* 98.

Vicious intentions: Frederick Seaton Siebert, *Freedom of the Press in England, 1476–1776* (Urbana: University of Illinois Press, 1965), 273.

153   *Government officials found ways around:* Ibid.

John Peter Zenger: Most histories of the colonial press discuss the facts surrounding the Zenger trial. The first and most important source is James Alexander, *A Brief Narrative of the Case and Trial of John Peter Zenger, Printer of the New York Weekly Journal,* ed. Stanley Nider Katz, 2nd ed. (1736; reprint, Cambridge, Mass.: Harvard University Press, 1972). All information in this section without specific citation comes from David Copeland, "The Zenger Trial," *Media Studies Journal* (Spring/Summer 2000): 2–7.

154   *THE DEFENDER: Pennsylvania Gazette* (Philadelphia), May 18, 1738.

155   *Only the wicked Governours of Men: New-York Weekly Journal,* December 17, 1733, January 28, 1733/1734, and November 11, 1734.

156   *Notoriously known to be true:* Alexander, *A Brief Narrative of the Case and Trial of John Peter Zenger,* 75.

I must insist: Ibid., 91, 93.

157   *I only intend:* Ibid., 91.

158   *Truth will always prevail: New-York Weekly Journal,* November 12, 1733.

I beg leave to insist: Alexander, *A Brief Narrative of the Case and Trial of John Peter Zenger,* 84.

Better than the law: Pennsylvania Gazette (Philadelphia), May 18, 1738.

158 *I cannot think it proper:* Alexander, *A Brief Narrative of the Case and Trial of John Peter Zenger,* 62.

Questioning and discussing individuals: Smith, *Printers and Press Freedom,* 11.

159 *Men who injure and oppress the people:* Alexander, *A Brief Narrative of the Case and Trial of John Peter Zenger,* 99.

The people are the only censors: The Writings of Thomas Jefferson, Memorial Edition, 20 vols. (Washington, D.C., 1903–1904), 6:58.

161 *The* principal pillar *in a free Government:* Quotes taken from Alexander's articles that appeared in the *Pennsylvania Gazette* (Philadelphia), November 17–December 8, 1737.

In 1742, the Council of Massachusetts: Leonard W. Levy, *Emergence of a Free Press* (New York: Oxford University Press, 1985), 32–33.

Destructive *of THE LIBERTY: South-Carolina Gazette* (Charleston), March 30, 1747, in Martin, *The Free and Open Press,* 53.

George Clinton ordered: Levy, *Emergence of a Free Press,* 45–46.

162 *In 1741, South Carolina authorities:* Julie Hedgepeth Williams, *The Significance of the Printed Word in Early America* (Westport, Conn.: Greenwood, 1999), 89–90.

New York printer Hugh Gaine: Alfred Lawrence Lorenz, *Hugh Gaine: A Colonial Printer-Editor's Odyssey to Loyalism* (Carbondale: Southern Illinois University Press, 1972), 18–20.

The Massachusetts assembly ordered: Duniway, *The Development of Freedom of the Press in Massachusetts,* 116–18.

164 *More than 1,200:* Larry D. Eldridge, *A Distant Heritage: The Growth of Free Speech in Early America* (New York: New York University Press, 1994), 3.

I get my living, to print: DeArmond, *Andrew Bradford,* 5, note 16.

165 *Defoe did not need to argue:* Williams, *The Significance of the Printed Word in Early America,* 110–11.

The exposing . . . of publick Wickedness: New-England Courant (Boston), September 11, 1721.

166 *Even Errors made publick: New-England Courant* (Boston), December 4, 1721, November 20, 1721.

Clear'd the Head: South-Carolina Gazette (Charleston), February 17, 1733.

For ourselves, we declare: Independent Advertiser (Boston), January 4, 1748.

167 *The* Independent Advertiser *was also: Independent Advertiser* (Boston), January 9, 1749. See Martin, *The Free and Open Press,* 57.

169 *The Liberty of the Press is a Subject: New-York Weekly Journal,* November 12 and 19, 1733.

170 *THE FREEDOM OF SPEECH: Pennsylvania Gazette* (Philadelphia), November 17 and December 1, 1737. The essay appeared over four consecutive weeks, the conclusion running on December 8.

171 *This privilege, which we call the* Liberty: *Boston Gazette, or Country Journal,* June 2, 1755.

172 *Printers do continually discourage: Pennsylvania Gazette* (Philadelphia), December 1, 1737.

As the eighteenth century progressed: Smith, *Printers and Press Freedom,* 36.

173 *The Great Awakening provided:* Martin, *The Free and Open Press,* 56.

It pitted: Henry. F. May, *The Enlightenment in America* (Oxford: Oxford University Press, 1976), xiv.

174 *In 1738 . . . only about 133 pamphlets:* Numbers based on the bibliographic listings in Charles Evans, *American Bibliography,* 14 vols. (Chicago, 1904), 2:109–326; and Roger P. Bristol, *Supplement to Charles Evans' American Bibliography* (Charlottesville: University Press of Virginia, 1970), 58–78.

During Whitefield's first preaching tour: David A. Copeland, *Colonial American Newspapers: Character and Content* (Newark: University of Delaware Press, 1997), 291–93.

174   *In which people were encouraged:* Harry S. Stout, *The New England Soul: Preaching and Religious Culture in Colonial New England* (New York: Oxford University Press, 1986), 193.

175   *The common topic of conversation:* Thomas, *The History of Printing in America,* 568.

    Traveling with Whitefield was William Seward: See Frank Lambert, "'Pedlar of Divinity': George Whitefield and the Great Awakening," *Journal of American History* 77 (1990): 812–37; Copeland, *Colonial American Newspapers,* 215–23; David A. Copeland, *Debating the Issues in Colonial Newspapers* (Westport, Conn.: Greenwood, 2000), 94–108.

176   *Jews were granted religious liberty: Pennsylvania Gazette* (Philadelphia), August 21, 1755; *American Weekly Mercury* (Philadelphia), July 17, 1740.

    IT is evident that Religion: New-York Mercury, May 12, 1755.

180   *Meer Mechanics:* Stephen Botein, "'Meer Mechanics' and an Open Press: The Business and Political Strategies of Colonial American Printers," in *Perspectives in American History* 9, eds. Donald Fleming and Bernard Bailyn (Cambridge, Mass.: Harvard University Press, 1975).

CHAPTER SEVEN

183   *Community separate from Britain:* This idea is also proposed in Richard L. Merritt, *Symbols of American Community, 1735–1775* (New Haven, Conn.: Yale University Press, 1966).

    Newspapers created a space: Michael Schudson, *The Good Citizen: A History of American Civic Life* (Cambridge, Mass.: Harvard University Press, 1998), 38.

184   *It was by means of News papers:* John Holt to Samuel Adams, January 29, 1776, quoted in Arthur M. Schlesinger, *Prelude to Independence: The Newspaper War in Britain, 1764–1776* (New York: Alfred A. Knopf, 1958), 284.

185   *Well-crafted essays:* Benjamin Franklin, *Autobiography,* eds. J. A. Leo Lemay and P. M. Zall (New York: W. W. Norton, 1986), 50.

185   *Twenty-five pseudonyms:* Philip Davidson, *Propaganda and the American Revolution, 1763–1783* (Chapel Hill: University of North Carolina Press, 1941), 5.

From the time of the reformation: John Adams, "A Dissertation on the Canon and the Feudal Law," quoted in Michael Warner, *The Letters of the Republic* (Cambridge, Mass.: Harvard University Press, 1990), 2.

186   *By which the public opinion was enlightened:* John Adams to Thomas Jefferson, 1815, quoted in Bernard Bailyn, *The Ideological Origins of the American Revolution* (Cambridge, Mass.: Harvard University Press, 1967), 1.

Necessary & important Alarms: Quoted in Ward L. Miner, *William Goddard, Newspaperman* (Durham, N.C.: Duke University Press, 1962), 126.

The public sphere: Jürgen Habermas, *The Structural Transformation of the Public Sphere: An Inquiry into a Category of Bourgeois Society,* trans. Thomas Burger (Cambridge, Mass: Harvard University Press, 1989).

Twenty thousand publications: Meiling Hazelton, "'Mony Choaks': The Quaker Critique of the Seventeenth-Century Public Sphere," *Modern Philology* 98 (2000): 253.

187   *A "reasoning public":* Habermas, *The Structural Transformation of the Public Sphere,* 29.

The great advantage: Ibid., 87.

188   *The gen'ral source:* Typically, printers promoted their newspapers in assorted ways, especially at the beginning of a new year. Any time, however, was acceptable. This line of verse appeared in numerous American papers in 1770. They include *Virginia Gazette* (Williamsburg, Purdie, and Dixon), January 22, 1770; *New-York Gazette: or the Weekly Post-Boy,* April 16, 1770; *New-York Journal; or the General Advertiser,* April 19, 1770; *New-London Gazette,* May 25, 1770; *Providence Gazette; and Country Journal,* July 7, 1770.

How common is it to see: New-York Weekly Post-Boy, November 8, 1756, quoted in Jeffery A. Smith, *Printers and Press Free-*

dom: The Ideology of Early American Journalism (New York: Oxford University Press, 1988), 130.

188 *Impression of a unified front:* Jean Sgard, "Journale und Journalisten im Zeitalter der Aufklärung," in H. U. Gumbrecht, R. Reichardt, and T. Schleich, eds., *Sozialgeschichte der Aufklärung in Frankreich* (Munich, 1981), in Hanna Barker and Simon Burrows, eds., *Press, Politics and the Public Sphere in Europe and North America, 1760–1820* (Cambridge: Cambridge University Press, 2002), 12.

189 *Should be encouraged:* Quoted in Warner, *The Letters of the Republic,* 71.

Plans to establish public schools: David A. Copeland, *Debating the Issues in Colonial Newspapers* (Westport, Conn.: Greenwood, 2000), 142–64.

190 *The Main Subject of the Publick Attention: Boston Evening-Post,* March 15, 1757.

The most important event: Fred Anderson, *Crucible of War: The Seven Years' War and the Fate of Empire in British North America, 1754–1766* (New York: Alfred A. Knopf, 2000), xv.

These taxes led to protests: David A. Copeland, *The French and Indian War,* The Greenwood Library of American War Reporting, ed. David A. Copeland, 8 vols. (Westport, Conn.: Greenwood, 2005), 1:10. Portions of this and the next paragraphs are adapted from this work.

The Seven Years' War also rearranged: Anderson, *Crucible of War,* xvi.

The great running story: Frank Luther Mott, *American Journalism, A History: 1690–1960,* 3rd ed. (New York: Macmillan, 1962), 52.

191 *We cannot forbear to express: Maryland Gazette* (Annapolis), March 14, 1754. The announcement first appeared in *Virginia Gazette* (Williamsburg), February 16, 1754.

Unity in opposition: The following discussion of America's press effort during the French and Indian War comes from David Copeland, "'JOIN, or DIE': America's Press during the French and Indian War," *Journalism History* 24 (1998): 112–21.

192   *Appointed deputy postmasters:* Franklin and Hunter were first appointed postmasters in 1753. See *New-York Mercury,* November 19, 1753.

You will see all about him: Quoted in Harry S. Stout, *The Divine Dramatist: George Whitefield and the Rise of Modern Evangelism* (Grand Rapids, Mich.: Wm. B. Eerdmans, 1991), 286.

Countrymen! . . . I need only repeat: "The Virginia Centinel, no. 1." The "Centinel" wrote a series of essays on the dangers of the invading French and Indians to the American colonies. The essay was first printed in the *Virginia Gazette* (Williamsburg), April 30, 1756, which is no longer extant. Other papers throughout the colonies ran the warnings as well. This version comes from the *Maryland Gazette* (Annapolis), August 12, 1756. The same essay also appeared in the *New-York Gazette,* June 14, 1756; *Boston News-Letter,* June 24, 1756, and July 1, 1756; *Connecticut Gazette* (New Haven), June 26, 1756; and *Boston Evening-Post,* June 28, 1756.

Increased the demand: Isaiah Thomas, *The History of Printing in America* (1810; reprint, New York: Weathervane, 1970), 304.

193   *So necessary at this Juncture:* William Goddard, quoted in Miner, *William Goddard, Newspaperman,* 24.

By 1760, and the capitulation: Copeland, "'JOIN, or DIE,'" 118.

The plan called for all colonies: "The Albany Plan of Union," in Benjamin Franklin, *Writings* (New York: Library of America, 1987), 378–82.

194   *I hope, and pray:* New-York Mercury, September 23, 1754.

Ye cannot be saved: Pennsylvania Gazette (Philadelphia), August 29, 1754.

195   *We shall gradually consume: South-Carolina Gazette* (Charleston), June 20, 1754.

195 *More concern'd . . . its own Defence: New-York Mercury,* September 16, 1754, supplement.

To the great Satisfaction: Boston Weekly News-Letter, May 15, 1755.

196 *The melancholly Accounts: New-York Mercury,* September 22, 1755.

Such is our Situation: New-York Mercury, January 20, 1755.

197 *Parker added an essay:* Smith, *Printers and Press Freedom,* 130; Leonard W. Levy, *Emergence of a Free Press* (New York: Oxford University Press, 1985), 45–46.

The Moravian settlement at Gnadenhutten: Copeland, *The French and Indian War,* 8 vols., 1:97–98.

Franklin sidestepped the governor: Smith, *Printers and Press Freedom,* 131.

198 *Needless public Expences: Connecticut Gazette* (New Haven), May 15, 1756.

The fatal Stamp: *Boston Evening-Post,* January 10, 1757.

In New York, printers did the same: Boston-Gazette, and Country Journal, May 2, 1757; *New-York Gazette; or, the Weekly Post-Boy,* October 17, 1757.

199 *THE* Liberty *of the* Press: *New-York Mercury,* March 22, 1756.

200 *Propagandists of revolution:* Davidson, *Propaganda and the American Revolution,* 225. Eliot is quoted here from November 14, 1766, correspondence.

Britons wondered what the massive sacrifice: Edmund S. Morgan and Helen M. Morgan, *The Stamp Act Crisis: Prologue to Revolution* (Chapel Hill: University of North Carolina Press, 1953), 7.

201 *A GOOD PIECE: Maryland Gazette* (Annapolis), April 28, 1763.

We shall complete our Empire: New-York Mercury, May 3, 1762.

To send you all: Francis Bernard to John Pownall, July 11, 1764, quoted in Schlesinger, *Prelude to Independence,* 67.

202 *What difficulties have occurr'd:* Massachusetts Historical Society, *Collections,* 6th series, 9 (1897), 22.

202   *Upon every paper:* Quoted in Copeland, *Debating the Issues in Colonial Newspapers,* 193.

203   *The sole end of government:* Quoted in Schlesinger, *Prelude to Independence,* 41–42.

   He will never pay: Boston Evening-Post, November 4, 1765.

   Ye ruthless crew: New-York Mercury, October 21, 1765.

   'Tis G———le calls: Boston-Gazette, and Country Journal, November 4, 1765.

   HAVE the Sole Rights: Maryland Gazette (Annapolis), July 4, 1765. According to Morgan and Morgan, *The Stamp Act Crisis,* 94, what appeared in the *Gazette* differed from the resolves printed by the House of Burgesses.

204   *Every falshood that malice could invent:* Quoted in Schlesinger, *Prelude to Independence,* 72–73.

   Print every Thing that is Libelous: Quoted in Levy, *Emergence of a Free Press,* 65.

   Governor Francis Fauquier: Morgan and Morgan, *The Stamp Act Crisis,* 97.

   New York locked up Alexander MacDougall: Thomas, *The History of Printing in America,* 466–70.

205   *Cooking up paragraphs:* John Adams, *The Works of John Adams, with a Life of the Author, Notes and Illustrations,* ed. C. F. Adams, 10 vols. (Boston, 1850–1856), 2:219, quoted in Davidson, *Propaganda and the American Revolution,* 227.

   To the Inhabitants of the Province: Boston-Gazette, and Country Journal, October 7, 1765.

   Man, in a state of nature: Boston-Gazette, and Country Journal, March 9, 1767.

206   *It is a standing Maxim: Boston-Gazette, and Country Journal,* October 14, 1765.

   RANK Slavery: Boston-Gazette, and Country Journal, November 4, 1765, supplement.

   NO government can have a RIGHT: Boston-Gazette, and Country Journal, November 18, 1765.

207   *THERE is nothing so fretting: Boston-Gazette, and Country Journal,* March 14, 1768.

207   *The battle surrounding the Stamp Act:* Levy, *Emergence of a Free Press,* 67.

By loading the press: Boston-Gazette, and Country Journal, August 26, 1765.

208   *A most unfortunate affair: Boston Chronicle,* March 8, 1770. Mein's note to Hutchinson quoted in Levy, *Emergence of a Free Press,* 68.

209   *There could not have been got together:* Quoted in Hiller B. Zobel, *The Boston Massacre* (New York: W. W. Norton, 1970), 110.

To the cause of truth: New-York Journal; or the General Advertiser, January 5, 1775.

210   *If ten mens voyces be louder:* Richard Baxter, "To the Reader," *Aphorismes of Justification* (1649), in William Haller, ed., *Liberty and Reformation in the Puritan Revolution* (New York: Columbia University Press, 1955), 2.

Patriot printers, it seems: Robert W. T. Martin, *The Free and Open Press: The Founding of American Democratic Press Liberty, 1640–1800* (New York: New York University Press, 2001), 87.

Even though news of an event: In 1760, a story appeared in the *New-Hampshire Gazette* on August 29, less than three weeks after it ran in the *South-Carolina Gazette* in Charleston. The New Hampshire paper credited its South Carolina counterpart for the story. Information could not be physically transmitted much faster than that in the era of wind sail and horse travel.

211   *Let these* truths *be indelibly impressed: Pennsylvania Chronicle, and Universal Advertiser* (Philadelphia), February 15, 1768.

Printers in America began to discard: Stephen Botein, "Printers and the American Revolution," in Bernard Bailyn and John B. Hench, eds., *The Press & the American Revolution* (Boston: Northeastern University Press, 1981), 45.

212   *Nearly 100,000:* Francis G. Walett, *Patriots, Loyalists & Printers* (Worcester, Mass.: American Antiquarian Society, 1976), 74.

212   *Can they be friends: Rivington's New-York Gazetteer; or Connecticut, New-Jersey, Hudson's River, and Quebec Weekly Advertiser,* December 2, 1773.

Seed of sedition: Massachusetts Gazette and Boston Post-Boy, January 1, 1773.

In Philadelphia, William Smith: New-York Gazette; and the Weekly Mercury, April 1, 1776.

Patriots accepted nothing less: Levy, *Emergence of a Free Press,* 173.

213   *The last right we shall mention:* "To the Inhabitants of the Province of Quebec," October 24, 1774, quoted in Richard Buell Jr., "Freedom of the Press in Revolutionary America: The Evolution of Libertarianism, 1760–1820," in Bernard Bailyn and John B. Hench, eds., *The Press & the American Revolution* (Boston: Northeastern University Press, 1981), 61–62.

If you print: Levy, *Emergence of a Free Press,* 175.

Congress refused to punish: Dwight L. Teeter, "Press Freedom and the Public Printing: Pennsylvania, 1775–1783," *Journalism Quarterly* 45 (1968): 445–51.

Of the Use, Abuse: William Livingston, "*Of the Use, Abuse, and* LIBERTY OF THE PRESS," *Independent Reflector,* August 30, 1753, in William Livingston, *The Independent Reflector or Weekly Essays on Sundry Important Subjects More particularly adapted to the Province of New-York,* ed. Milton M. Klein (Cambridge, Mass.: Harvard University Press, 1963), 341.

214   *But how great is the Absurdity:* William Livingston, "The Absurdity of the civil Magistrate's interfering in Matters of Religion," August 9, 1753, in William Livingston, *The Independent Reflector or Weekly Essays on Sundry Important Subjects More particularly adapted to the Province of New-York,* ed. Milton M. Klein (Cambridge, Mass.: Harvard University Press, 1963), 313.

Buell proposed that the hostilities: Buell, "Freedom of the Press in Revolutionary America," 62, 76, 82.

CHAPTER EIGHT

215 *If we knew what freedom of the press meant:* Dwight L. Teeter, "Decent Animadversions: Notes toward a History of Free Press Theory," in Donovan H. Bond and W. Reynolds McLeod, eds., *Newsletters to Newspapers: Eighteenth Century Journalism* (Morgantown: School of Journalism, West Virginia University, 1977), 237.

Few of us, I believe: Quoted in Leonard W. Levy, *Emergence of a Free Press* (New York: Oxford University Press, 1985), 204.

What is the liberty of the press?: Publius [Alexander Hamilton], *The Federalist Papers, No. 84: Certain General and Miscellaneous Objections to the Constitution Considered and Answered,* http://thomas.loc.gov/home/histdox/fed_84.html. The final eight letters of *The Federalist Papers* appeared in *The Federalist II* (New York: J. and A. McLean, May 28, 1788). They were published in a single bound volume.

216 *Considerable Lattitude: Independent Gazetteer; or, the Chronicle of Freedom* (Philadelphia), April 13, 1782.

Heaven grant that the FREEDOM: Massachusetts Spy: or, Worchester Gazette, April 3, 1788, quoted in Clyde Augustus Duniway, *The Development of Freedom of the Press in Massachusetts* (Cambridge, Mass.: Harvard University Press, 1906; reprint, New York: Burt Franklin, 1969), 136.

The liberty of the press is indeed: William Blackstone, *Commentaries of the Laws of England, 1765–1769,* ed. William Carey Jones, 4 vols. (San Francisco: Bancroft-Whitenet, 1916), 4:152.

The Liberty of the Press is doubtless: Quoted in Duniway, *The Development of Freedom of the Press in Massachusetts*, 125.

217 *Levy also explained:* Levy, *Emergence of a Free Press,* 186.

Print every Thing that is Libelous: Quoted in Levy, *Emergence of a Free Press,* 65.

Bulwarks of Liberty: Section XII, *Virginia Declaration of Rights* (1776).

218 *'Tis common freedome:* Anonymous [William Walwyn], *The Compassionate Samaritane Vnbinding The Conscience, and pourring Oyle into the wounds which have been made upon the Separation: recommending their future welfare to the serious thoughts, and carefull endeavours of all who love the peace and vnity of Commonwealths men, or desire the vnanimous prosecution for the Common Enemie, or who follow our Saviours rule, to doe unto others, what they would have other doe unto them* (London, 1644), 5–6, 78–79, in William Haller, ed., *Tracts on Liberty in the Puritan Revolution, 1638–1647,* 3 vols. (New York: Columbia University Press, 1934; reprint, New York: Octagon Books, 1965), 3:67, 103–4.

219 *Noble or other, tag and rag:* Anonymous, *An Admonition to the Parliament* (London, 1572), in Barrington R. White, *The English Puritan Tradition* (Nashville, Tenn.: Broadman, 1980), 31.

220 *The art of Printing:* Gabriel Plattes, *A Descripton of the Famous Kingdome of Macaria* (1641), quoted in Elizabeth L. Eisenstein, *The Printing Press as an Agent of Change,* 2 vols. (Cambridge: Cambridge University Press, 1979), 1:305.

Stopping the establishment of Anglicanism: Patricia U. Bonomi, *Under the Cope of Heaven: Religion, Society, and Politics in Colonial America* (New York: Oxford University Press, 1986), 187–216.

221 *Bookshops thrived:* Iona Italia, *The Rise of Literary Journalism in the Eighteenth Century: Anxious Employment* (London: Routledge, 2005), 8.

224 *THE* Liberty *of the* Press: *New-York Mercury,* March 22, 1756.

226 *A free people:* Cato [John Trenchard and Thomas Gordon], "Of Freedom Of Speech: That The Same Is Inseparable From Publick Liberty," *London Journal,* February 4, 1721, in *Cato's Letters, or Essays on Liberty, Civil and Religious, and Other Important Subjects,* ed. Ronald Hamowy, 4 vols. (Indianapolis: Liberty Fund, 1995), 1:74.

BIBLIOGRAPHY

NEWSPAPERS

American Weekly Mercury (Philadelphia)
Boston Chronicle
Boston Evening-Post
Boston Gazette
Boston Gazette, or Country Journal
Boston News-Letter
Connecticut Gazette (New Haven)
Independent Advertiser (Boston)
Independent Gazetteer; or, the Chronicle of Freedom (Philadelphia)
Maryland Gazette (Annapolis)
Massachusetts Gazette and Boston Post-Boy
Massachusetts Spy: or, Worchester Gazette
New-England Courant (Boston)
New-Hampshire Gazette (Portsmouth)
New-London Gazette
New-York Gazette
New-York Gazette; and the Weekly Mercury
New-York Gazette; or, the Weekly Post-Boy
New-York Journal; or the General Advertiser
New-York Mercury
New-York Weekly Journal
Pennsylvania Chronicle, and Universal Advertiser (Philadelphia)
Pennsylvania Gazette (Philadelphia)
Providence Gazette; and Country Journal
Publick Occurrences Both Forreign and Domestick (Boston)
Rivington's New-York Gazetteer; or Connecticut, New-Jersey, Hudson's River, and Quebec Weekly Advertiser

South-Carolina Gazette (Charleston)
Virginia Gazette (Williamsburg)

PRIMARY DOCUMENTS

Addison, Joseph, and Richard Steele. *The Spectator, No. 245* (London), August 12, 1712. In Joseph Addison and Richard Steele, *Selections from* The Tatler *and* The Spectator, 2nd ed. Introduction by Robert J. Allen. Fort Worth, Tex.: Holt, Rinehart and Winston, 1957.

Baxter, Richard. *Plain Scripture Proof.* London, 1651.

Blackstone, William. *Commentaries of the Laws of England, 1765–1769.* 4 vols. Ed. William Carey Jones. San Francisco: Bancroft-Whitenet, 1916.

The Book of the General Lawes and Libertyes. Cambridge, 1660.

Franklin, Benjamin. "The Albany Plan of Union." In Benjamin Franklin, *Writings.* New York: Library of America, 1987.

———. *Autobiography.* Eds. J. A. Leo Lemay and P. M. Zall. New York: W. W. Norton, 1986.

Frith, John. *A pistle to the Christian reader: the reuelation of antichrist.* Antwerp: H. Luft Hesse, 1529.

———. *The articles wherefore Johann Frith died which he wrote in newgatae the 23 daye of June the yere of oure Lorde 1533.* Monster [Münster]: C. Willems, 1533.

Helwys, Thomas. *A Short Declaration of the mistery of iniquity.* 1612; reprint, London: Kingsgate Press, 1935.

Hobbes, Thomas. *Leviathan or the Matter, forme and Power of a Commonwealth Ecclesiasticall and Civil.* London, 1651. In *Leviathan, with Selected Variants from the Latin Edition of 1668.* Ed. Edwin Curley. Indianapolis: Hackett, 1994.

Keach, Benjamin. *Tropologia: A Key to open Scripture Metaphors.* London, 1681.

Locke, John. *A Letter Concerning Toleration.* 1685, 1689. In *John Locke on Politics and Education,* Introduction by Howard R. Penniman. Roslyn, N.Y.: Walter J. Black, 1947.

———. *The Second Treatise of Government.* Introduction by Thomas P. Peardon. Indianapolis: Bobbs-Merrill, 1952.

———. *Two Treatises of Government*. Ed. Thomas Hollis. London: A. Millar, 1764.

Milton, John. *Areopagitica: A Speech of Mr. John Milton for the Liberty of Unlicens'd Printing, to the Parliament of England* (London, 1644). *The Works of John Milton*. 20 vols. New York: Columbia University Press, 1931.

Publius [Alexander Hamilton]. *The Federalist Papers, No. 84: Certain General and Miscellaneous Objections to the Constitution Considered and Answered. Federalist II*. New York: J. and A. McLean, May 28, 1788, http://thomas.loc.gov/home/histdox/fed_84 .html.

Virginia Declaration of Rights (1776).

Williams, Roger. *The Bloudy Tenent of Persecution for Cause of Conscience Discussed in a Conference between Peace and Truth*. London, 1644.

Winthrop, John. *History of New England, 1630–1649*. Ed. James Kendall Hosmer. 2 vols. New York: Charles Scribner's, 1908; reprint, New York: Barnes and Noble, 1946.

———. *The History of New England from 1630 to 1649*. Ed. James Savage. 2 vols. Boston: Little, Brown, 1853.

PRIMARY DOCUMENT COLLECTIONS

Adams, John. *The Works of John Adams, with a Life of the Author, Notes and Illustrations*. Ed. C. F. Adams. 10 vols. Boston, 1850–1856.

Addison, Joseph, and Richard Steele. *The Spectator*. Ed. Donald F. Bond. 5 vols. Oxford: Clarendon, 1965.

Alexander, James. *A Brief Narrative of the Case and Trial of John Peter Zenger, Printer of the New York Weekly Journal*. Ed. Stanley Nider Katz. 2nd ed. 1736; reprint, Cambridge, Mass.: Harvard University Press, 1972.

Browning, Andrew, ed. *English Historical Documents, 1660–1714*. New York: Oxford University Press, 1953.

Haller, William, ed. *Tracts on Liberty in the Puritan Revolution, 1638–1647*. 3 vols. New York: Columbia University Press, 1934; reprint, New York: Octagon Books, 1965.

Haller, William, and Godfrey Davies, eds. *The Leveller Tracts, 1647–1653.* New York: Columbia University Press, 1944; reprint, Gloucester, Mass: Peter Smith, 1964.

Hughes, Paul L., and Robert F. Fries, eds. *Crown and Parliament in Tudor-Stuart England: A Documentary Constitutional History, 1485–1714.* New York: G. P. Putnam's Sons, 1959.

Jefferson, Thomas. *The Writings of Thomas Jefferson.* Memorial Edition. 20 vols. Washington, D.C., 1903–1904.

Livingston, William. *The Independent Reflector or Weekly Essays on Sundry Important Subjects More particularly adapted to the Province of New-York.* Ed. Milton M. Klein. Cambridge, Mass.: Harvard University Press, 1963.

Nashe, Thomas. *The Works of Thomas Nashe.* Ed. Ronald B. McKerrow. London: Sidgwick, 1910.

Payne, William L., ed. *The Best of Defoe's Review: An Anthology.* New York: Columbia University Press, 1951.

Steele, Robert. *Tudor and Stuart Proclamations, 1485–1714.* Oxford: Oxford University Press, 1910.

Trenchard, John, and Thomas Gordon. *Cato's Letters, or Essays on Liberty, Civil and Religious, and Other Important Subjects.* Ed. Ronald Hamowy. 4 vols. Indianapolis: Liberty Fund, 1995.

Underhill, Edward Bean, ed. *Tracts on Liberty of Conscience, 1614–1661.* London: Hanserd Knollys Society, 1846.

SECONDARY SOURCES

Achinstein, Susan. *Literature and Dissent in Milton's England.* Cambridge: Cambridge University Press, 2003.

Anderson, Fred. *Crucible of War: The Seven Years' War and the Fate of Empire in British North America, 1754–1766.* New York: Alfred A. Knopf, 2000.

Andrews, Charles M., ed. *Narratives of the Insurrections, 1657–1690.* New York: Charles Scribner's Sons, 1915.

Aurner, Nellie Slayton. *Caxton: Mirrour of Fifteenth-Century Letters.* New York: Russell and Russell, 1965.

Aylmer, G. E., ed. *The Levellers in the English Revolution.* London: Thames and Hudson, 1975.

Bailyn, Bernard. *The Ideological Origins of the American Revolution.* Cambridge, Mass.: Harvard University Press, 1967.

Barker, Hannah, and Simon Burrows, eds. *Press, Politics and the Public Sphere in Europe and North America, 1760–1820.* Cambridge: Cambridge University Press, 2002.

Blanchard, Margaret A. "Turning Worlds Upside Down: Freedom of Expression through the Revolution." Unpublished manuscript, 1992.

Bleyer, Willard Grosvenor. *Main Currents in the History of American Journalism.* Boston: Houghton Mifflin, 1927.

Bond, Richmond P. *New Letters to the Tatler and Spectator.* Austin: University of Texas Press, 1959.

Bonomi, Patricia U. *Under the Cope of Heaven: Religion, Society, and Politics in Colonial America.* New York: Oxford University Press, 1986.

Botein, Stephen. "'Meer Mechanics' and an Open Press: The Business and Political Strategies of Colonial American Printers." In *Perspectives in American History* 9, eds. Donald Fleming and Bernard Bailyn. Cambridge, Mass.: Harvard University Press, 1975.

———. "Printers and the American Revolution." In Bernard Bailyn and John B. Hench, eds., *The Press & the American Revolution.* Boston: Northeastern University Press, 1981.

Bristol, Roger P. *Supplement to Charles Evans' American Bibliography.* Charlottesville: University Press of Virginia, 1970.

Brown, Gillian. *The Consent of the Governed: The Lockean Legacy in Early American Culture.* Cambridge, Mass.: Harvard University Press, 2001.

Brown, Richard D. *Knowledge Is Power: The Diffusion of Information in Early America, 1700–1865.* New York: Oxford University Press, 1989.

Bush, Douglas. *John Milton: A Sketch of His Life and Writings.* New York: Macmillan, 1964.

Chalklin, Christopher. *The Rise of the English Town, 1650–1800.* Cambridge: Cambridge University Press, 2001.

Clark, Charles E. *The Public Prints: The Newspaper in Anglo-American Culture, 1665–1740*. New York: Oxford University Press, 1994.

Clark, Sandra. *The Elizabethan Pamphleteers: Popular Moralistic Pamphlets, 1580–1640*. Rutherford, N.J.: Farleigh Dickinson University Press, 1985.

Clebsch, William A. *England's Earliest Protestants, 1520–1535*. New Haven, Conn.: Yale University Press, 1964.

Clyde, William M. *The Struggle for the Freedom of the Press from Caxton to Cromwell*. London: Oxford University Press, 1934; reprint, New York: Burt Franklin, 1970.

Copeland, David A. *Benjamin Keach and the Development of Baptist Traditions in Seventeenth-Century England*. Lewiston, N.Y.: Edward Mellen Press, 2001.

———. *Colonial American Newspapers: Character and Content*. Newark: University of Delaware Press, 1997.

———. *Debating the Issues in Colonial Newspapers*. Westport, Conn.: Greenwood, 2000.

———. *The French and Indian War*. The Greenwood Library of American War Reporting. Ed. David A. Copeland, 8 vols. Westport, Conn.: Greenwood, 2005.

———. "'JOIN, or DIE': America's Press during the French and Indian War." *Journalism History* 24 (1998): 112–21.

———. "The Zenger Trial." *Media Studies Journal* (Spring/Summer 2000): 2–7.

Davidson, Philip. *Propaganda and the American Revolution, 1763–1783*. Chapel Hill: University of North Carolina Press, 1941.

Davis, Richard Beale. *A Colonial Southern Bookshelf: Reading in the Eighteenth Century*. Athens: University of Georgia Press, 1979.

DeArmond, Anna Janney. *Andrew Bradford: Colonial Journalist*. Newark: University of Delaware Press, 1949.

Dexter, Henry Martyn. *As to Roger Williams, and his 'Banishment' from Massachusetts Plantation*. Boston: Congregational Publishing Society, 1876.

Dickens, A. G. *Reformation and Society in Sixteenth-Century Europe.* London: Thames and Hudson, 1966.

Dowley, Tim, ed. *The History of Christianity.* Grand Rapids, Mich.: Wm. B. Eerdmans, 1977.

Duffy, John. *Epidemics in Colonial America.* Baton Rouge: Louisiana State University Press, 1953.

Duniway, Clyde Augustus. *The Development of Freedom of the Press in Massachusetts.* Cambridge, Mass.: Harvard University Press, 1906; reprint, New York: Burt Franklin, 1969.

Edwards, David L. *Christian England.* 3 vols. Grand Rapids, Mich.: Wm. B. Eerdmans, 1980.

Eisenstein, Elizabeth L. *The Printing Press as an Agent of Change.* 2 vols. Cambridge: Cambridge University Press, 1979.

Eldridge, Larry D. *A Distant Heritage: The Growth of Free Speech in Early America.* New York: New York University Press, 1994.

Emery, Michael, and Edwin Emery. *The Press and America: An Interpretive History of the Mass Media.* 6th ed. Englewood Cliffs, N.J.: Prentice Hall, 1988.

Evans, Charles. *American Bibliography.* 14 vols. Chicago, 1904.

Fischer, David Hackett. *Albion's Seed: Four British Folkways in America.* New York: Oxford University Press, 1989.

Frank, Joseph. *The Beginnings of the English Newspaper, 1620–1660.* Cambridge, Mass.: Harvard University Press, 1961.

Goodell, A. C. *Proceedings of the Massachusetts Historical Society.* June 1893.

Gordon, Walter M. "A Scholastic Problem in Thomas More's Controversy with John Frith." *Harvard Theological Review* 69 (January 1976): 131–49.

Griffin, Dustin H. *Regaining Paradise: Milton and the Eighteenth Century.* Cambridge: Cambridge University Press, 1986.

Habermas, Jürgen. *The Structural Transformation of the Public Sphere: An Inquiry into a Category of Bourgeois Society.* Trans. Thomas Burger. Cambridge, Mass.: Harvard University Press, 1989.

Haller, William, ed. *Liberty and Reformation in the Puritan Revolution.* New York: Columbia University Press, 1955.

Hamburger, Philip. "The Development of the Law of Seditious Libel and the Control of the Press." *Stanford Law Review* 37 (1985): 661–765.

Hazelton, Meiling. "'Mony Choaks': The Quaker Critique of the Seventeenth-Century Public Sphere." *Modern Philology* 98 (2000): 251–70.

Hill, Christopher. *The Century of Revolution, 1603–1714.* Edinburgh: Thomas Nelson, 1961.

———. *Milton and the English Revolution.* New York: Penguin, 1979.

Hill, Douglas. *The English to New England.* New York: Clarkson N. Potter, 1975.

Historical Statistics of the United States: Colonial Times to 1970. Washington, D. C.: U.S. Department of Commerce, 1975.

Hofstadter, Richard, and Walter P. Metzger. *The Development of Academic Freedom in the United States.* New York: Columbia University Press, 1955.

Hudson, Frederic. *Journalism in the United States, from 1690–1872.* New York: J. and J. Harper, 1873.

Huffman, Clifford Chalmers. *Elizabethan Impressions: John Wolfe and His Press.* New York: AMS Press, 1988.

Hutchinson, Thomas. *The History of Massachusetts, from the first Settlement thereof in 1628, until the year 1750.* 3rd ed. 2 vols. Boston, 1795; reprint, Cambridge, Mass.: Harvard University Press, 1936.

Hyman, Harold M. *To Try Men's Souls: Loyalty Tests in American History.* Berkeley: University of California Press, 1959.

Italia, Iona. *The Rise of Literary Journalism in the Eighteenth Century: Anxious Employment.* London: Routledge, 2005.

Kittelson, James M. *Luther the Reformer: The Story of the Man and His Career.* Minneapolis: Augsburg, 1986.

Knappen, Marshall M. *Tudor Puritanism.* Chicago: University of Chicago Press, 1939; reprint, Gloucester, Mass.: Peter Smith, 1963.

Kobre, Sidney. *The Development of the Colonial Newspaper.* 1944; reprint, Gloucester, Mass.: Peter Smith, 1960.

Lambert, Frank. "'Pedlar of Divinity': George Whitefield and the Great Awakening." *Journal of American History* 77 (1990): 812–37.

Lee, James Melvin. *History of American Journalism.* Garden City, N.J.: Garden City Publishing, 1917.

Levy, Leonard W. *Emergence of a Free Press.* Oxford: Oxford University Press, 1985.

Lewalski, Barbara Kiefer. *The Life of John Milton: A Critical Biography.* Malden, Mass.: Blackwell, 2000.

Lorenz, Alfred Lawrence. *Hugh Gaine: A Colonial Printer-Editor's Odyssey to Loyalism.* Carbondale: Southern Illinois University Press, 1972.

Lunt, W. E. *History of England.* 4th ed. New York: Harper and Row, 1957.

Martin, Robert W. T. *The Free and Open Press: The Founding of American Democratic Press Liberty, 1640–1800.* New York: New York University Press, 2001.

Masson, David. *The Life of John Milton Narrated in Connexion with the Political, Ecclesiastical, and Literary History of His Time.* 7 vols. 1875; reprint, Gloucester, Mass.: Peter Smith, 1965.

May, Henry F. *The Enlightenment in America.* Oxford: Oxford University Press, 1976.

Mayton, William T. "Seditious Libel and the Lost Guarantee of a Freedom of Expression." *Columbia Law Review* 84 (1984): 91–142.

McGee, J. Sears. *The Godly Man in Stuart England: Anglicans, and Puritans, and the Two Tables, 1620–1670.* New Haven, Conn.: Yale University Press, 1976.

Merritt, Richard L. *Symbols of American Community, 1735–1775.* New Haven, Conn.: Yale University Press, 1966.

Miner, Ward L. *William Goddard, Newspaperman.* Durham, N.C.: Duke University Press, 1962.

Morgan, Edmund S., and Helen M. Morgan. *The Stamp Act Crisis: Prologue to Revolution.* Chapel Hill: University of North Carolina Press, 1953.

Morton, A. L. *The World of the Ranters: Religious Radicalism in the English Revolution*. London: Lawrence and Wishart, 1970.

Mott, Frank Luther. *American Journalism, A History: 1690–1960*. 3rd ed. New York: Macmillan, 1962.

Nord, David Paul. *Faith in Reading: Religious Publishing and the Birth of Mass Media in America*. New York: Oxford University Press, 2004.

―――. "Teleology and the News: The Religious Roots of American Journalism, 1630–1730." *Journal of American History* 77 (1990): 9–38.

Orwell, George, and Reginald Reynolds, eds. *British Pamphleteers*. 10 vols. London: Allan Wingate, 1948.

Painter, George D. *William Caxton: A Biography*. New York: G. P. Putnam's, 1977.

Parker, William Riley. *Milton: A Biography*. 2nd ed. Oxford: Oxford University Press, 1996.

Parramore, Thomas C. *Carolina Quest*. Englewood Cliffs, N.J.: Prentice-Hall, 1978.

Payne, George Henry. *History of Journalism in the United States*. 1920; reprint, Westport, Conn.: Greenwood, 1970.

Pease, Theodore Calvin. *The Leveller Movement: A Study in the History and Political Theory of the English Great Civil War*. Washington, D.C.: American Historical Association, 1916; reprint, Gloucester, Mass.: Peter Smith, 1965.

Penninger, Freida Elaine. *William Caxton*. Boston: Twayne, 1979.

"A Population History of London: The Demography of Urban Growth." *The Proceedings of the Old Bailey,* http://www.oldbaileyonline.org/history/london-life/Population%20History%200f%20London.html (accessed July 19, 2005).

Ridley, Jasper. *Statesman and Saint: Cardinal Wolsey, Sir Thomas More, and the Politics of Henry VIII*. New York: Viking, 1982.

Robbins, Caroline. *The Eighteenth-Century Commonwealthman*. Cambridge, Mass.: Harvard University Press, 1959.

Russell, Conrad. *The Crisis of Parliaments: English History, 1509–1660*. Oxford: Oxford University Press, 1971.

Schlesinger, Arthur M. *Prelude to Independence: The Newspaper War in Britain, 1764–1776.* New York: Alfred A. Knopf, 1958.

Schudson, Michael. *The Good Citizen: A History of American Civic Life.* Cambridge, Mass.: Harvard University Press, 1998.

Sensabaugh, George F. *Milton in Early America.* Princeton, N.J.: Princeton University Press, 1964.

Shaaber, M. A. *Some Forerunners of the Newspaper in England, 1476–1622.* Philadelphia: University of Pennsylvania Press, 1929; reprint, New York: Octagon Books, 1966.

Shaw, Howard. *The Levellers.* New York: Harper and Row, 1968.

Shields, David S. *Oracles of Empire: Poetry, Politics, and Commerce in British America, 1690–1750.* Chicago: University of Chicago Press, 1990.

Siebert, Fredrick Seaton. *Freedom of the Press in England, 1476–1776.* Urbana: University of Illinois Press, 1965.

Sloan, Wm. David, and Julie Hedgepeth Williams. *The Early American Press, 1690–1783.* Westport, Conn.: Greenwood, 1994.

Smith, Jeffery A. *Printers and Press Freedom: The Ideology of Early American Journalism.* Oxford: Oxford University Press, 1988.

Snyder, Henry L. "Newsletters in England, 1689–1715, with Special Reference to John Dyer—A Byway in the History of England." In Donovan H. Bond and W. Reynolds McLeod, eds., *Newsletters to Newspapers: Eighteenth-Century Journalism.* Morganton: West Virginia University, 1977.

Stephens, Mitchell. *A History of News: From the Drum to the Satellite.* New York: Viking, 1988.

Stout, Harry S. *The Divine Dramatist: George Whitefield and the Rise of Modern Evangelism.* Grand Rapids, Mich.: Wm. B. Eerdmans, 1991.

———. *The New England Soul: Preaching and Religious Culture in Colonial New England.* New York: Oxford University Press, 1986.

Sutherland, James. *The Restoration Newspaper and Its Development.* Cambridge: Cambridge University Press, 1986.

Teeter, Dwight L. "Decent Animadversions: Notes toward a History of Free Press Theory." In Donovan H. Bond and W.

Reynolds McLeod, eds., *Newsletters to Newspapers: Eighteenth Century Journalism*. Morgantown: School of Journalism, West Virginia University, 1977.

————. "Press Freedom and the Public Printing: Pennsylvania, 1775–1783." *Journalism Quarterly* 45 (1968): 445–51.

Thomas, Isaiah. *The History of Printing in America*. 1810; reprint, New York: Weathervane, 1970.

Tindall, George Brown. *America: A Narrative History*. New York: W. W. Norton, 1984.

Voss, Paul J. *Elizabethan News Pamphlets: Shakespeare, Spenser, Marlowe & the Birth of Journalism*. Pittsburgh: Duquesne University Press, 2001.

Walett, Francis G. *Patriots, Loyalists & Printers*. Worcester, Mass.: American Antiquarian Society, 1976.

Warner, Michael. *The Letters of the Republic*. Cambridge, Mass.: Harvard University Press, 1990.

White, B. R. *The English Baptists of the Seventeenth Century*. London: Baptist Historical Society, 1983.

White, Barrington R. *The English Puritan Tradition*. Nashville, Tenn.: Broadman, 1980.

Williams, Julie Hedgepeth. *The Significance of the Printed Word in Early America: Colonists' Thoughts on the Role of the Press*. Westport, Conn.: Greenwood, 1999.

Wilson, A. N. *The Life of John Milton*. New York: Oxford University Press, 1983.

Wroth, Lawrence C. *The Colonial Printer*. Portland, Maine: Southworth-Anthoensen Press, 1938; reprint, New York: Dover, 1994.

Zobel, Hiller B. *The Boston Massacre*. New York: W. W. Norton, 1970.

INDEX

Hyde, Robert, 69

impartiality and the press,
    166–72
Independent Advertiser, 166–67,
    180
Independent Reflector, 213–14
information circles, 132–33
inoculation controversy, 144–48
Iran-Contra scandal, xvi
Isaacson, Walter, xiv–xv

James I, 6, 36–39, 54, 103, 105;
    on freedom of speech, 39
James II, 50–51, 71
Jamestown, 104
Jefferson, Thomas, x–xi, 91–92,
    159–60
Johnson, Marmaduke, 121
"JOIN, or DIE," 191
Journal of Occurrences, 209
jury trials, 149–50, 152, 153–63

Keach, Benjamin, 11–12, 49–50
Keith, George, 125
King William's War, 130
Kobre, Sidney, 134

Laud, William, 39–40, 103, 118
Laws of Ecclesiastical Polity, The,
    91
Leonard, Daniel, 212
Leonard, J. William, xiv
L'Estrange, Roger, 69–70
Letter Concerning Toleration, A, 54
Levellers, 17, 44–45, 77–82, 84,
    91, 106, 113, 157, 220; and
    the level society, 80–82
Leviathan, 17, 88–90

Levy, Leonard, 125–26, 207,
    212–13, 217
Lexington and Concord, 209
liberty of conscience, 3, 9,
    105–6, 223; in America,
    126–27; England, 21–52,
    72–73, 75–76, 77–82, 87;
    and the Great Awakening,
    172–77
licensing, 6, 44–45, 49, 51–52,
    61–63, 65, 95, 152, 164; in
    America, 121–37; and
    Boston's first newspapers,
    140–44; ends, 70, 92–93,
    120; in Pennsylvania, 151;
    and *Publick Occurrences,*
    130–31
Licensing Act, 152
Lilburne, John, 17, 41–42,
    44–47, 63, 65, 76, 77–82,
    84, 113
literacy in America, 108
Livingston, William, 3, 9, 189,
    213–14
Locke, John, 3, 11, 12, 17, 46,
    54, 64, 76, 83, 98, 106, 126,
    158, 205, 209, 220, 223;
    theory of government,
    90–95
London Gazette, 95, 137
London Journal, 13, 97, 98, 100,
    165, 178
Lord Baltimore, 118
Louis XIV, 131
loyalty oaths, 117–18
Lushington, Thomas, 58
Luther, Martin, 5–6, 10, 23–24,
    93; Ninety-Five Theses,
    23–24, 218

David A. Copeland is the A. J. Fletcher Professor of Communications in the School of Communications at Elon University, Elon, North Carolina. He is the author of *The Antebellum Era; The Function of Newspapers in Society: A Global Perspective; Benjamin Keach and the Development of Baptist Traditions in Seventeenth-Century England; Debating the Issues in Colonial Newspapers;* and *Colonial American Newspapers: Character and Content,* and he is the general editor of the Greenwood Library of American War Reporting.

Daniel Schorr is a senior news analyst for National Public Radio and a former correspondent for CBS News (1953–1976) and CNN (1979–1985). He is the author of *Clearing the Air* and *Staying Tuned: A Life in Journalism.*